YEARS

SIMON &
SCHUSTER
PAPERBACKS

ONE WEEK TO CHANGE THE WORLD

AN ORAL HISTORY OF THE 1999 WTO PROTESTS

DW GIBSON

Simon & Schuster Paperbacks

NEW YORK   LONDON   TORONTO
SYDNEY   NEW DELHI

An Imprint of Simon & Schuster, LLC
1230 Avenue of the Americas
New York, NY 10020

First Simon & Schuster trade paperback edition June 2024

SIMON & SCHUSTER PAPERBACKS and colophon are registered trade-
marks of Simon & Schuster, LLC

Simon & Schuster: Celebrating 100 Years of Publishing in 2024

For information about special discounts for bulk purchases,
please contact Simon & Schuster Special Sales at 1-866-506-1949
or business@simonandschuster.com.

The Simon & Schuster Speakers Bureau can bring authors to your
live event. For more information or to book an event, contact the
Simon & Schuster Speakers Bureau at 1-866-248-3049
or visit our website at www.simonspeakers.com.

Text design by Paul Dippolito

Manufactured in the United States of America

1 3 5 7 9 10 8 6 4 2

Library of Congress Cataloging-in-Publication Data has been applied for.

ISBN 978-1-6680-3356-2
ISBN 978-1-6680-3357-9 (ebook)

For MJ Sieber and Mike Tryon—
thank god you're still around

and in memory of Sanjay Iyer and
Terry Guerin—I miss you every day

Each person is characterized by their role or position in 1999. Brief bios, as well as descriptions of organizations mentioned in the text, can be referenced at the back of the book.

BEFORE

Lori Wallach, Director of Global Trade Watch: The fight was over the World Trade Organization.

Julia Hughes, vice president of the United States Association of Importers of Textiles and Apparel: A large part of establishing the WTO in 1995 was to create a participative, consensus-based international organization—not unlike the United Nations. It was created to establish rules of the road for international trade and to have a way to enforce those rules when countries go rogue.

Pascal Lamy, EU trade commissioner: The WTO, like many other international organizations, has always been about the acceptance of reduced sovereignty in the name of the common good. Something like: "Given the problems we all have, I accept that we constrain my country's sovereignty in the name of global benefit."

Victor Menotti, program coordinator for the International Forum on Globalization: The WTO was there to move power from the local and national level into a set of global rules written by the world's largest corporations at the exclusion of civil society. That raises concerns for a lot of people.

John Nichols, reporter for the *Nation*: It was establishing the ability to supersede and effectively overrule what the nation-state might do. So even if you won the legislative battle at home, you could be overridden at the global level.

Lori Wallach: The rules being written were things like, "You can only have this much food safety, anything higher is a trade barrier." Or, "This labeling system you have, it's an illegal trade barrier." Or, "You can't have this kind of investment rule, you can't regulate services." All of it is viewed by the WTO as illegal trade barriers.

Deborah James, organizer for Global Exchange: People didn't realize that under the rules of the WTO it's illegal to ban products based on production methods. One of the only things you're allowed to ban is prison labor. But if you say, "We don't want these products in our country because they're made under exploitative conditions, or because they're made in ways that damage the environment," it's actually illegal to say we don't want those products circulating in our country.

We were telling people this in 1999 and they'd say, "Well, we should be able to decide those things."

And we were saying, "Yeah, that's why we don't like the WTO!"

Celia Alario, media liaison at the Independent Media Center: People were seeing the ways in which everybody was affected, no matter what issues were important to you—the environment, human rights, social justice, sweatshop issues—this unchecked globalization and trade was going to affect all of us.

Lori Wallach: It was a battle of ideology. One was a vision of a single constitution for global corporate governance, which is what the first director of the WTO had said was needed. The alternative was making trade rules for countries according to what was interesting to *their* people and *their* governments, rules about what they would do when they decided to trade—not one-size-fits-all, top-down, corporate dictates.

Ralph Nader, founder of Public Citizen: There is no such thing as a free market. Can you have a free market when you have monopolistic practices? Can you have a free market when you have big business subordinating small business in all kinds of ways? One-sided franchise agreements? Can you have a free market when you have corporations who often love intricate regulations—not very onerous, mind you, but intricate—and they have the accountants and lawyers to do the work of compliance? Small businesses can't afford that, so they go out of business. Large corporations have propagandized the innocent and the ignorant in our society into accepting the idea of free markets. That's the way they legitimize what they do.

Colin Hines, founding member of the International Forum on Globalization: Margaret Thatcher's most corrosive four-letter word, TINA—There Is No Alternative—was totally absorbed by, not just the status quo people who did well out of it, but also by the intellectually lazy who just said, "Well, you know, globalization's like gravity."

Celia Alario: We were being told, "The train had left the station. There is no turning back. This is the way the world is going to be."

Vandana Shiva, founding member of the International Forum on Globalization: We realized if we don't tell our plural stories—what happened to Indian farmers, what happened to the Southeast Asian countries, what happened to Africa—we will get the typical story of all boats rising. And all boats weren't rising, some boats were actually sinking.

Julia Hughes: The creation of the WTO wasn't the end of the job. Processes needed to be put in place that would help bring people together. So, built into the creation of the WTO was the concept of the ministerial. Talking about "ministers" is more European-speak—the WTO is, after all, based in Geneva. We don't use that phrase here in the U.S. We have a U.S. trade representative and that person's equivalent in other countries would likely be a trade minister. Most other countries around the world use that title, "minister." So the conferences, which are usually every two years, are called ministerials and the idea of the ministerial is to force countries face-to-face to discuss issues, to keep governments engaged and not just have the Geneva-based community—which is an incestuous thing, the Geneva crowd—making all the decisions. The idea behind the ministerials is to make sure home capitals and officials are also engaged. The objective going into the 1999 ministerial was to expand on the original framework that was set up four years earlier.

Tetteh Hormeku, coordinator for the Africa Trade Network: By 1999, African civil society organizations like ours had come to be very, very unhappy with the way the WTO was evolving. We discovered that the original agreements that were signed were problematic—to put it mildly—especially for Africa. But also, at that point, the big countries, the European Union, Japan, Canada and the U.S.—"the Quad"—were hell-bent on expanding the agenda further. So, we were opposed to the agreement that was signed already and even more opposed to the effort to expand the agenda.

David Solnit, cofounder of Art and Revolution: At the beginning of 1999, when we heard that the WTO ministerial was coming to the

U.S., I thought, "Okay, this is our chance to step up like the Zapatistas did, like people in Africa and other parts of the world have."

Lori Wallach: It was either going to be in Seattle, San Diego, or Honolulu.

Ron Judd, president of the King County Labor Council: I had a dream about WTO coming to Seattle—people thought I was crazy. Everybody goes, "How do you know that?"

I go, "Just what my gut tells me. Here's my conclusion." And I walked them through my assessment of why everybody just loves free trade in Washington State, from our congressional delegation, to our statewide elected leaders, to all of our local, regional, urban leaguers, right down to the county commissioners. Per capita, we're the most trade-dependent state in the country. The meetings were going to be between Thanksgiving and Christmas, so the common view was no one's going to show up to protest, all they're going to do is cut ribbons and celebrate how good free trade is and use Washington and Seattle as the symbol of that. I said, "The great thing is, they don't know we're going to plan something that's going to shock the shit out of them!"

Colin Hines: Prime Minister Harold Macmillan, a very old, duffer-y guy from the sixties, was asked, "What's the most frightening thing in politics?"

He said, "Events, dear boy, events."

Mike Dolan, field director for Global Trade Watch: I had already been in touch with folks in San Diego and I had been in touch with folks in Seattle. Hawai'i would have been hell in terms of organizing—impossible. As much as I'd love it, no thank you—just the buses alone. If they picked San Diego, I knew I'd be putting a lot of energy into a cross-border mobilization. But Seattle was a home-court advantage. The labor movement was there, all the environmentalists, militant liberals.

Victor Menotti: We knew that if they picked Seattle, the forest issues would be big—the Timber Wars were still quite fresh in that region.

four waters, organizer with the Direct Action Network: In 1996, a lot of us came together in Humboldt for what was called the Timber Wars. When Seattle came up, I had been working with Julia Butterfly almost two years at that point. She had been living in a two-hundred-foot-tall, one-thousand-year-old California redwood tree for 738 days in order to prevent it from being harvested.

Jim Flynn, organizer with Earth First!: Somebody once said that you need twenty-five people on the ground for every person in the tree to bring that person food and water. Then there is all the media work that's got to be done. If you go sit in a tree, nobody will know—or they can do whatever they want to you—so you have to create a media situation so that the cops or the loggers themselves don't do something really bad, just attack you in the middle of the night.

Hilary McQuie, organizer with the Direct Action Network: The traumatized militant forest activists in the Northwest were such an important strand of what came together in Seattle. I had done a little bit with Earth First! back in the day. Those Eugene, Oregon, tree sits-in—people ended up getting beaten up and getting their hearts broken—those sit-ins really created this energy.

Jim Flynn: A friend took me to some hot springs in the old-growth forest near Portland and that really changed my life, just being in an amazing place like that. I fell in love. Then I saw a bumper sticker on a car that said EARTH FIRST! I said to my friend, "What's that?"

She said, "It's an environmental group that is not afraid to break the law to get their point across."

I said to myself, "Well, I don't mind breaking the law."

I was a juvenile delinquent. Joining Earth First! was like putting on an old pair of blue jeans. I was meant for it. It felt very comfortable. It was a community that I could jive with. I had a respect and love for nature, giving voice to the voiceless, fighting the good fight even though victory is never guaranteed and rarely achieved. It's still fighting the good fight. I quickly became a backpack activist, going from campaign to campaign in a car pool with a bunch of people. It just became the social calendar for me and other people that built community.

Earth First! is pretty well-known in Eugene. There are anarchists involved. We had lots of connections in the community and some people started to see signs on some trees downtown. This was an area where the local annual Eugene celebration took place. It was nothing but a parking lot but in all the medians were huge trees, redwoods included. We knew one of the city council members, a ninety-year-old woman who was disgusted that they were going to cut the trees down before it could even get talked about. So she alerted us.

A group of us conspired to sit in the trees. That was really the entire plan. We thought it would delay the tree cutting until the next Monday night when there could be a council meeting. Not that we had a lot of faith in council meetings, but it's what we had at the time.

So, in the wee hours of the morning, two women started a catfight outside a bar right next to the parking lot with the trees. It drew all the security guards and allowed the rest of us to get up into the trees. There were fifteen to twenty people who climbed at least four different trees. Most of them were in one huge oak.

At dawn, the police showed up with gas masks on their hips. There had been no confrontation and hardly any communication at this point. The tree with most of the people in it got threatened with pepper spray and they all came down, dragging their feet. Since the police were there with riot gear, the public noticed—people were waking up, word was getting out. Now there are hundreds of people. It's becoming a big scene and people are getting angry.

They got most of the people out of the trees. This one guy, they got a ladder and used a couple cans of pepper spray on him, mainly focusing on his hands. It's a skin irritant as well as a lung irritant. Eventually, he chose to come down.

That left me alone in a tree, a sweetgum. I took a firmer stance. I developed a position where I could stand relatively comfortably and then wrap each arm around a different branch until I felt like they couldn't just pull me off. They tried. They went up I don't know how many times. Each time the torture got more intense. They were twisting my feet. They were pulling my hair. They were trying pain holds.

Eventually they had a fireman in a bucket lift and he grabbed the back of my hair and yanked down like he was working out in the gym. He was snapping my head back like a Pez dispenser, causing a lifelong neck injury. They used over twenty cans of pepper spray on me.

They used up all the pepper spray they could get from Eugene, Lane County, and neighboring Springfield. The pain compliance holds and the pepper spray, nothing worked. It was getting more and more intense and I remained nonviolent.

The police and people on the street are going wild. *Long pause.* It's hard to relive this sometimes. *Crying.* It was getting more and more intense. There was a huge crowd, close to 1,000 people, but by this time I could barely open my eyes because they had pepper-sprayed my face. I was blind. I had a lot of supporters on the ground. I couldn't see them, but I could hear them. One said, "They're moving in with more pepper spray," or "They are moving out." I knew some of them by their voices. *Crying.* They were screaming at the cops because they were so outraged.

I don't want to discount chemical weapons but, in this case, it was mainly cayenne pepper, which has a pain effect but also has a numbing effect in some ways. They were wasting their time by respraying me with the same stuff once I was already drenched. I had my back to them the whole time. Eventually, I said, "Is that cayenne all you've got? Don't you have any habañero?" They did not appreciate that and started using Mace. Mace was a hell of a lot worse for me. Mace causes all your mucus membranes to start gushing out. I was still able to resist that. Not that I was looking for glory but, on some level, I recognized that I was the last line of defense at that point.

They cut up one of my pants legs all the way to my inner thigh and they were spraying my inner thigh but they weren't spraying my groin. People say that they pepper-sprayed my balls. They did not pepper-spray my balls.

They started cutting branches away from around me so they could get closer. Eventually, they got to where they could literally put their hands around me. They got a belt around my waist and attached the belt to the bucket on the lift. Then they yanked me. The first time they did it, I almost passed out. I had a really good grip around these two branches but they yanked me with the bucket and it bent me in half right in the stomach area.

They were escalating so I knew the second time would be harder. I knew that if I tried to resist, I would go flying off of there. I couldn't resist anymore. The second time they did it, I let go and they took me down in the bucket to the ground. I was completely drenched in pepper spray. It was about a six-hour ordeal from dawn until early afternoon, June 1, 1997.

The cops had to put me in a patrol car so they wanted to rinse me off first. They took a fire hose to me because I was dripping with pepper spray and Mace. The pepper spray is oil-based, so spraying me with water had limited effectiveness. It spread the pepper spray to places that it hadn't already been. So they put me in an ambulance and took me to a hospital. Then I was sent to jail. All of my skin had fully absorbed the pepper spray. It was thirty-six hours of sitting in a jail cell, just marinating. Even one week later when I took a bath, it all just re-electrified. It was like I got into a spicy bath. It was soaked into my skin. My hands were orange for one week. By the time they got me out of my tree, they had cut all the other trees down. My tree was the lone tree from what I heard. I didn't see it, but as soon as I was gone, they cut it down.

John Zerzan, Black Bloc organizer: There was an energy that was emerging in Eugene, I would say as far back as the Unabomber phenomenon. In '95 it was huge. You couldn't get away from it. Right after Kaczynski was captured in '96, I started overhearing these conversations. These kids were just down with Ted. He had just been arrested. We were going to send him some money for books. They understood the critique of technology and a technological society. They were completely in accord with it. I was just amazed. I started to see that it was way ahead of what we might have thought was brewing. It annoyed the left. I could see that too. They weren't then—and still are not now—interested in the critique of a technological society.

At the same time, the forest defense was going strong. There was a lot of that building up, getting more militant and getting more folks involved in tree-sitting. There were protests and demonstrations in Eugene around that time especially starting in 1997, your standard street stuff. You could just feel that something was going on.

Suzanne Savoie, Black Bloc organizer: Y2K was coming up so there was a lot of passion around primitive skills and decentralizing, living more natural lifestyles and trying to do away with corporate control of your life. I think that because Y2K was looming, there was this my-thology about we're going to actually be able to break down the global system. I think the juxtaposition with Y2K at the same time that the WTO meeting was happening made it a really interesting time. We were seeing the writing on the wall, the kind of slow-motion apoc-alypse that was going to lead to the destruction of biodiversity and upend cultures and take away indigenous rights. People said, "Well, maybe we actually have an opportunity to turn the ship around right now before things get worse. We have an opportunity right now to try to live more sustainable lives, more in line with the capacity of this planet." There was this feeling that we could do this.

Norm Stamper, chief of the Seattle Police Department: There was Y2K—remember that? Everyone was telling me, "Oh shit, Norm, do you realize how much of our systems are out of date? Computeriza-tion and the internet are deeply embedded with everything we do. It's going to blow up!"

Ed Joiner, assistant chief of the Seattle Police Department: We had a lot of concerns about what was going to happen when the clock ticked midnight in 1999.

Patrick Collins, National Guard operations officer: Everybody was worried about Y2K. The National Guard was told that they were going to be on alert for Y2K and we had to put together this elaborate plan for how we were going to mobilize people if the end of the world came.

Suzanne Savoie: It was its own kind of weird phenomenon. We were at the turning point of a millennium. That was significant. It felt like we have the opportunity right now to reevaluate our relationship with technology, our relationship with corporations, our relationship with the inequality and social justice and environmental issues in the world right now, at this change of the millennia. It was a wake-up call. Like, "We've got to do this!" It was us saying at this point in the trajectory of humanity, here at the new millennium, we have an opportunity to change course. I was younger then and everybody says you always are a lot more hopeful when you're younger. But it gave you hope that you were actually going to be able to change something, change the planet, change the course of history.

*   *   *

Mike Dolan: I was in Washington, D.C., at the offices of Public Citizen—on the edge of my seat, waiting to find out which city was going to host this thing.

Lori Wallach: We had a contact in Geneva who was supposed to call me the minute the decision was made about where the ministerial would take place. I got a phone call at two or three in the morning D.C. time. We found out it was Seattle and immediately got phone chains going.

Victor Menotti: When Seattle was announced, we pounced on contacts and identifying issues that would get people involved.

Mike Dolan: The announcement came down and I picked up the phone and started making calls. I was reserving venues and hotel rooms and really grabbing space like crazy. The WTO guys had the Sheraton and the Westin. I wasn't really interested in those rooms anyway, but I needed to find rooms—any rooms. I was putting down deposits on my credit cards. I was like, "I'll deal with this shit later but, right now, I need the rooms." I got a whole youth hostel, 140 beds.

Lori Wallach: In the middle of the night in Seattle, we started calling hotels and putting down deposits. We originally put them on personal credit cards, significant others' credit cards, parents' credit cards, roommates' credit cards—just to hold venues. All this had to be done quickly because governments would be doing the same thing. By the time the sun rose in D.C.—much less in Seattle—we already had cornered a lot of the market. In organizing, real estate is power.

David Solnit: My initial thought was that it would be in San Diego and that it would be easy to get people there from all the cold parts of the country in November. Just show them a picture of a beach and they'll come. Then they chose Seattle. There was Boeing and Microsoft on the host committee, so I think it was the big engines of corporate globalization.

Pat Davis, chairperson for Seattle Host: I was president of the Washington Council on International Trade, and we formed a group called Seattle Host and our role was to facilitate the services that were necessary to host the WTO ministerial—the space, the transportation, the hotel accommodations. We also helped inform the public on the importance of trade. We had to persuade the members of Washington Council on International Trade to help pay for it—they were the Boeings and Microsofts and all those, big-time. They had to be persuaded that this had to be funded.

Nick Licata, Seattle City Council member: The council was not part of the budget process. It was a backroom deal, playing out between the civic leaders, Bill Gates, heads of the Chamber. Paul Schell, the mayor, was a Democrat but very comfortable with the business community and knew them very well.

Pam Schell, Seattle's first lady: Money didn't matter to Paul. He was a preacher's kid, the oldest one, and had a great sense of responsibility. He really did everything constantly saying, "This is public service. I'm in here for public service."

Nick Licata: The business community in Seattle, for the most part, is socially liberal. They're still into the market economy but they're not totally free market. They are large organizations that are concerned about profits, and they're concerned about trade and that's where they're focused. They saw the WTO as a good thing because it was dollar signs. Ca-ching, ca-ching. Seattle is a major port city. A lot of people don't know that. I think they all thought they'd be able to puff up their feathers as the major corporate businesses in Seattle that sponsored the WTO.

Pam Schell: Paul really wanted to see Seattle do well through the WTO, even before he was mayor. He'd been port commissioner and was part of the decision-making that they should go after the opportunity of hosting the WTO. He was an advocate of Clinton's free trade. But he was also very tolerant of other positions.

Charles Mandigo, regional assistant specialist for the FBI: Seattle was going to put their mark on the world by hosting the WTO. The mayor, the city itself, was saying, "We're becoming a global force here." You've got Starbucks, you've got Microsoft, you've got Boeing, you've got Amazon coming up—they're all out front. Seattle was definitely prime time. This is going to be the cherry on the sundae. What could go wrong?

Ralph Nader: The WTO is having a meeting in Seattle—wow—we're going to really give them an experience. At Public Citizen, we were among the first to raise the banner against these trade agreements. I recruited Lori Wallach, who helped start the Citizens Trade Campaign. I saw the WTO right from the beginning as an attempt to pull down treaties. They pull down the higher standards of our country in labor, consumer rights, and the environment.

Noam Chomsky, professor at the Massachusetts Institute of Technology: In the 1990s, the few people who were paying attention to the Clinton trade agreements could see what was happening. We were writing about it, but didn't reach the general public. They weren't aware that Clinton was carrying forward Reagan's neoliberal programs in a particularly brutal way. You could see it if you looked, but who looks? I mean, who even knows, for example—even today—that NAFTA was rammed through in violation of U.S. law? The U.S. law requires that labor be consulted on any international labor agreement. They weren't. In fact, they weren't even notified until the last minute; it was all in secret. The effect of Seattle was to bring these issues to a much broader audience. Then you start getting people interested, concerned, maybe try to do something.

Maud Daudon, deputy mayor of Seattle: At first it was very exciting. This is a huge deal happening in our city and it's an important dialogue to have. It's important to talk about the issues of globalization and it felt like a significant thing for Seattle and a proud moment for the city. There'd been a series of other meetings in Seattle that were not as big as the WTO meeting but they were in the arena of international trade issues. The city was positioning itself as a hub of activity in global trade, partly because we have great ports and we were competing with other West Coast ports.

Pat Davis: Seattle is a port town. I was elected port commissioner in 1986, the first woman—shock and awe to downtown. *Laughs.* I was not from the establishment. Washington State is the only state in the union which elects its port commissioners. Trade was in so many people's lives, so many businesses, small and large, and the membership of Washington Council on International Trade wasn't just Boeing and Microsoft. It was a lot of small businesses that did trade. They were all selling abroad, to Asia particularly, and so they came on board along with the governor and other leaders of the time. In those days, Seattle was small enough that we knew each other, but it was large enough to get things done. It was just the right time.

Gary Locke, governor of Washington: We endorsed it. We were supportive of it and various units of our state government were involved in the advocacy and tangential planning. I thought it was very important that we host big-subject conferences. It's important to bring world leaders together to talk about coordination of their economies and trade with each other and trade as a way of creating jobs and lifting the lives of people.

Kim Thayil, guitarist for Soundgarden and the No WTO Combo: Seattle's always had this provincial rent-a-culture attitude, where it understands itself through the rest of the world. I had a roommate who coined the term *rent-a-culture*, and we all started using it—it was hilarious—because Seattle never really understood itself on its own terms. It saw itself often from external sources: What do people in New York say about Seattle? What do people in LA say about Seattle? What do people in London say about Seattle?

Charles R. Cross, editor of the *Rocket*: When people think of Seattle in their minds, they're often thinking of the early '90s—*Singles*, the grunge world, which was an analog world. By the time of the WTO, a transition was happening. Big companies were really becoming the drivers of the city. Boeing had been the biggest employer but by 1999, Microsoft was becoming by far the biggest economic engine in the area. There were a lot of tech workers and a lot of yuppies. Housing prices were going up dramatically. Seattle musicians who had lived in $200 or $300 apartments on Capitol Hill were now priced out of Seattle because there were a lot of developments and redevelopments that had started.

Matt Griffin, managing partner at the Pine Street Group: At the beginning of the '90s, downtown was a pretty good mess. There was a feeling that we have to launch an effort to get people back downtown and take back our city. So I was part of a team that ended up doing the three-block project that became the Pacific Place Shopping Center. Once we announced that, Nike went forward with a store and there were a bunch of other buildings that went forward, that added to the synergy, added to that momentum that we established. There were a bunch of local people that put their heart and put their money in it.

Steve Koehler, chair of the Downtown Seattle Association: There was quite a bit of resurgence at that point in time. I think a lot of major retailers came into the city as a result of that. Then it was just a matter of keeping that going.

Charles R. Cross: It was the beginning of the change from this cheap-old Seattle to a Seattle that would become pretty unaffordable. There was tension already between the artistic community and the tech over-lords. By 1999, almost all the early clubs that had been happening for grunge and many of the places that people identified with the '80s had gone out of business or been redeveloped. Seattle was an extremely business-friendly place. It felt like Bill Gates was the true mayor of Seattle.

Kim Thayil: I knew Seattle from the '80s but was gone for a lot of the '90s. It's like if you're home with a plant that you're watering every day, you may not notice it growing because it grows incrementally. But if you're gone and you come back, you know it's changed, you know that plant is not the way it was when you left. When I came back after Soundgarden broke up in '97, Seattle had changed. There were more people, it was busier, there was dysfunction. The city was going through transition. It had grown, but its sense of self hadn't seemed to have grown with it. It was a big city with a little-city attitude. The gangly kid whose pants are too short.

*　　*　　*

Lori Wallach: Mike Dolan was dispatched early to find an office. He reached out to groups to figure out who would be our core. The vision I had was that this was going to be one of those moments where the policy and the politics needed to be incredibly synergistic, or it could be catastrophic. We had to make it synergistic.

Mike Dolan: The reason for the Citizens Trade Campaign was to bring in labor, environment, human rights and faith-based groups, plus the family farmers—all the constituents that have a stake in globalization.

Lori Wallach: We created the Citizens Trade Campaign, this cross-sectoral coalition of all these groups that typically would not hang out together but rather fight each other. The entire fucking multinational corporate lobby for the first time in history is united for this goddamn trade agreement. If we don't unite with the other side, we are going to get played royally and lose.

Mike Dolan: I was the CTC's field director and what I did from '95 to '99 was build the sinews and muscles of that coalition that Lori envisioned. I had state chapters all around the country. I had to build that so that in '99, I could go to all those coalitions and say, you've got to come to Seattle.

I was involved in different pedigrees of organizing, strands from the lateral-anarchy-consensus-decision-making approach, to hierarchical-labor. Being in between those two worlds, it was like an alchemy; the whole was greater than the sum of its parts. The challenge was getting those different traditions of organizing melding and working together. I was the reviled reformist from Washington, D.C.—*laughs*—but I'm actually pretty good at reading the room.

David Solnit: There were different worldviews and different politics. Labor was trying to get a seat at the table, and we were basically saying, "Do you want to turn the table over?" The WTO's entire existence and trajectory from NAFTA is not reformable. They've shut down every opportunity for any kind of democratic, civil society participation. It exists to concentrate power, wealth, and overrule all the things we fight to protect, our communities and the planet. We were calling out capitalism and corporate globalization. We saw ourselves linked to the global anticapitalist movement with the Zapatistas and the People's Global Action.

Han Shan, program director for Ruckus Society: As privileged First World solidarity activists, a lot of us were responding to calls that have been coming from the Global South. There were people who'd been working on these issues in all these different forms for decades—you could go back hundreds of years and talk about colonialism.

Pascal Lamy: One of the arguments at the time was against forcing developing nations to renounce their own policies because it was bad: "Everybody should remain sovereign and given that we live in a global market capitalist system, the big guys are imposing rules on the small guys that basically benefit capitalism. We should not push developing countries to reduce their tariffs on things which they need to produce at home because it's good for the population. Who are you to tell me that, as a nation, my policies are good or bad?"

Of course, there is asymmetry between rich countries and poor countries in terms of the ability to draw the benefits of international division of labor, which is why we had a big principle that rich countries should open proportionately more, and give poor countries time for building capacity. When they will be developed in the future, the world will be the same for everybody, a future paradise of all countries being similarly developed.

Tetteh Hormeku: There were the African civil society expectations for Seattle and then there were the African government delegation expectations for Seattle. African civil society believed that the previous agreement should be denounced and thrown out of the window so that it did not apply. But African governments said, "Oh, no, no, no. We can't say we should throw everything out. We should say that these are our suggestions for repairing what exactly should be repaired." This African position was supported by many, many other developing countries, especially India. You might say that the majority of the developing countries were in no mood for launching a new round of negotiations in Seattle. Whereas, the U.S. and the EU, Japan, and Canada, the Quad, were very intent on expanding the WTO to cover issues, which—in everybody's conclusion—had nothing to do with trade. They wanted to cover things like an investment agreement. But issues around investments are not a question of exchange or trade among countries. It's really about a sovereign policy of government, as it pertains to foreign investment. They wanted to have a new agreement on competition policy. Again, it has nothing to do with trade. It's about the government's right to establish competition policy. Most of all, they wanted to cover government procurement under the idea that all African countries and developing countries are so corrupt that we don't do our government procurement correctly. What they really wanted was for African and developing countries to open up their government procurement for the big international corporations to be able to bid. Again, that was not the WTO's role.

Vandana Shiva: We know what *free trade* means. The first free trade agreement written was by the East India Company. It means asymmetric trade. It means extraction. It means transfer of wealth. Not only does concentration of economic power grow but military power is used to support it. I think the issues that brought people to Seattle are issues that are still the most important issues of our times.

Lori Wallach: You would expect an amazing protest in Korea, farmers against corporate trade agreements, or you expect India to have mass street protests. Even in Europe, there was still more of a direct action culture, more nonviolent civil disobedience. But for it to happen in the U.S., after all these years of really extremely subdued public movements—I didn't think that was doable. The people who get credit for that are the people in the Direct Action Network.

John Sellers, executive director of Ruckus Society: The Direct Action Network was a network of networks. It was all the individuals and organizations that wanted to take action against the WTO and shut down the ministerial. There were so many folks who turned up that the Direct Action Network became a whole bunch of affiliated collectives.

I think that lefties get pretty cannibalistic about defining "direct action." Like those super-radicals who say, "Well, your action wasn't a direct action because you weren't directly at the means of destruction and your action was highly symbolic. You just hung a banner! That's nothing. That's bullshit. Plus, when you got in jail you negotiated! You ate the Man's food! You didn't hunger strike like we did." Everybody eats each other alive about who can have the most radical definition of direct action.

For me, direct action is intervening with an injustice. I don't want to alienate anybody who's taking a risk and standing up to an injustice. I grew up in Pennsylvania, where there's Quakers so, for me, the idea of direct action is that notion of bearing witness. When you see an injustice taking place, you have a fundamental choice. You can do nothing and accept the responsibility for doing nothing, or you can act to intervene with it. Direct action, to me, it's something about putting your body out there, putting your body on the line.

Dana Schuerholz, cofounder of Art and Revolution: Direct action is the people's voices being heard when something is not in the interest of human beings, the planet, and what sustains us. Sometimes it does take the form of civil disobedience and you get arrested because you will not be silent and just go along. If stopping traffic is a way to get people to pay attention, then so be it. If we have to hang a big banner or climb on board a boat and get arrested to draw media attention, we'll do it. There are so many levels of direct action. It's really about shouting, "Wake up! Look! Listen! Pay attention!"

Hilary McQuie: The first Direct Action Network meeting was huge. We had something like two hundred people—this was by spring. And for a while it was highly local. We were sometimes going to meetings with the NGOs but the vision they had was, you know, labor and mainstream environmental groups and the trade nerds from D.C. That was what they thought was going to be the big thing. I think it started to become apparent that it was going to be a lot bigger than that because there were so many different threads.

Mike Dolan: In the Direct Action Network, I was a little bit controversial. I was a reformist, the "D.C. guy," and the Direct Action Network was on the more radical side in that continuum. They were anarchists and radicals and militants and they were suspect of my NGO credentials. That was an organizing cultural divide that I had to negotiate every single freaking week.

Lori Wallach: I learned about direct action and was radicalized by the notion that sometimes you just need to be fucking ungovernable. You must physically interrupt power. That methodology we learned from our Latin American partners. That was not where I came from. I came from a political culture of protesting to make people pay attention. That was also the Ralph Nader methodology—or you sue them. The Latin American methodology was that if you did any of those things, you may disappear. The first thing you do is fuck the place up! You start by smashing things, becoming ungovernable and scaring the living crap out of the elites so they realize they have to make settlements with you. You don't start by asking nicely. For many people around the world, there is still a very high cost to protest. Part of what led us to realize that Seattle had to be a moment was because it was, relatively speaking, safe to do it there. The likelihood that someone would be kidnapped or murdered to make examples of them, dropping someone from a helicopter, is not something we had to deal with. In so many other places, that was not the case. We felt an obligation because the U.S. had helped cause the problem of the WTO and we were in a safe place to take it down.

*   *   *

Jim Pugel, captain for the Seattle Police Department: One of the reasons I was promoted to the rank of captain in April of 1999 was because I had done work in some different parts of the city with protests. None of them had really ever amounted to anything. Perhaps a presidential visit or a scrum of people trying to get at the president or something like that, but Ed Joiner—he was my boss at the time—he said, "You're going to be in charge of the small international trade conference. We don't really know what it is but the majority of events are going to be in your precinct, so we're going to have you be the field commander." Initially we were going to have between thirty and sixty officers, which was a fair amount based on a small event. That was April. We didn't have any idea.

David Solnit: I had moved up to Seattle for about six months to help organize. I was with Art and Revolution. We trained artists and performers how to organize and we trained activists how to use art and theater. We were one of the groups that the Direct Action Network grew out of. There had been a network of radical groups around the country that had been collaborating on sweatshops, unions, environmental struggles—using art and theater. There was a network of Art and Revolution groups up and down the West Coast, friendly groups. In the Bay Area we had unions and also environmental groups that were looking at how the WTO would undermine environmental standards and protections.

Yalonda Sinde, organizer with the Community Coalition for Environmental Justice: We worked on water quality, food security, housing, all kinds of civil rights issues. There were all kinds of people involved in CCEJ, but a lot of the work was done by high school, college-age students, early twentysomething and thirtysomethings who were passionate about globalization because we saw it as a root cause of the problems we were having. The main issue was corporations—the way workers were being treated. Most—if not all—of the people who volunteered with us were low-wage workers. People saw globalization as corporate control, and they already had enough control.

Mainly our role was organizing people of color on a grassroots level, getting more of the general public educated. What is the WTO? How does it affect your life? We had a lot of teach-ins and wanted to be a visible presence, having boots on the ground. Our whole goal was to get people educated and involved in fighting globalization.

Skip Spitzer, organizer with the Direct Action Network: People were coming to the action from wherever they're coming from, arriving with needs. Even if you were coming from Seattle, you still have needs. People needed to get oriented. People needed a place to stay, people needed to know what was happening. People needed training. People needed a space to build puppets, make signs. People needed to

get around. People needed to be safe from potential raids by police—
we had all these needs.

David Solnit: We rented a warehouse at 420 Denny Way and called
it our Convergence Center. We adopted both the term *convergence*
and the language of convergence. It was big, so we had space for
everything—meetings, training sessions. The landlord didn't realize
what exactly we were doing there. We said we were a community arts
organization and said that we were going to be doing art with the
community, which is definitely part of what we did.

Jim Pugel: They rented a warehouse in Seattle, unbeknownst to us,
where they camped out, where they prepared food, prepared their
street theater—massive stuff. Costumes and everything.

Lisa Fithian, organizer with the Direct Action Network: The Convergence Center, it was the hub, the heart, the place that everyone
could come. Today's language is a lot about the culture of belonging
but that space was a culture of care. You could get food there. You
could get legal attention there. You could get medical support there.
You could get childcare support there, you could meet people. The
model of organizing that we were using in Seattle, which has a long
history in our country, was really building the culture and the relationships that are needed—and the vision and the skills—to shut down
something on a big scale.

David Taylor, organizer with the Direct Action Network: The Convergence Center was the lifeblood where everyone physically went.
This is pre-living-on-the-internet. You couldn't get a text that says,
"Come here, we're doing this." You had to go to the space to find out
what was happening.

Larry Mayes, deputy chief of the King County Sheriff's Office: From
the beginning, Mayor Schell saw this as a great opportunity for the
city, and himself, to showcase the city—how accommodating, how fair
in terms of welcoming the WTO delegates and welcoming the protesters. He stated publicly many times during the planning sessions

that he wanted to treat both groups the same, that he felt it would be a peaceful demonstration, a peaceful discourse and exchange of information and ideas between these two groups.

Maude Daudon: I was in very close contact with the police department throughout the entire planning effort. Norm Stamper was the chief at the time, and there was Ed Joiner—what an amazing human being. I just admired the way he handled himself and his composure.

Ed Joiner: I was in no way concerned because we'd had quite a number of events in Seattle over the years and they had gone off quite well. We were aware that the WTO and some of these other international organizations were a rather sensitive issue in other countries where they'd had some pretty sizable demonstrations.

David Solnit: There had been an international network of people initiated by the Zapatistas who had been doing a series of global gatherings at the G8 in Birmingham, U.K., and at the WTO in Geneva, Switzerland. I spent time in Europe where youth movements were already engaged in addressing corporate globalization, doing mobilizations around the IMF and World Bank. There were a few folks addressing it in North America but movements in Europe really got it a lot deeper than we did. Honestly, European movements are often more sophisticated, the people are, around economics. When they knocked two years off retirement in France, one million people were striking and mobilizing every week.

Norm Stamper: I was insisting on rigorous planning and Joiner, who was my deputy chief, was very good at thinking logistically and smartly. He and I had issues. Joiner gave me the hardest time as one of my assistants and yet he says that I'm the best chief he ever worked for. I thought that was really sweet.

Ron Griffin, captain for the King County Sheriff's Office: At my first meeting, Seattle PD said they were expecting 5,000 to 10,000 demonstrators. And the way they were going to handle that was to use gas. Their term was "use a lot of gas."

By spring when the sheriff's department had been brought into the planning, one of our chiefs rang the alarm bell: "Hey, this thing is coming to town. It looks big and we should get our stuff together."

Annette Sandberg, chief of Washington State Patrol: Certainly by spring we were having meetings, the federal people were involved, the FBI and all other federal law enforcement agencies, and they tried to bring everybody together—Seattle PD, county, State Patrol. It was alphabet soup, as far as all the people who were there.

We really tried to be strategic about the best way to approach the conference and the best way to approach the people who were going to be there to protest. We knew that there were going to be diverse representatives there. How do we make that happen so that everybody will be able to participate yet, at the same time, make sure that the conference is able to convene?

The State Patrol, we stayed out of the middle of it initially and just watched. It was supposed to be Seattle Police's show. Obviously, there was some federal involvement just because of the State Department and the people that were coming in for the conference, the president. But the security itself was supposed to be the responsibility of the city. They said, "Hey, we got it. We'll call you if we need help. Be ready. But you sit out there." And that's kind of what we did.

Ron Griffin: It was April and I am fat, dumb, and happy in my office, when the chief calls me and says, "Hey, Ron, I want you to take this role in putting together civil response teams." That's what they were called at the time. The name of the team has changed several times, trying to find the political proper mix. It used to be the "riot squad" back in the day.

I was directed to meet with the Seattle Police Department, bi-weekly meetings. Right away the understanding was that a fair number of protesters were starting to circulate on the internet, which was nothing like we have today.

Maude Daudon: It was the first time the internet could be used as an organizing device. You had people from all over the world preparing to come to Seattle.

Pam Schell: We didn't realize how many people were coming from out of town. We began to talk to relatives who said, "Oh, my nephew, who we never saw for the last ten years, has suddenly asked if he can come stay with me." All these young students came from Eugene to protest, and a whole smarter group of people than the city had ever dealt with before.

John Sellers: We had some of the best online ride boards and house-sharing boards that had ever been tried. We were preparing to get 10,000 people to the city—and accommodations after they arrived.

David Taylor: I knew a little bit about tech, so I put a lot of energy into the digital presence. This was a very early point of that world, way before Twitter. This was when email and LISTSERVs were pretty innovative tactics.

When I built the website for the Direct Action Network—I forget what it was, it was a URL that was ten miles long—mostly what I did was take the work that other organizers were doing and created a lot of the outreach materials. I basically transcribed all of it and built that out into a website, and took all of the information we were getting on logistics and how to plug in and getting those things up on LIST-SERVs.

Yalonda Sinde: The internet was a big part of our organizing but we didn't have Zoom and all that. It was a lot through emails. We were able to reach more people that way and educate them.

John Sellers: The Ruckus Society became the training hub for a lot of the direct action movement. Ruckus wasn't a campaigning organization; we were a training organization that was functioning as a freelance action team.

Nina Narelle, organizer with the Direct Action Network: Ruckus was really small, ragtag, mostly white, mostly folks who came out of the environmental movement. After Greenpeace shut down their direct action campaign in the United States, a bunch of those people said, "We need another way to become trained activists." We would travel around and do these pop-up camps for different campaigns or organizations and teach them things like direct action but also campaign strategies, media strategies, having a police liaison, how to use a police scanner, how to use two-way radios.

John Sellers: Ruckus Society existed as its own organization next to the Direct Action Network, but we certainly interfaced with it and had representation there. We were represented in the spokescouncil.

The spokescouncil model was adopted from longtime successful models of organizing coming out of the Spanish Civil War, the *grupos de afinidad*. The Direct Action Network had chosen a *grupos de afinidad*—or "affinity group"—structure in order to make concrete, coordinated plans for shutting down the WTO meetings.

Skip Spitzer: The idea is that anybody in an affinity group can sit behind their spokesperson at a spokescouncil meeting, usually at the Convergence Center, and they can pass notes or make comments to their spokesperson—they can still be involved in the process. It's a representative form of decision-making.

Nina Narelle: Each affinity group varied in size, maybe ten to twenty people on average. Each group was made up of people who were committed to staying together, looking out for each other—it's a group of people who establish high relational trust before they go protest together. It has a couple functions. One, you do your best to always stick with those people; you're not alone in a crowd, which can be really scary and, in some cases, dangerous. Usually, affinity groups will negotiate before they protest and find alignment about what kind of experience they are hoping to have. An affinity group might be like, "We are all planning to bring our children, snacks, water bottles and if it gets crazy, we're all out right away." Another affinity group might say, "We're open to getting arrested today. If that happens, we've got someone at home, we all have that phone number on our arms and we have a plan so that if we end up in jail, we can communicate that to people we care about. We have time off from our jobs figured out in advance." Another affinity group might say, "We are planning to lock our necks to this bridge with a bike lock and we are not leaving until they saw it off." Within the affinity group, depending on what you're planning to do, there are really specific roles. There will be one person responsible for keeping an eye on health and safety for the group. Someone will talk to the media.

Kevin Danaher, cofounder of Global Exchange: What we recommended was to try to have the members of the affinity group be people that you did LSD with or got really stoned with or really drunk with—you know who they are. A lot of it is about trust. If you've got twenty people circling a limousine locking arms and sitting down, there is a chance that limousine driver might decide to run you over. You've got to really trust the people that you're with.

David Taylor: Hundreds of people could be in the spokescouncil meetings. It was crucial for us to have these highly trained facilitators that could manage these processes—it's not a mild thing. We had some amazing facilitators, Nadine Bloch and Lisa Fithian and all of those people who had been doing this in the antinuclear movement and in earlier movements, they had the long-running skills to manage these processes, the group decision-making within a decentralized manner.

Lisa Fithian: We were doing nonviolent, direct action training. How to mentally prepare, emotionally prepare, physically prepare. At the Convergence Center, we would often get people into small group work. There's also a lot of physicality to it, practicing blockades, practicing role plays of civil disobedience, having the police come on you, practicing marches. It's putting people in the experience of doing something that's very dynamic so that they can, one, see how their body's responding and, two, think through in advance how you might want to be in these situations and how you and your crew best prepare.

four waters: Nobody was the boss. That's not an insignificant thing. It's a pretty remarkable thing. We sat in a circle and we had consensus about how we were going to deal with things and these were difficult things. The idea that you would have a conversation with so many people and be able to move forward is insane but we did it. I feel like that needs to be said.

Skip Spitzer: Consensus process, at first glance seems like it could be a process that could either take forever, or run into the problem of not getting unanimous agreement from everybody. Those things notwithstanding, the United Nations, when it's coming up with an agreement or a treaty, that's all done by consensus. It's a process of going through proposals. It's not about trying to find an idea or a decision that everybody thinks is good; it's about finding an idea that everybody can accept. It emphasizes hearing what people don't like about it, and you can express those concerns on a spectrum, all the way up to "this violates core principles that I believe in and I, under no circumstances, can support it"—and everything in the middle. By identifying those concerns, you're often able to revise a proposal in such a way that it becomes acceptable to everybody. You have a clear decision that everybody felt like they're part of. Everybody has a sense of ownership, and nobody objects to the point that they're not willing to support, as opposed to, say, a majority rule process where you literally have close to fifty percent of people involved in the process tremendously unhappy with the decision. Consensus is the ability to create a broad sense of ownership and to include as many voices as you can elicit in that process. It gives great power to people trying to make the world better.

Lisa Fithian: These alternative models and processes that we use are one of the ways we get outside of the dominant culture in this country, the sort of white supremacists, hierarchical, top-down—all that stuff. When people get a taste of that, it's like, "Oh, there's another way to do things. We don't have to just elect somebody and have them tell us what to do." We have not only a practice but also a language for reclaiming power as an active person in the world, as a decision-maker who can collectively make decisions about how they'll put themselves in a protest, or what will happen to their bodies on that day, how they'll work with other people. It's a refreshing and liberating way of being because that's not what we normally get.

four waters: Because so many of the organizers had been working together before Seattle, I think there was a lot of cohesion in a way that would not have happened otherwise. That doesn't mean that we all got along. It doesn't mean that we all agreed. There were conflicts but there was cohesion and unified understanding and a unified goal.

Nadine Bloch, facilitator with Ruckus Society: We had taken a map of the city and divided it into pie wedges identifying who was going to blockade which key intersection.

Nina Narelle: If you were in an affinity group that volunteered to be in wedge X, for example, one person from your affinity group would sit in the spokescouncil and negotiate what was going to happen in that wedge of the city and how the blockades were going to be set up.

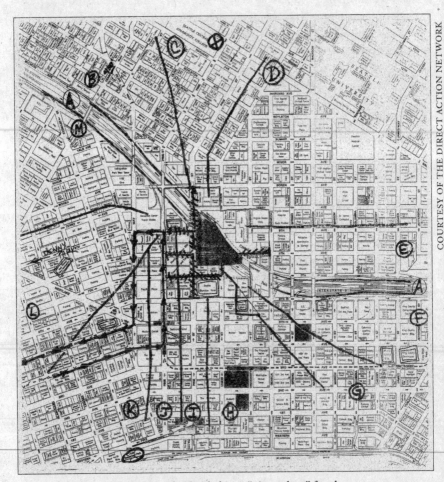

A map of Seattle, divided into "pie wedges" for the purposes of blocking access to the WTO ministerial.

Kevin Danaher: I went into the Seattle Convention Center months ahead of the conference in a nice suit and I said to them, "My trade organization is thinking of renting this building for a big conference. Could I have the floor plans so we know how to plan our event?" *Laughs.* We knew exactly where all the entrances were. There were thirteen intersections around the convention hall that we needed to block in order to make it successful. We had guys dressed as bike messengers that were taking photographs of all the intersections and all the doorways and we used those photographs in the planning sessions so that everybody knew ahead of time who was in charge of what intersection and we made sure that there were enough people out there to block that intersection.

Hilary McQuie: There were just so many particulars in Seattle—the geography of the city itself, how small the center is. Capitol Hill created this barrier on one side, the water on the other side, and that made it really easy to shut down the meeting. That was pretty rare.

Celia Alario: Because of the one-way streets and the tightness of downtown and a bunch of other factors, taking all the intersections, that would probably never work in another city.

John Nichols: The people who decided to locate the WTO in Seattle made a terrible geographical mistake. Downtown is sort of a punch bowl. You've got the hills coming down, and then you've got that center of the city there. By its nature, it's actually a very small area in which protests were going to occur and the ministerial itself was going to occur. Unless the police could keep all of the protesters out of that area, lock it down completely, there was going to be a confrontation. There was going to be an intensity.

David Taylor: The framework was very straightforward, which was, we're going to try and identify enough affinity groups beforehand, get them assigned to take on different areas so we can encircle the convention center and do a blockade. It was a very, very tactically focus. We were going to do that and hope that the mass mobilization support of labor and what students were doing would support the lockdown and that everything would flow together naturally.

Lisa Fithian: We'd set people up to go do scouting to figure out where they wanted to do their blockade and come back to the spokescouncil meeting. The spokescouncil process would always be figuring out which affinity groups are doing what, getting a sense of the numbers, figuring out which pie slices on the map were getting adopted, and with how many people, more or less, so that other people had the benefit of knowing where there were gaps. The whole process of the spokescouncil was making sure that we were getting the coverage that we needed to be successful. You might have five, ten, fifteen different affinity groups who have a plan in the same slice, so that they could then coordinate together to make sure they wouldn't trip each other up.

Nadine Boch: We let affinity groups make autonomous decisions so then even if some of us were infiltrated, the hope was that not all of us were infiltrated.

Jim Pugel: We have a unique ordinance within the city of Seattle that's called the Investigations Ordinance. It restricts the collection of information based on a person's political ideology, religion, or sexual orientation. Since this was seen as a political event, we were very hampered within the city limits in gathering much information. All we could do was get open-source information. The internet back then was pretty primitive.

David Reichert, King County sheriff: We did infiltrate some of the groups. The Seattle Police Department had very constricted parameters placed around the ability of their intelligence unit to gather info but we had an intelligence unit that could operate under the county ordinance of collecting intelligence.

My intelligence unit notified me that they had information that there were going to be some riots during the WTO. Yes, most of the organizations involved were there for peaceful protests but we had information that anarchists from Oregon, specifically Eugene, were going to be making their way up to Seattle and cause problems within the peaceful protest. We had information that there would be some vandalism and destruction of property. Technically we were not allowed to share that information. However, we did find a legal avenue where we could maneuver that information into the Seattle Police Department.

Kevin Danaher: We had internal meetings in buildings where a team of electronics guys would go through and scan the rooms for any listening devices. That's how cautious we were about not having infiltrators.

David Reichert: Any time that you're gathering information on U.S. citizens, you have to really follow the law very strictly. Our team knew that. We were following the guidelines of the King County ordinance, which was strictly within the guidelines of our constitution.

We had at least one person who was able to, I would say, become a member of the group—who was able to get close enough to the anarchist group when they arrived in Seattle.

I did this a little bit during the Green River Killer case, years later—this was a pretty gruesome serial killer: forty-nine confirmed victims, mostly vulnerable females. For that case, if I wanted to interview people on the street, pimps, prostitutes, drug dealers, alcoholics, and homeless people, I would dress in very sloppy clothes, have a few drinks—so there's alcohol on my breath. Maybe douse some alcohol on my clothes. I'd stand in a soup line and just listen to the chatter. If there's a person there that I may have recognized from previous visits to prostitution areas, I may grab my bowl of soup and sit down next to that person and casually start up a conversation about his life, where they were from, how they survive. Then working around to, "Hey, have you heard about the Green River Killer?" That sort of thing.

A person working intel has to dress in a way where a group wouldn't be suspicious, maybe have a beard, maybe be a little unkempt. Or maybe they need to look more like a college student or whatever environment they're trying to get next to. *Infiltrate* might be a strong word. It's just a way to create this association with a person to where they feel comfortable enough to share and talk freely about some of their activities.

Kevin Danaher: There was an evening when we were hanging around having some drinks, smoking some joints, about four or five of us—this was still months before the protests. And this old white guy comes up and says, "You know what we should do at the WTO? We should get guns and shoot the first motherfucker in a limousine that we see!" Everybody just drifted away from him. He was not one of us.

Lisa Fithian: You can do closed organizing and think you're secure but, no, you're not. The way we built some security into the mix was that it wasn't like anyone knew, centrally, who was doing what, where, or exactly when. The only thing that everyone knew was that on the first morning of the WTO meetings, all the groups were going to deploy to wherever they were deploying to, whether it was a lockdown or whatever—boom.

Mike Dolan: I started meeting with the cops to get permits. I'm the Tom Hayden guy, trying to get the permits. *Laughs.* As opposed to the Abbie Hoffman types, Han Shan, John Sellers: "We don't need no freaking permits!" We had our own version of the Chicago Seven going, and so my relationship with the mayor's office, with the city, with the cops started early. And I have to say it was a really good relationship with Laurie Brown.

Laurie Brown, special assistant to Mayor Paul Schell: Mike Dolan is an interesting character. I met him in the months leading up to the protests, when the mayor asked me to get involved in the dialogue between the city and the demonstrators—in part because of my background in labor.

I spent roughly fifteen years as a union organizer. I had quit high school in my junior year to hitchhike out west. I hopped on freight trains. I was a straight-A student but was a hippie and involved with left politics and decided that school wasn't relevant for me. My mom was a single mom at that point in time. My dad had committed suicide when I was thirteen. She told me, "You know what's best."

When Paul Schell was running for mayor, I was watching him on TV. He had a lot of information wrong about city employees and I was representing city employees at the time. He didn't know what he was talking about—not philosophically, I was very taken with him philosophically, in terms of his values and his attitude towards city employees and workers in general—but he just didn't have the facts right.

I called his campaign and introduced myself and said, "This is me as an individual, not me representing the coalition of unions. I'm happy to sit down with a staff person and give some background information so that Paul can be better prepared when he's asked questions regarding certain city policies that impact employees."

They called me back and said, "Paul wants to have coffee with you." It was a really exciting meeting and he ended up offering me a job four times and I turned it down four times because I had no interest in working in an elected official's office. I was really happy doing my union work. But finally, I was convinced that it was an opportunity. Paul definitely opened a door for me. I loved Paul. I remained friends with him until his death. He had a certain amount of wealth but he was not pretentious. He was loyal. He was incredibly smart. He was a very savvy businessperson. He was not a savvy politician and I honestly don't think that he enjoyed it. He didn't have a lot of patience for the political gamesmanship, which served him well at times and other times, well, it was the reason he didn't become a career politician. He was just a real person. It was a great environment to work in. He would have all the staff over to his waterfront property and have barbecues.

Pam Schell: We loved Seattle. We chose it. We came from New York for a small city. He thought of it as being the Boston of the West, that it's restrained and a lovely city. He loved Seattle. He loved the employees. He got up in the morning at six to leave. He'd be walking around the office before people had come to their desks, so that they knew that he was totally engaged, and the morale was really good.

Ron Judd: Paul Schell was a friend of mine. He was a port commissioner for years. I did a lot of union collective bargaining and organizing in the maritime side and Paul was a huge supporter of ours as the port commissioner and that's one of the reasons why we supported him as mayor.

Before the WTO protests, I suggested we start having dialogue about the intensity on the street and how things are like powder kegs. We were meeting with the city once a month. It was controversial but we tried so hard to say up front, "We don't want to surprise anybody. We're going to be doing major protests."

Many people on the other side were dear personal friends. Maud

Daudon was a dear friend. We were very involved in electoral politics. Those relationships helped with communication.

Maud Daudon: Paul was very reluctant to be viewed as a hard-liner against protesters. I also think on the flip side he was very excited and supportive of the business community's interest in doing something that would put Seattle in this global position. He used to talk about his vision for Seattle as sort of the Geneva of America, that it was a place where people could convene and have big discussions and talk about the future. To find that right path between globalization and job preservation he had an ideology around inclusiveness. He saw this future for Seattle kind of like the Emerald City, this beautiful place where you could have disagreement and dissonance and yet get to something harmonious and good for everybody.

Laurie Brown: Paul, himself, and most people in his office were all very liberal and progressive. They participated in various demonstrations themselves in their youth. Some of them were quite youthful even in the mayor's office. It was a group of idealists who believed that protesting should be able to happen.

Charles Mandigo: They made no allowance for security. Particularly, there was no funding and that put limitations on the Seattle Police Department and their ability to do pre-exercises, consultants, planning—all that kind of stuff. Having said that, the attitude in Seattle PD was they had prior experience with demonstrations. They said, "Hey, we've had these before. We know how to do it. We meet with the demonstrating participants. We work out the agreements in advance, the protocol, who's going to do what." The PD basically said, "We already have our plans in place. We're not going to change our plans."

Jim Pugel: I was a political science major and I'd studied one of the biggest labor protests ever, the Wobblies back in the early 1900s in Seattle and San Francisco and Oakland. That was the last really big kick-ass one that Seattle had experienced.

Maude Daudon: Seattle had a strong history of demonstrations.

Jim Pugel: In Seattle, we were always taught to go out and meet with the protest organizers, see what they want their message to be. Before the WTO there'd been protests about human rights in China, at the Chinese consulate, and they wanted to break some ceramic things. We said, "Okay, cool. But let us put down a tarp the color of the street so it looks like it's street still. Then you can break your stuff and we can just roll it up real quick and get traffic going." So that's how we would work with these folks.

Ed Joiner: I think that's one of the reasons that Seattle got the bid in the first place, the fact that we had a reputation for being able to have protests—even sensitive ones—and not have any real conflict.

David Solnit: Once we had locked in how we wanted to do things, we approached NGOs like the Rainforest Action Network, Global Exchange, Mike Dolan at Public Citizen. My experience working with NGOs is that they have a hierarchical way of operating, so we wanted to lock in our affinity group model before we went to these NGOs. There was creative tension.

Mike Dolan: Remember, I was the NGO guy. Fortunately, I'm going to bed every night after a couple of games of pool and some beers with one of the main anarchists! Ruby, my kid, is in fact the love child of the Battle in Seattle.

Celia Alario: There was more than one love child that came out of Seattle—I think I know of at least a dozen.

Hilary McQuie: I met Mike when I was ten years old. He was my older brother's good friend. I've known him forever. We were friendly. He hit on me a couple of times when I was younger. *Laughs.* I wasn't interested. When he came to Seattle, he really was an important instigator of things—I'll give him that. He had that East Coast energy, which after living in Seattle for a while, I really appreciated because Seattle men are super boring.

Mike Dolan: She was my direct action mama! She was a pagan and anarchist and awesome. We were together that whole year. That connection led to Ruby but also allowed her to know about what the reviled reformists like me were doing and it allowed me to know what was up—and what the needs were—with the Direct Action Network. That was a real symbiotic and romantic aspect.

Hilary McQuie: With Michael, we had good communication. Some of those groups that were NGOs understood the direct action world but I think for the most part that labor and the NGOs really underestimated us. But there was communication for sure—and we were organizing openly. We weren't trying to hide what we were doing. We told the cops we were going to shut down the meeting.

Kevin Danaher: Our principle of unity was that we were going to nonviolently try to shut them down. It wasn't asking for reform, it was abolition. We abolished slavery. We abolished prohibition on women voting. We abolished certain civil rights abuses. These institutions need to be abolished. They are bad institutions. But the protesting conduct has to be nonviolent.

Denis Moynihan, media liaison for the Independent Media Center: There were two goals, actually. One was to shut down the ministerial, and one was to make "the WTO" a household phrase.

*   *   *

Mike Dolan: When I wasn't in Seattle, I was in other places in the country saying, "Come to Seattle!" Let me give you an example:

I was on the road outside of Phoenix, talking to some of these United We Stand, America Reform Party Perot-tista types—we're having pie at Denny's. And their critique was always "Big government, big government." This was their boogeyman. I said, "Look, actually, big government is not the enemy. If you really want to dig down, it's the small focal shift. The enemy, actually, is big transnational corporations who are *buying* governments. These governments are really following an agenda that is dictated to them by large corporations. There's something wrong with our democracy there."

When you see somebody sitting across the Denny's table make that small focal shift, it's like scales falling off their eyes. It's a certain epiphany to realize that our common interests on behalf of local control, labor rights, wages, consumer protection—whatever it is, we've identified some issues that we share in common that are part of globalization. But let's identify correctly who the enemies are.

Eating pie at Denny's outside of Phoenix with those cats—that's what I live to do. Having those conversations and making those mobilizations. People can remove, just for a minute, the media-driven polarization and see underneath that shtick, underneath that narrative, there is actually work that we can do together.

David Solnit: We did a "Stop the WTO" road show. We were trying to figure out how to explain corporate globalization and the WTO to ordinary people in a way that didn't sound like a college economics lecture. We created a street theater performance using puppets and music to tell the story of the WTO.

I came out of the antiwar movement when they brought draft registration back in the '70s. I had also organized in the '80s and I learned how to make puppets and started rethinking how we did demonstrations. I wanted to make them more participatory theater with artmaking. That percolated for me through the late '80s and into the '90s.

In the mid-'90s, I brought puppetry to active resistance and into Art and Revolution. It was a different language. There was big inspiration from the Zapatistas, who were a movement that didn't have boring leftist manifestos. They actually used poetry and had a sense of theater and spectacle.

Dana Schuerholz: The purpose of the artist is to shift cultural norms, shift conversations, and inspire people to feel and take notice and open their eyes whether it's through photographs or puppets or street theater. It's one thing to stand in streets and block traffic and say, "Stop the war!" That is totally important but it's also important to have different ways to reach people's hearts. Puppets transcend the frame of a human being. They're larger than life. In that way, they allow us to transcend for a moment. We have to feel something when we see this art in the streets. Taking art out of museums and galleries is essential. Puppetry inspires us to think outside of reality and dream about what is possible. It's fun and funny and gets people's attention.

Nadine Bloch: I'm an artist too. I've built giant puppets like Solnit does and I walk on stilts. I train people to do all kinds of crazy shit. In Seattle, there was a real emphasis on taking inspiration from the Global South and the Zapatistas and a lot of the other movements from the world to incorporate the artistic pieces that could really bring joy into the revolution. Make the space more enticing and interesting to people and really celebrate another world which we thought was not only possible but essential.

Lisa Fithian: The direct action element always brings the energy, attracts young people, but it is also the primary way in which we're building culture. Because all of these movements have to have culture—the songs, the music, the visuals. Culture's life. And we're dealing with a culture of death in the U.S. We need to have an alternative. So, we were embodying a culture of life.

Kevin Danaher: I started going out to college campuses and I would start by saying, "How many people here were at Woodstock in 1969?" I would put my hand up and say, "Oh, I'm the only one? Oh, that's right, you're too young." *Laughs.* "But there's something coming that's going to be even better than Woodstock—the WTO protest in Seattle," and I'd get them all fired up. People understood that the WTO was writing a constitution for the planet and the only interests at the table were corporate interests.

David Solnit: An organizer named Chie Abad joined us on the road show. She had been working in a sweatshop and had her life threatened when she tried to organize a union.

Chie Abad, organizer with Global Exchange: I worked in Saipan. I came from the Philippines to grow, earn more money. In Saipan, clothes are made, they use the label "Made in the USA" but the conditions are worse. We used to work more than fourteen hours a day in a bad situation. It's only $3.15 an hour. When we do overnight work, they fed us only with a cup of noodle soup.

All the factories were affected. We had limited bathroom break, we have to finish a certain quantity of work per hour, and you cannot be pregnant—they fire you. We have to pay the housing. They call these barracks. The barracks look like a shanty. When it rains, it pours. No hot water. And the room is squalid. It's only bed space. Like double bunk space, triple bunk space.

I started organizing a movement in Saipan. I wore undercover video camera, filming the condition of the workers. It was a very tiny camera. The lens of the camera is as big as a point of a ballpen. I put it in the bottom hole of the colored T-shirt. Then the recorder attached to the waistline of my short pants. I feel very confident because I told myself that this is it. I can do whatever I can do to expose everything that's going on here.

I was already out of Saipan when they put it on the television. I didn't tell everybody that I'm leaving Saipan. I just keep quiet—that's it.

I came to the U.S. for the first time in 1999. I saw there's lots of homeless people. It surprised me because people always talk about the U.S. being very rich—the glory of the United States.

Global Exchange is first to get me here in the States. They petitioned me to be one of their staff. Medea Benjamin did everything, give me documentation—Medea's like my mom. I don't have relatives here in the states. Only she. I used to live with her for six months without paying anything. She fed me even though I'm receiving a salary. She said "Keep it, Chie. When you move out of this house, you need three months to pay deposit, security deposit." She took really good care of me.

We filed the one-billion-dollar class-action lawsuit against all the leading brand names here in the States. They closed almost all the garment factories in Saipan and moved them to China or other countries.

David Solnit: Chie would tell her story and she would do it as part of our street theater. We had cardboard sewing machines, songs, puppets of the WTO holding the earth in one hand and a fork in the other. We traveled all the way from Santa Cruz to Vancouver, B.C. We would usually follow the performance with a workshop on nonviolent, direct actions and also on street theater, how to make puppets and art. A lot of groups were mobilizing by having a group of people come to your town, do a performance, invite everyone and follow it up with training.

NGOs and labor were also mobilizing. Although not always on the same page completely, we were complementary.

Ron Judd: I was going around the country and talking and teaching and writing about union cities and union communities. Union cities equal union communities.

Part of my role in the AFL-CIO was building community coalitions. Me and about five other more progressive leaders at the local level were building power, not just through unions and organizing but through coalition building. There was a big transitional moment to pivot more towards grassroots organizing. WTO fit right into that.

Jim Hightower, host of *Hightower's Radio Lowdown*: I had been one of the first progressive forces, media-wise, to be talking about this issue. I can't remember how many shows we did on the WTO that year. I knew the American people would be shocked if they knew what it entailed and how much sovereignty it was taking from us.

Ralph Nader: With these global agreements, disputes are outside national jurisdictions. That should be a violation of our Constitution. How can we have a country take us to the World Trade Organization in Geneva for a closed-door judiciary procedure? If we lose, the appeal is internal so it's a rubber-stamp appeal within the WTO. That's the way the corporations have tailored judiciary. You don't have standing, you're just a citizen.

Celia Alario: People were saying, "In our little town of Burlington, Vermont, we are not going to let any company that uses sweatshop labor have a storefront on our main street." Or, "On our college campus, if you are a pizza company and you are known for doing bad things, we're not going to let you in our cafeteria." That kind of proactive methodology, like a policy that incentivizes small businesses for women of color.

Now here come global agreements from the WTO and it's clear it's a horrible blueprint to strip us of those powers, to take away that agency that we have as the little town or county—or the U.S. government—to make these choices on behalf of good things in the world and make choices against the bad things of the world.

Nick Licata: I got resolutions passed before the WTO came to the city. One was basically expressing our ability to regulate laws, environmental and labor laws. People were willing to go along with that. It passed unanimously. I had focused in on how the WTO could ignore or over-run or overrule local environmental protection legislation. That struck a responsive chord amongst all the council members. They were very concerned about local control of the Seattle environment.

Chie Abad: I kept on talking to universities and colleges and schools. We tried to get cities to sign up with the "sweat-free" movement. The schools, government offices, the fire department, and the police department procured their clothing with the cheap labor. But it should be sweat-free. The police uniforms, and even the flags that they fly over the public schools and public office buildings should be sweat-free. And the hospital gowns that they use in public hospitals, it should be sweat-free. Because all procurement is millions and millions of dollars. I am one of the organizers of this movement. Seattle was the beginning.

Lori Wallach: The U.S. was the mother ship of neoliberalism. They had gotten a lot of other countries to follow along, but if we could show that people in the United States, in the belly of the beast, said "no" to this version of globalization, the *human beings*—not the military, not the corporations, not trade negotiators—but the people, if we could say no then that would have an incredibly powerful enzymatic effect on the fight inside the WTO negotiating suites during the ministerial. That's value-added to what was going to happen behind closed doors.

Ron Judd: We wanted to make a statement to the world that people should pay attention to these agreements. There are policy implications that will affect potentially every man, woman, and child on the planet and they do these deals behind closed doors with very little transparency about it. When you dig deep into the prioritization of those decisions, it comes down to capitalism and not community and not the interest of the planet. We needed to have a dialogue in Seattle so the rest of the world starts paying attention. That was our underlying mantra.

Mike Dolan: The unions that were part of the Citizens Trade Campaign in those days included the steelworkers, included the Teamsters, the International Association of Machinists—all these unions were already part of the civil society critique of NAFTA and the WTO. The AFL-CIO is a federation and you have to approach them differently. You have to go through Judd, the guy on the ground in Seattle.

So Judd goes to D.C. and literally sits outside John Sweeney's office—the president of the AFL-CIO—until he'll meet with him. He told me about this later, how hard it was to get an audience with Sweeney to make the case for a larger labor mobilization. Ron Judd was crucial.

Ron Judd: A few of the unions within AFL-CIO were comfortable with getting in the streets but the D.C. leadership had this inside strategy, lobbying and trying to engage policymakers directly. But I'm a street heat organizer. I wanted to know how we could put pressure in the streets so that when you try to have a conversation inside the WTO, something has changed, it's a different dynamic. It took a while for some of them to get their brain around what I was talking about. Some unions were well ahead of me and some unions are more conservative. It's just the nature of a big organization like the AFL-CIO. I tried to connect with every type of personality. Whenever anyone said to me, "Well, we'd like to keep the action on the inside, working the delegates," I would say, "Yes, absolutely. But wouldn't you also like to have some muscle and voice on the outside to support that?"

David Solnit: The national labor leadership was not down with the Direct Action Network but Ron Judd, who had a background in environmentalism and direct action, was actually working well with us and being supportive.

The city that mobilized perhaps the most people for the Direct Action Network was Portland—the longshoremen, steelworkers as well.

Nina Narelle: As the momentum and coalition building was happening, I spent several months living in a car traveling around helping people organize momentum towards the protests and teaching people about direct action so that they could teach other people about direct action and build a groundswell momentum.

Victor Menotti: I was working with the International Forum on Globalization, which was doing public education on the WTO. We had already done some of our flagship teach-ins in New York and Washington and a few other places. So I got involved in engaging everyday people about the WTO and what it would be deciding that was going to change your life.

Colin Hines: The IFG teach-ins were very exciting, charged events. We always had a very large number of speakers but we kept them to five or ten minutes at the most. Predominantly, we tried to do focused aspects of the problem of globalization. People explained the adverse effects on America, the adverse effects on Europe, and then said something about what we ought to do. Martin Khor would speak about what was happening in Asia. Vandana Shiva would talk about what was happening with seeds and foods in India. We had to move to bigger venues because people were hungry to know. They knew that globalization wasn't good but it was big and complicated. We were not only giving them information but the confidence of being in a big group. "Hey, it's not just my little group in one town. There's a lot of people here."

Vandana Shiva: Before IFG, I organized the farmers of India because in 1984, Punjab erupted in violence. The city of Bhopal had a disaster when a pesticide plant owned by Union Carbide leaked. I was compelled to pay attention to why so many people were dying. What are we doing in agriculture that requires these pesticides that push farmers into death?

In the U.S. you are two percent farmers. In India we still have nearly sixty percent farmers. Agriculture's too important to be put into a free trade agreement and seeds are not inventions and shouldn't be patented. So, we were mobilizing against WTO and our rallies used to be 200,000 to 500,000.

I got invited to this discussion on what new biotechnologies would mean for the world, for the environment, for farming, for health. The chemical industry was there. They said, "Our future profits lie in seed patents and owning and patenting seed. To do that we have to adopt tools of genetic engineering. But it's not enough that we have patents in rich countries in the North—most farmers are in the South—we have to have a global regime of intellectual property, IP." This is what became the trade-related intellectual property rights issue. I was following this from 1987 onwards. Many of us from different parts of the world were looking at what was going on in this free trade agreement which had been called "the new constitution of the world."

Celia Alario: We were laying out all the things that we already knew were problematic, the things we'd already seen, listening at these teach-ins, watching Lori Wallach throw the NAFTA book around. She was sort of famous for that. She would show up with this big giant book and she would gesticulate wildly and end up throwing it around on the stage.

Lori Wallach: It wasn't NAFTA text—it was the text of the WTO. I threw it off the stage.

Celia Alario: She was really helpful at making this stuff understandable, really boiling it down for all of us when it could seem like a bunch of mumbo jumbo.

Lori Wallach: I'm famous for coming up with the Dracula strategy: dragging everything into sunshine. Basically, what I would say is, "Friends, this is a text that was written to be entirely impenetrable, but here is a dirty little secret: most of this is not about trade. Yes, there are some tariff cuts but, frankly, what they're talking about for Seattle and what most of the chapters of the WTO proposed agreements are about is a slow-motion coup d'état against democratic governance. This is twenty different agreements of one-size-fits-all crazy corporate neoliberalism. Democracy is thrown under the bus. Imposed rule."

People would start to laugh, and I would say, "No, seriously! It implores every country to have a twenty-year monopoly for big pharma. Or let's talk about food safety. Remember how we banned DDT thirty-five years ago? The WTO requires us to use the food rules of the Codex Alimentarius. 'What the hell is that,' you ask? Well, get the barf bag ready because that is an agreement that basically requires that every country allow imports of food with pesticides we've long banned. Yes, ladies and gentlemen, DDT will be back. They think if they write it out in trade language, they'll get away with imposing all the stuff that has nothing to do with trade but is going to ruin our lives."

I would go through these concrete examples that had to do with schools, tax dollars, jobs and tell them that this is a con job. I am a recovering trade attorney. I can translate this shit for you and it's not very complicated. My value-add to this whole movement was being a Harvard-trained wonk—I really actually know what all this technical shit means. Also, I have some basic instincts about what is compelling and how to communicate, in part from working in television news. You've got ninety seconds, if you're lucky. So I would tell everyone, "This is a bunch of corporations, behind closed doors with fancy language, basically rigging these rules to get their way over you. It's corporate enforceable governance. There are sanctions in place if you don't change your domestic laws. Who the hell elected these people? These rules did not come down from Mount Sinai like the Ten Commandments. It's just a slow-motion coup d'état."

People realized, "Oh my god, I'm getting fucked with my pants on!" The crowd would be riled up and go, "That sucks!"

I'd say, "Who wants something different?"

They'd chant, "Different!"

I'd be like, "Okay, let's get rid of this," and I would Frisbee the text.

* * *

Yalonda Sinde: You know, organizers are really very serious, skilled people. It was not something you just jumped into without training, without knowing the strategies. We would look at the chain of decision-making on a particular problem to see who we would target in terms of pressure and demonstrations or letter writing. We tried all kinds of tactics, borrowing a lot from the civil rights movement as an example of how to make social change and policy.

My dad was a Black Panther. We were around people who had been mentored by people in civil rights, marched with César Chávez. At that time, it was even more dangerous, when the police would really shoot you at a protest. They weren't shooting rubber bullets in the '60s and '70s—they were killing.

Elmer Dixon, senior consultant for Executive Diversity Services: In '67 Stokely Carmichael came to Seattle. He was the national spokesperson and chairman of SNCC, the Student Nonviolent Coordinating Committee. Stokely spoke at our high school, Garfield High School, and it was packed with black young people from all over the city. As he had done across the country, he ignited a new flame in us. It was the birth of the Black Power movement, which was different from the civil rights movement. It was taking it to a different level. That's the place where most of us got our consciousness and awareness of who we were and what the struggle was about.

I joined SNCC and became the cochair that fall. I and a few of my buddies started the first high school Black Student Union on the West Coast. The following spring, we were asked to help Franklin High School organize a Black Student Union because they were being mistreated. I was a senior in high school and I went with Aaron, my brother, and met with the students. We immediately marched across the street, took over the principal's office, kicked everybody out, and took over the school. The next day they called and said that they could have a BSU.

Days later, we were arrested. I was in my geometry class. I went to the juvenile hall. When I got there, the TV was blaring that King had just been assassinated. A couple of nights later my brother and I snuck through a back door and went to a secluded and exclusive golf club community and burned a big "BP" on the thirteenth hole.

A couple days after that, we attended the West Coast Conference of Black Student Unions at San Francisco State University, where the keynote speaker that night was none other than Bobby Seale of the Black Panther Party. After he gave the most fiery speech that we had ever heard, we made a beeline to Chairman Bobby Seale and said, "We want to start a chapter of the Black Panther Party."

Aaron Dixon, Central House founder: Bobby Seale came to Seattle and met with us, along with other Panther officials. He met with us for about three days. Twenty people all came to my parents' house. We had a real big house.

When he finished, he asked the question, "Who is going to be the captain?" Everybody pointed at me. I don't know why. I was kind of shy, but I became the captain at nineteen years old. I was still a college student at the University of Washington. I became the captain of the first chapter of the Black Panther Party outside of the state of California.

Elmer Dixon: When Chairman Bobby came to our mother's house, he laid down the rules of the Black Panther Party. He said that we needed to do two things: read twice a day and attend political education classes once a week. We needed two weapons and 1,000 rounds of ammunition. He said, "They're coming for you."

Our struggle—we didn't call it a social justice movement—we were building a revolutionary movement. The revolution that we were building was a very different thing. It was not a riot. It was not a demonstration. It was not any of that. We started programs throughout the community, survival programs for the "Pending Revolution"—that's what we called it. We had five breakfast programs in Seattle with 2,000 kids a week. We started a free medical clinic in 1970. We were doing political education. We were organizing in communities on a daily basis. Our lives were on the line. We were under constant threat of assassination. Our office was sandbagged. We had thousands of rounds of ammunition, bulletproof vests, gas masks. We took direct action. We didn't wait and ask for permission. We didn't demonstrate for the right to do it. We went out and did it.

Yalonda Sinde: These people risked their lives. When you learn from someone who was there at that time, you feel like if they can do *that*, I can do *this*. We felt it was our duty to continue the movement in a nonviolent way. These young people that were getting involved knew their history. You could ask them about anything and they knew about it. They understood how the world worked. If you're going to fight something you need to know everything about it. We analyzed the WTO, we understood the ins and outs of it. Who was involved? What were their names, what countries? How was it benefiting those countries to pass these trade rules?

Julia Hughes: Before the WTO there was only GATT—the General Agreement on Tariffs and Trade, which goes back to the 1940s—and there was no system for resolving trade disputes. If the U.S. said, "We're doing X," and another country wanted to challenge it, the U.S.

was going to do whatever they wanted. The idea within the WTO was that there would be a way to have checks and balances and have objective decisions made when there were trade disputes. Maybe you can't force countries to give up, say, subsidies, but if there are subsidies or government actions that distort trade, there is a way for other countries to file a dispute and get a resolution.

Kevin Danaher: Jim Hightower in Texas has a great saying. He says, "Capital is like cow manure: concentrated in a big pile, it stinks; you spread it out evenly, it makes things grow." The democratization of capital. When people talk about what socialism is, one element is that you democratize capital. You let the workers and the community decide things like building new highways versus mass transit and neighborhood clinics versus a big fancy hospital.

Jim Hightower: One of our real enemies was Bill Clinton—who I had supported! It's like a farmer friend told me, "I don't mind losing when we lose, but I hate losing when we win." The moderate Democrats—whatever they call themselves—they were big on this international trade and the New Order. There was great anger at Clinton, and then Al Gore got sucked up into it too. They're talking about the one world economy and how good that was going to be for everybody. But in reality, it became about the oppression of global corporations.

James P. Hoffa, Teamsters general president: We talked to the Clinton administration but they were hell-bent on doing this—NAFTA, WTO—and they were telling everybody, "Oh, this is going to be wonderful for America. They're going to buy our goods."

And we said, "That's not going to happen." We were starting to see NAFTA lead to an exodus of American jobs to Mexico and to the Third World. So we saw the WTO ministerial meeting in Seattle as an opportunity for labor to go there. We were very involved in trade along with the steelworkers—we all wanted to get very involved in this.

David Solnit: We invited a few folks to join us on our road show. We were in touch with a steelworker from Spokane who had been locked out of Kaiser Aluminum when Charles Hurwitz, the junk bonds guy, bought the company and tried to liquidate its assets and eliminate employees' retirements. Employees went on strike, and he locked them out.

Mike Dolan: There was this particular alliance between labor and the environmentalists, based around their shared opposition to Maxxam, a holding company that owned Pacific Lumber, outside of Seattle, where Julia Butterfly was up in her perch, not coming out of the tree. They also owned the steel plant out in Spokane where there was a steelworker strike. So the environmentalists and steelworkers had common cause.

Tracy Katelman, organizer with the Alliance for Sustainable Jobs and the Environment: Charles Hurwitz had bought Pacific Lumber. We were fighting his company, Maxxam, over the Headwaters Forest Reserve, the last of the ancient redwoods up on the north coast. We eventually joined Don and the steelworkers because they were also fighting Maxxam, which had locked out the workers at Kaiser Aluminum. Out of that, we started the Alliance for Sustainable Jobs and the Environment.

Don Kegley, organizer with the Alliance for Sustainable Jobs and the Environment: This was a new thing that was happening between labor and environmentalists. The cultures are a little different. I'm a third-generation steelworker. I've been a steelworker my whole life. We went on strike at Kaiser Aluminum but this was different than a regular strike because they immediately locked us out. A lockout means they kept the scabs and the striking employees were never going back. They had no idea what they were doing. Whenever the steelworkers have a strike, they don't sit on their hands. They gave us 3,500 employees when they locked us out. Our lawyers filed a lawsuit on day two of the lockout and then the battles began.

Tracy Katelman: When I met with the steelworkers there was an instant connection. I've always been a bridge builder in my organizing. Someone told me that I'd be a good union organizer. *Laughs.*

Don Kegley: Tracy came with a hell of a reputation. They were saying, "She's controlling." I was thinking that's not always bad—that's good,

I'm willing to go with that. She has real talents. When we started to interact with each other, we knew it would work. Everybody around us wasn't so sure. We found out from environmental groups that had joined our alliance that there was going to be this protest in Seattle. They understood that the WTO was not good for anybody. It's not good for the environment. It's not good for workers. If they were going to be in Seattle, we were going to be in Seattle.

I joined what they call the Road Warrior Group, going around the whole country trying to find support and get people on our side. We had never been on strike at our plant at Kaiser Aluminum in our existence—never! When they locked us out, international labor knew that if this guy were to succeed at Kaiser Aluminum, one of the largest aluminum companies in the world, every aluminum company in the country would face the same thing. You're talking about hundreds of thousands of people being affected.

Mike Dolan: So there was, if you will, a horizontal, this geographical thing—people coming from all over the country, people coming from all over the world.

Ed Joiner: I personally met with the leadership of virtually every protest group that we could find from the Teamsters all the way on down. We did not meet with the anarchists. They refused to meet with us. We met with all of the other groups that were there that intended to protest. Then we went over their needs. We designated individual sites at each of the venues where the protesters would be allowed, and everybody agreed with that. We went through that whole process of trying to dampen down the prospects of any serious confrontations way ahead of time.

Jim Pugel: John Sellers and Han Shan, they seemed to be the most knowledgeable about what could happen. They, of course, weren't telling us much. We also met with AFL-CIO. We worked with them nonstop. Weekly meetings. I met continually with the Church Council of Greater Seattle because they were going to have marches and silent sit-ins. We worked with the National Lawyers Guild; they were somewhat obnoxious. Not necessarily obnoxious but righteous. Ah man, we worked with everyone.

Ron Judd: We started meeting once every two weeks and then it was once a week and then it was multiple times a week as we got closer. The Seattle Police Department brought in Washington State Patrol and other police, other federal agencies came in and started having a presence, like the FBI and Secret Service, because we had all these important dignitaries coming in. Everybody's so interested in knowing, "What the hell are the protesters up to again?"

We were trying to be transparent and sharing with them—while not disclosing our exact tactics. Just saying, "We should reach agreement, in principle, about how we're going to behave on the street when we're facing eyeball to eyeball." We kept saying, "It's not about you, we don't want to fight you in the streets. It's about the message that we want to send to the international media so that the people around the world understand."

James P. Hoffa: We met with Gary Locke. We told him what we were doing. We were very up front with him.

Gary Locke: We knew that many of the labor leaders and advocacy groups, concerned about workers' rights and so forth, were going to protest and there was a large rally that was permitted. I very much support people's rights to express their viewpoints and so I had no problem with the rallies that were being planned.

Ed Joiner: I remember the Teamsters union in particular because that was going to be one of the largest single groups and we talked about the fact that this was going to be a great opportunity to have a sizable protest and it could be a very positive opportunity for them. I said, "You know, if this thing goes sideways, it's going to be a real black mark on the message that you're trying to convey."

They said, "We fully understand. We intend to make sure we have our own people throughout the demonstration"—because some people were coming from quite some ways away—"we will do everything we can to minimize any potential conflict."

Gary Locke: I'm very good friends with many of the labor leaders and some of the religious leaders that were going to be involved in the planned protests. I really felt that having these protests, or rallies, would help stimulate the debate and deepen the discussion about the benefits and the drawbacks of trade. Especially the need for worker retraining and helping dislocated industries and communities. I've always felt that governments have not done enough to help people who are adversely affected by trade.

Ed Joiner: I chaired a committee where we met with all of the chiefs and the sheriff, or their designee, and went through that whole planning process in terms of what we were going to be doing, what kind of assistance we could use. We went through that week after week after week.

I felt we had done everything we could do, from our side, to be prepared. It really depended on the cooperation of the various protest groups and if they kept their word, we could probably have a sizable protest but a peaceful one. That had always been the history of Seattle.

Larry Mayes: By summer, SPD still had not solidified what they wanted from us. We had offered up as many as 150 crowd-control-trained officers, plus air support, K-9, motorcycles and SWAT—all key support elements for a major event like this. They declined.

Ron Griffin: I had very little understanding of the internet at the time, but we had people—detectives, intelligence—who were monitoring it. The intelligence that we had grew. Every week, I would get a new number. It started off with 5,000 protesters. Now, we've got 10,000. Now we've got 15,000. Now, we've got 20,000, 30,000.

Larry Mayes: There is an absolute tenet to planning for large-scale demonstrations—that is, you plan for worst-case scenario every time. You don't necessarily have to use all those resources, all those plans, but if things go south, you better have planned for them, trained for them, and staged for them. My folks were concerned that was not happening to the degree that it should. We had early intel that some of these protest groups were maybe going to attempt to shut down the meetings.

Maud Daudon: The mayor really believed that it was critical that people had their say and he did not want to be the mayor to shut that down. That was his political judgment at the time, or his philosophical judgment. He was not a typical mayor in that he was not a super-political animal. He said what he thought, and he really did what he thought was best, so he was a very unusual kind of elected official, in that sense.

Ron Griffin: Mayor Schell put SPD in a bad spot because of the policies that he decided to adopt. He did not want a big police plan. He did not want barricades to help direct the flow of individuals. So their hands were tied to begin with.

Laurie Brown: Maud Daudon was the deputy mayor involved in all the planning. She was, for all intents and purposes, my day-to-day supervisor. Paul had one hundred percent confidence in Maud.

Maud Daudon: As I started to learn more, as the weeks went on and we got closer to the actual event, I inserted myself a little bit more. Because I began to hear, especially from external labor people, that they were getting a sense this was going to be really, really big and the demonstrations were going to be unlike anything Seattle had ever seen.

Nick Licata: The progressives on the City Council, we were the most critical, the most concerned about the environment, social disruption, the priorities of the WTO. I think our message was let's not let the city give the WTO a blank check and let's not just go endorse it because we have some serious problems with it. But we were in the minority.

Paul Schell was an individual I liked. At one time he claimed to be an antiwar protester. He was a constant liberal in many senses, both socially and somewhat economically, but he came out of the business community. He was going to go ahead with the effort to host the WTO and he didn't want the council to mess around with it.

Steve Koehler: The Downtown Seattle Association was an activist organization for downtown prosperity. I was chair at the time and all we ever really tried to do was keep the economy going, make sure that downtown was healthy, vibrant. We had a voice in the WTO planning process, but it wasn't listened to. It was, "Hey, we got this covered.

We're under control. Nothing bad is going to happen, da da da da. Don't worry about it."

We were focused on "What are we going to do about the possible protesting? What are we going to do about the marchers? How is that going to be handled?" We were strongly advocating for keeping the pathway of those marchers from being able to get between the venues and the hotels.

Larry Mayes: You had 5,000 WTO delegates coming to Seattle to discuss global economic and financial issues that were going to impact millions of citizens throughout the world without their input. We had accurate numbers of at least 40,000 people, one of the largest protest events ever in the country, coming to Seattle. Paul Schell believed that he could take both of those groups and place them in close proximity in downtown Seattle and pull off a peaceful exchange of ideas. Paul Schell's fantasy world presented a large gap to reaching reality. It was irrational. I can't explain it. There should have been a huge perimeter around the delegate venues, their hotels, the restaurants in that area. Instead, they placed the protesters on the same streets in the same vicinity.

Steve Koehler: The one thing I'll never forget is the mayor saying, "This is Seattle. We're different." He allowed the marchers to get between the hotel and the venue. I think if some of that could have been prevented it might not have blown up as much as it actually did. I think we were just really naïve that that wasn't going to happen—naivety particularly from the mayor was a problem.

*   *   *

Helene Cooper, reporter for the _Wall Street Journal_: Trade was a big beat at the _Journal_ in the 1990s. They cared more about it than they did about foreign policy because they're a business newspaper. By summer I had turned my attention to Seattle. I met with Lori Wallach at Public Citizen and she told me there's a guy named Mike Dolan. She was like, "This WTO in Seattle's going to be fucked-up. You need to be paying attention."

So, I go to Mike and say, "I'm going to come to Seattle with you and do a story."

Mike Dolan: Helene Cooper came out and spent a few days with me. By that time I was talking to everybody—and I was learning the whole time. It's not like this whole thing was born whole out of my head. More and more shit just came along that I thought were good ideas.

John Nichols: Somebody would call Mike up and say, "Hey, we're thinking of doing a balloon drop."
"Yes!"
"We're thinking of doing a march at midnight."
"Yes!"
"We're thinking of rappelling off the sides of buildings."
"Yes!"
He would get excited about every idea. As a result, people would keep bringing him ideas. There's a dialectic that occurs in that. Because maybe the first idea was just okay. But over time, you get to a really good idea. And Dolan's in the middle of all of it. Because of his enthusiasm, he was somebody people felt they had a connection with. They tended to trust him.

I have a picture of Mike where he had a cell phone on each ear. This was 1999 when cell phones were less sophisticated. But he had one on each ear and was talking to somebody. After I took the picture, he said, "Yeah, if I'm going to get brain cancer, I'd better get it on both sides."

Jim Hightower: Mike Dolan is completely insane—but he's *our* insane guy!

John Nichols: Dolan never suggested he was the leader—and I don't think he was. Again, this was a consortium. Anytime you have a leaderless movement, what they really mean is that there are many leaders. The truth of the matter is that in Seattle, there were many folks who could be referred to as a leader of some aspect of the protest. You had everybody from anarchists, who, of course, aren't supposed to have leaders, but in fact do, to labor union folks, the environmental folks. There's a lot of different people. But when you've got somebody who's a trusted touchstone for all these different folks, that person's got to have their ego in relatively good control. Dolan is a very dynamic person. He comes in a room, you know he's there. He's definitely present. He's loud, funny, and engaged and all this. But if it was time for everybody to give their ideas, he wasn't necessarily going to be the first one to get up there and say, "Well, here's what we're going to do." Instead, he'd create a conversation. Then he brought a lot of other people in. He may have played a coordinating role but he didn't necessarily play a dominant role.

Mike Dolan: The summer was fraught as more and more folks were getting involved. I want to say this as nicely as possible: When progressives get together—particularly in a place like Seattle, which is pretty fucking touchy-feely—it can be pretty frustrating. Organizers like me, particularly in a type of pressure-cooker situation where there is a hard date, the end of November when the WTO was going down, it's important to distinguish between what is important—because everything is fucking important!—and what's *essential*. I had to use that lens.

David Solnit: We had a mixed relationship with a lot of NGOs and established labor. We ended up organizing with them and had some tension, and at times there was even counterorganizing. We were aware of the fraught relationship. We were making a bolder proposal. They wanted to march and go home. We wanted to shut down the WTO with massive civil disobedience so they couldn't make these decisions to wreck our communities and the planet.

Lori Wallach: What seemed possible was to put tens of thousands of people on the street for the labor rally and march and program of events. The Direct Action Network had a different vision of what they could physically do, something we had not seen done in this country for a hell of a long time. It didn't even seem possible. But if we were going to actually change the course of history, if we were going to make the contribution as American civil society that was necessary, given what the fuck our government was doing for ill, if we were going to be able to balance any of that and help change the outcome, it was going to have to be an incredible spectacle.

Nadine Bloch: The activist community—as opposed to the labor unions and formal NGOs—they are different. There was a realization that if we could put bodies in the streets, that would be strategically critical to support the inside strategy that the NGOs had. The inside and the outside were both important and both needed.

Lori Wallach: The idea was basically to have an inside-outside game, and be involved in a bunch of stuff inside the ministerial too. The inside game was really a game for the developing countries but we could support it.

Mike Dolan: There was real symbiosis that we created with the inside-outside game, that tension, that monkeywrenching—you'll hear Lori use that term *monkeywrenching*. It was really important in Seattle.

Ron Judd: Some of the bigger divides about tactics and strategy and message were within the labor movement itself. *Laughs.*

Don Kegely: Richard Trumka, who was the AFL-CIO secretary-treasurer at that point, was probably the least excited about what we had been doing. He supported it but he had a lot of worries. While every union is its own entity, we all coalesced around this idea that our real strength is us sticking together no matter what. That "no matter what" includes even if you're really not into it. We can't say, "We're going to do this and if you don't want to support us, that's okay," because then there's no power. The power comes from being able to say that 160 million people in this country are behind us. That's where the power comes from.

Ron Judd: We had general presidents of large international unions that wanted to be far crazier, and we had others that wanted to be delegates at the conference. We ended up saying, "Maybe what we ought to do is have an inside-outside strategy." We've got to create a crack somewhere in the unity of the WTO. Part of the street presence should be so crazy and outrageous that those on the inside can do nothing but pay attention to what the hell is happening. Part of that is making sure that if they can get to their meeting that it's very difficult. Respectful but difficult.

Skip Spitzer: As time went on, it got to the point where there was just a constant line of people going into the Convergence Center and a constant line of people coming out. We had to constantly remind each other to not stop and say hello at the door because you just clogged up the whole works.

It was pretty spectacular to see how people could work without a strong hierarchical framework, make it more efficient. People got housing, medical care. You needed to get around Seattle? Sign out a bike. The Convergence Center was not only the backbone of the mobilization but, in a lot of ways, it was a microcosm of the kind of world that we actually like to live in. People work together. Everybody's voice matters. People are sharing what they can, repurposed resources, taking care of each other. It was a tremendously beautiful experience.

David Taylor: As the spokescouncil continued to meet, the decisions were about how to proceed tactically. So, moving from "We're doing a blockade" to "Now we're doing jail support. Who's managing the jail support shifts? We're going to do an occupation here at the Marriott while we're still doing jail support. Who's going to be in which places? How are we doing communications?"

That's how this affinity group model manages to work, because you have enough flexibility with the resources you have, with who's in the room. When everyone starts getting arrested, you can keep going. When you talk about a state of oppression, it's very, very good that you can't take the head off of anything.

There were some splinters in the Direct Action Network with folks that were more focused on property destruction but they were not as directly involved in the organizing. It was a different model. The model was always very traditional, nonviolent, direct action with the affinity group model.

John Zerzan: These folks in Seattle were having scores of meetings. There was a big lead-up. They organized and organized. Some of us went up there and we had a flyer. I don't remember specifically but, in general, it said that it was time for action. Standing around with a sign or having a nice parade, screw that! This is for real. Let's go. We went to this big warehouse space where all these meetings were being held.

There was a spokescouncil, I remember. They didn't let us in. They wouldn't let us participate or even pass out the flyer.

The way we saw it was that it was not a matter of democracy. You don't vote on what to do. It's a matter of autonomy. You do what you want to do, we'll do what we want to do. Don't mess with us. Go ahead and do whatever you want, including kneeling down, getting pepper-sprayed and beaten by the pigs. Go for it. That's not necessarily what we want to do.

David Taylor: The Black Bloc people didn't come near the Convergence Center and they understood that they were not supposed to be drawing the police toward the Convergence Center.

Ron Judd: We also understood that there was going to be an element of anarchists that would be coming into the organizing. I spent a lot of time chatting with them. It's like trying to hug an amoeba because there's no organizational structure there so it's everybody's a leader and nobody's a leader.

John Zerzan: Even though we're anarchists, at times we've been forbidden to use the word or if it is used, immediate associations and connotations are triggered. The term *Black Bloc* was just a tactical expedient. It was employed in Europe before the U.S. There has been a lot of silliness written about that as if it's an organization. "Are you a member of the Black Bloc?" *Laughs.* Well, there is no membership. You might be hoping for some chance to do some damage. If you have some experience or some spontaneous street smarts, it's called Black Bloc, but it's just a temporary thing that happens as a solidarity thing, as a protection thing. People are masked up together. They don't want to go to jail.

David Taylor: The Black Bloc came out of the Earth First! movement, and there was a division between those who were doing some more confrontational tactics, like property destruction, versus those who were not. Some of the more radical anarchist communities out of the Northwest were a bit more tactically focused and in-your-face. Then there was also a flavor of anarchist organizing that was "we're anarchists in that Mikhail Bakunin, political kind of way," versus "we are anarchists, smash the state." It's a different flavor and engagement—little-*a*, big-*A* kind of thing. There were a lot of people who were deeply involved in the Direct Action Network who identified as anarchists but you would never know that.

Charles R. Cross: I used to go to this place called the Globe for lunch every day. It was a collective. If you couldn't afford your food, they would pay for it. There was a five-dollar community bowl of rice and beans. If you could afford it, you'd put in a little extra money, and they'd give it to everybody who came in. There were communal tables and before the WTO, there were all these people who weren't paying who were there. Did I look at them and say, "These are anarchists who are going to start a riot"? Yes, I did! They were different than the Seattle hippies that were there. Seattle hippies are mellow. These anarchists were not. I overheard some of the conversations. It was as if Karl Marx was at the next table. I knew some shit was up, just by listening to these people.

Larry Mayes: As time moved on, we got more intel. And it became clear that the Eugene and Portland anarchists, now Antifa, were planning on attending also.

Suzanne Savoie: I think there are huge differences between what was happening in the 1990s and the 2000s in terms of anarchist–Black Bloc actions and the modern Antifa movement. They are quite different entities. I think conflating the two is a big error. Just because people put on black masks—or put on whatever-color masks, it doesn't have to be black—but people put on masks and take to the streets, it doesn't make them all one entity. Just because there are groups of people that do that doesn't mean they're all the same. I'd say when people conflate anarchists and Antifa they're basing that off of aesthetics more than actual political reality.

My main reason for being in Seattle was to fight corporate greed and the destruction of the planet. That was my personal passion. I'd been doing activism for a number of years, everything from local land use issues to protesting nuclear waste dumps in the desert, to animal rights and ecology-based issues. A couple years before Seattle, I lived in Wales, and that's where I got heavily involved in activism. The Reclaim the Streets movement was very strong; events were happening in major cities almost on a weekly basis. Reclaim the Streets was a very decentralized organization, a phenomenon where people were taking over the streets in their community, mainly with street theater, bikes, sit-down protests, music, putting on dance parties, raves, whatever—saying we're going to take over the streets from corporate America, corporate Europe, and we're going to reclaim it. It's going to become our own. People would dig up some areas and plant vegetables and do symbolic little gardens, trying to say, "We want to take the cities and turn them back into sustainable places where people can live. Not only sustainable for the planet but also in a way that's more socially just." It was a way for people to make a political statement while also having fun. When I got back to the U.S., every city I went to had Reclaim the Streets events happening very regularly—and not just big cities but medium-sized cities, too, from Santa Cruz to Eugene. A lot of that energy made its way to Seattle and it helped get people involved and excited.

Mike Dolan: Not everybody was interested at first. A lot of the work that I was doing was getting people interested. All the groups had to be invited—and inspired—to join in. The interest wasn't turnkey. I had to actually get people committed, invested. The Sierra Club was there and if you had asked me in February of '99 if we were going to be able to get the really big NGOs that supported NAFTA, I would have said, "I'm not sure." There's this whole Clinton problem because they're all Democrats.

Dan Seligman, Responsible Trade Program director for the Sierra Club: We had a close collaboration with Public Citizen and Mike and Lori Wallach but had message differences and tonal differences that we thought were important to keep the environmental community from fracturing excessively—and to be persuasive. Our audience, our target audience, was really these pro-trade Democrats on the West Coast. At a certain point, it really didn't help to align our message too closely with Ralph Nader and company. So we tried to have a little distance. We were kind of close to the Democratic Party, didn't want to burn down the house. Nader was not so averse to that. So there's a whole bunch of factors that created these different tonal emphases.

At the Sierra Club, we had a posture in the environmental community that was a little more independent of Washington thinking. We were a big mainstream conservation group like World Wildlife Fund, National Wildlife Federation, Natural Resources Defense Council. But there was a cleavage in the environmental community around trade, with the more policy-oriented, Washington-centered, expert environmental groups. There were a few of us who were more grassroots-oriented and kind of rigid in our thinking about all that the environmental movement had built in terms of domestic law and policy on air, water, food that we took to be in jeopardy—and were willing to duke it out for our principles.

Mike Dolan: It took some persuasion on my part to get them to throw in all together. But they did finally really turn out and did shit. And as soon as one group would buy-in it became easier to get the next group to buy-in, going up the reformist acuity ladder.

It was incremental all of '99, getting more and more buy-in. Each day was greater than the day before. The steelworkers were going to outdo the Teamsters, on and on. There were internal sectoral competitions like Friends of the Earth versus the Sierra Club.

David Taylor: The Direct Action Network had one message and one message only, which was shut down the WTO. That was the framing we had for everything. There was some cat-and-mouse stuff between us and the NGOs. We all were friends, we all had different frames, we all had different places to have meetings. There were definitely people in the Direct Action Network that were interning with Public Citizen. I would say it goes even further, where people were in the Direct Action office who were doing Black Bloc stuff—but we didn't know that they were doing it. So resources sort of trickled down and moved all the way through the pipeline.

Mike Dolan: It was a lot of work just getting venues all around town. Helene Cooper was at this meeting when I reserved the whole fucking church, this gargantuan Methodist church with all these great rooms downstairs for breakouts. The head preacher was a woman and she was impressed by my presentation and the fact that I had a *Wall Street Journal* reporter with me.

That church was so convenient. It was just right there—I had my office, my headquarters set up right downtown. It was perfect. And there were some in the faith-based community who dug the fact that I was going to design a symposium parallel to the WTO ministerial schedule. We had the days of the week scheduled out—Agriculture Day, Labor Day, Environmental Day—that was just a fiat by me and Lori Wallach, basically, on how we were going to organize the week. Each of those days there were different constituencies that I had been mobilizing all year who were now suddenly collaborating and working together to design those days, to make the critiques explicit and well choreographed.

Dan Seligman: Mike and Lori designed a protest schedule, wisely, and handed to us Environment Day, to be lead organizers of.

Celia Alario: It was smart because different types of groups and coalitions and networks were able to say, "This is my day."

Mike Dolan: Michael Ramos of the Washington Council of Churches, they were all like, "Yes, cool, Faith-Based Day."

Michael Ramos, organizer with the Washington Association of Churches: I was employed as a layperson by the Washington Association of Churches, which is the state ecumenical association. I was bringing the faith voice into a wider conversation that involved groups like Public Citizen, the labor movement, all the groups that were planning, in essence—a dimension of the 50,000-person protest.

I helped organize the Jubilee Campaign in the area—the call for debt cancellation for the world's poorest countries, part of a global movement—and that was coinciding with the WTO protests.

The international debt regime basically was foisted upon many countries. They had no ability, in many cases, to repay the debts they were accumulating. Jubilee called for debt cancellation in the spirit of the biblical mandate that every fiftieth year should be declared a jubilee and debt should be released, slaves should be made free, and people should be able to return to their land and families reunited. We wanted to raise this issue alongside other injustices and other forms of racist and structural oppression that the WTO, in its practice and its policies, was implementing.

*   *   *

Maud Daudon: I'd say it really was the last months before the event that it did feel like there was a little bit of a snowball going on. The police department did their usual thing with the protest movement folks, especially labor, because labor really did a lot of mobilization. They did things like negotiate the route. They always did these things with protests to make sure it worked for the protesters and worked for the city.

Jim Pugel: The AFL-CIO was going to have a march with tens of thousands of people. Busloads from all over the United States were going to come in and begin their march at the Seattle Center, come down Fourth Avenue, and because they were unions, they wanted to make a U-turn from Fourth Avenue on Union Street. The Secret Service said no way, that goes right into the convention center and that's exactly where all the delegates are going to be. We can't have them march up Union.

So I went to Maud Daudon and said let's rename Pine Street, which is two blocks north of Union; let's rename Pine Street for the day "Union Way." She actually got signs made up, legal street signs. They took down "Pine Street" signs and put up blue "Union Way" signs.

Maud Daudon: It was classic Seattle and, in retrospect, looked so naïve. It had been that kind of relationship that had been a trustful relationship probably since the '60s, between protesters and police in Seattle.

Laurie Brown: Maud Daudon was on top of it but she wasn't talking to me about it yet. I remember I was sitting in the office reading an article about the WTO and I said, "Oh, this could be something." That's when I started asking questions. I thought I better learn more about how prepared we needed to be and what I needed to do to help prepare city employees. I began working with the Human Resources folks and the Labor Relations folks to prepare employees because if things really got squirrelly, they may not be able to report to work. They might not be able to get into downtown buildings.

Eventually I was also asked to negotiate with Mike Dolan around the use of the Kingdome.

Mike Dolan: The Kingdome was a shuttered baseball stadium that didn't have a revenue stream. See, there was a guy named Bob with the musicians' union. He took me aside at one point and said, "Look, we really ought to do a concert."

What I know about putting on concerts would not fill a thimble, but I said, "Yes, we should totally do a concert!"

But shows are actually a pretty expensive proposition. We were going to need talent to donate or we'll pay their expenses and we're going to need a venue. Bob said, "You can get the Kingdome." And because it didn't have any real revenue stream, it became a thing I could actually get but the thing is, I never had the money to do that. And I hadn't closed the deal. That, however, didn't stop me from going into a meeting with Laurie Brown to say, "Yes, it's happening. This is going to happen. I'm sorry."

That was a bluff. You've got to be willing to gamble sometimes. That was just one big fucking gamble. I thought, "Can I get away with this?"

Laurie Brown: Mike was in a very strong negotiating position. I did think he had an agreement that they would be able to rent the Kingdome. I had direct marching orders to not let that happen because it was too close in proximity to where cocktail parties and WTO events for the delegates were going to be happening. We did not know that he did not actually have the money to rent the Kingdome.

Mike Dolan: Next door to the Kingdome, the WTO fat cats would be meeting on the same night. The Washington Council of Churches and Jubilee 2000 were already planning a hands-around-the-building thing. The city was getting anxious about the choreography. That's when they took me into this meeting and said, "Look, we don't want you to use the Kingdome."

I said, "Fuck you! I'm going to do it!"

They said, "No, come on, really."

I said, "Really, we're going to do it! For heaven's sake have a concert for people, a People's Gala, so that they won't be burning down the cocktail party a few blocks away! We're on the same page here."

They said, "No." But then they said, "How about if we offer you the Seattle Center?"

"The Seattle Center, huh? I'm going to need to talk to my people about this, but—"

"For free."

I went, "Oh, all right, well that's sweet." It did sweeten it up a little bit. But it wasn't like I jumped on it. I just said, "Maybe."

Then they said, "There's just a couple of things." One stipulation was that I had to let the mayor onstage.

I said, "Yeah, okay. He's got four minutes. Fine, I'll let the mayor on the stage." So, they got Mayor Paul Schell in the lineup. And they had one other stipulation.

Laurie Brown: Before I met with him, I went to the internet and researched him. I do my homework. I wasn't going to let my guy Paul Schell be out there with, like, a crazy man. So I said, "Who is this dude? What organization is he with? Who is affiliated with the organization?" On the website I found, you would go to the main page and it would link you to another organization and another. There was some wild stuff on there, things that I thought no way can the city cohost the People's Gala or enter into an agreement to allow them to use the Seattle Center if Mike Dolan's group is affiliated with some of these fringe groups.

Mike Dolan: They saw the link to David Solnit and Art and Revolution and a few others.

Laurie Brown: So I asked him, "Can you help me understand what your affiliation is with these organizations?" He downplayed it. I said, "It's a dealbreaker. They're not just protesting the WTO, they want to shut it down. There is no way that the mayor will agree to anything if your organization is affiliated with these wacko groups. What do we do about that?"

Mike Dolan: I said, "Okay," and I picked up my phone and called my IT people and said, "Sever the link to Art and Revolution."

Laurie Brown: He was very dramatic. He did it right then and there. I double-checked to make sure that it happened and it did.

David Solnit: Mike was actually dating someone in the Direct Action Network who made him put the links back on their website a few days later. There was tension there.

Laurie Brown: Why Mike Dolan wanted to be affiliated with them to begin with, I don't know. He's a very dramatic person, grandstands. He was having a good time. It apparently made him successful in his role.

Mike Dolan: It was really a cool moment when I was able to get them to give me the fucking Seattle Center—and have the sheriff's department in-kind contribution from the city. I'm not sure I could have pulled the Kingdome off, so they basically saved my ass with that deal. I had free security and the Seattle Center, which was cooler anyway. Then we got the Teamsters to donate some security. I was going to have the sheriff's department on the outside and the Teamsters on the inside. I was thinking, "God, is this going to be like Altamont?" *Laughs.*

Laurie Brown: For him to say that he pulled one over on the city, that we gave him the People's Gala space free with security services—technically that's true, but the city got what they wanted: the Kingdome was not used and Paul was given the opportunity to speak.

*   *   *

Mike Dolan: I should say a few things about money:

The labor money was coming in. AFL-CIO and the steelworkers rented, I don't know, 4,000 hotel rooms—something absurd. Similarly, you look at the environmental side, the Sierra Club was throwing some money in.

But what was also interesting is that Roger Milliken money was getting funneled through me to the Direct Action Network. And Milliken was this John Birch Society guy—a racist, South Carolina, anti-union textile magnate.

Ralph Nader: Lori Wallach was working with some right-wing people like Roger Milliken—it was the left-right coalition. The press blacked her out for years for that. I got blacked out too.

Mike Dolan: I think that encapsulates the left-right situation that played out in Seattle: through Lori and the Citizens Trade Campaign I was actually taking right-wing John Bircher money and passing it onto the militant left. *Laughs.*

Jim Hightower: I was actually on Alex Jones, the TV show, talking about the WTO. He wasn't completely crazy by then, and he was really focused on the WTO. Pat Buchanan was too. We had Pat Buchanan on our show because we wanted to make the point that this is not some lefty thing, just anticorporate hippiness, but this is a real political explosive moment.

Jello Biafra, lead vocalist for the Dead Kennedys and the No WTO Combo: I was just amazed how many types of people and types of organizations were pissed-off about the WTO and what NAFTA was already doing to people's lives, wiping out the jobs, wiping out their towns. A lot of the Rush Limbaugh suckers and the people who fall even for Pat Buchanan and Fox News and the rest of them, they're really on the same side we are and they don't know it. They are just people who are really frightened that they're not going to be able to put food on the table. They might not have a job. They might not have a home, especially a job that had any kind of meaningful work. What am I going to do? I'm frightened and I'm mad.

Nadine Bloch: People of different stripes from all over the country were trying to raise money to support the protests. There were people like Mike Dolan and Lori Wallach who had salaried jobs and were able to show up fully covered but a lot of us lived very low on the chain, if you will. There were lots of us living on couches and floors. Sometimes there were small stipends that were offered to main organizers. Ruckus was instrumental in raising some money.

John Sellers: Dame Anita Roddick, the founder of the Body Shop, who is no longer with us, she and I were pretty good friends. She gave us 100,000 GBP to go bananas in Seattle. I met with other donors and was working to raise money to grant out to all these different affinity groups to give them $2,000 to do whatever they were going to do to block their intersections.

Lori Wallach: The money for Seattle was a lot less than the corporate guys thought because there was an enormous amount of genius organizing. There were some 5,000 home stays. There was an enormous number of volunteer car pools. Obviously, venues had to be rented. Comms systems had to be rented. It was largely foundation money and individual money. There were some lefty musicians, artists, TV folks who had written $20,000 and $30,000 checks or in-kind had done a fundraiser. A lot of it was labor money for the hard expenses.

David Taylor: These budgets were not big numbers, tens of thousands of dollars; it was definitely hand-to-mouth. There was also a lot of passing of the hat at the Convergence Center. We did raise a couple large-dollar donations for the Direct Action Network. And we had ads in some political magazines for people just mailing in checks. We had mailing lists for environmental groups and those checks would come in, very grassroots stuff. A couple thousand bucks would come in and we'd have that petty cash and we'd use that for giving money to Food Not Bombs to go buy what they needed. Or we gave some money to some folks that were setting up some squats.

David Reichert: The anarchists took over a vacant building—several floors, downtown.

David Taylor: That was a political action. Squatting was a big thing in the anarchist community.

Larry Mayes: The building that housed the anarchists was at the intersection of Virginia Street and Ninth Avenue, about a block from Seattle PD's West Precinct. There were about 150 them squatting there. It was a run-down building with only a couple of operating businesses in it on the first floor.

Jim Brunner, reporter for the *Seattle Times*: I got interested in these guys and I managed to convince them to let me into their building and do a tour and talk with a bunch of them. It was a stand-alone story and I think I led with "These are the rules that the anarchists have"—because they had this list of rules. I think it was no drugs, no graffiti, and smoking only on the roof. And they went by pseudonyms like Sergeant Pepper Spray. They had walkie-talkies, communication to get in. It was very clandestine. They were mostly young people who felt like this was something that gave their life some meaning.

Larry Mayes: Law enforcement knew early on this was the anarchists' operations headquarters and wanted to close it down, make arrests, and stop the coordinated vandalism, looting, and violent protests. The political decision by Schell and Stamper not to do so fit perfectly with all the other crazy decisions made by them and the political establishment in Seattle.

Jim Brunner: The interesting thing is that building was a block from the SPD precinct there and they didn't do anything to stop it. Basically they were like, "Well, we know where these guys are at least, and we can watch them."

Michael Ramos: On one level, the WTO protesters, at least at the planning stages, were given a wide latitude or berth in terms of setting up the event, which would not have been granted to certain groups, particularly people of color.

four waters: Civil disobedience having to do with environmental issues and global economic issues has almost always been dominated by white, fairly comfortable, well-off people. This has been an ongoing issue. This was a conversation that we were having in Humboldt in '96, not just looking at black or Latino but especially Native Americans. We were trying to figure out how to make those relationships work, recognizing that they are in a much more vulnerable position and recognizing that our wealth, our privilege, allows us to get up and go if things become uncomfortable. Often times we think of privilege as money but privilege is choice. You have a choice to leave a situation that is no longer healthy or no longer safe. You can be momentarily economically disadvantaged if you went to college, for instance, but the very option of going to college is a choice that a lot of people don't have. This has been an ongoing issue.

Mike Dolan: I was looking across many constituencies, different sectors, the faith-based groups, the family-farm groups—and I was counting numbers. My whole fucking organizing pedigree made me look at the bottom line, the numbers, "How many you got?" This was a standard-issue, United Farm Workers model. I was making my important-versus-essential distinctions as much as anything based on that criterion. I didn't ever say to anyone, "Who are you bringing? How many you got?" I didn't ever say that but that's what I was looking at. I made my logistical and resource decisions based on that. And I was definitely criticized for not doing the communities of color right—like, in a big fucking way. I was the white guy with a law degree who's got the money—because I had a budget—and people thought I was not adequately sensitive to organizing communities of color. One person insists to this day that I hired her because she was a token. She was the only gay woman of color on my staff. I got a real intro to identarian politics. My analysis is class. Identity stuff, the feminists, communities of color—I was never against any of that organizing, it was just that they never thought that I was paying them enough attention, showing them enough love. It became clear to me that I was going to remain controversial, so I just had to own it.

Yalonda Sinde: I remember there was tension around some of the bigger organizations taking credit for everything and making it look like they organized the whole thing and it just made us kind of invisible. We talked about that a lot and about how marginalized we were feeling. Also some of it was media spin. We were characterized as these street thugs and troublemakers and these other folks were characterized as the real leaders. Some of it wasn't the fault of the mainstream; it was just that the media liked that story line that we were just rabble-rousers, bandwagoners. We were really educated, sophisticated, professional organizers and activists. We were no joke.

Mike Dolan: There is nothing that I can do about being the white NGO guy from D.C. I wanted to try to make it as smooth as possible but there was no way that I was going to come out smelling good. I just had to eat it and focus on doing stuff that I needed to do to get to where we needed to be. Nobody could argue with what I was doing at a logistical level—getting the church, getting the hotel rooms, securing the venues. I brought shit to the table. Even if I was fucking up rhetorically and giving off a bad white-guy vibe, I was able to rent the allegiance of different groups. I don't want it all to sound terribly transactional because it was empowering. People wanted in. Every week it was busier and bigger and better than the week before. There was a real momentum to the whole thing. I just kept telling myself, "Don't fuck up!"

*   *   *

Jello Biafra: I came up with "don't hate the media, become the media" in a spoken-word piece against the first Gulf War back in the early '90s. It tapped a vein. That seven-inch 45 was selling out. And that was the line: "Don't hate the media, become the media."

Celia Alario: The other world that was possible in 1999, from a media perspective, was that anybody could go out with some audio equipment or some video equipment—they didn't need to be affiliated with any media outlet—and they could tell their story.

John Sellers: The Independent Media Center was getting set up to do what social media does now: people-powered media, telling our own stories and not allowing ourselves to be filtered by the corporate media.

Celia Alario: I go downtown to this storefront, which is the Independent Media Center-to-be. There's still paper on the glass windows. I knock and knock and somebody answers. It's Jeff Pearlstein. I ask him, "What the heck is going on?" And he's laying high-speed internet cable, which I am really excited to see.

I get down on my hands and knees with him, and I spend the next two hours laying internet cable all over this giant space with him, trying to convince him that it would make sense to have a phone or two where the corporate media could call into this space. Because of course, what they were creating with the Independent Media Center was an answer to the corporate media; it was the antithesis of the corporate media. This is where you can get all sparkly and starry-eyed with unicorns and rainbows about what the internet was supposed to do. It was supposed to be democratizing technology and leveling the playing field and empowering people to tell their own story, and someday, it would be on par with the three old white guys who, by appointment at six o'clock every night, would tell you what you needed to care about. It was supposed to be that something else was possible.

Suffice to say, everybody was not a fan of the mainstream, corporate media. My job was to convince Jeff and then have him convince his collective that we should be able to be inside there relaying to corporate media what we were doing. It was a very hard sell but eventually we convinced them. We had a couple of fax lines, and we ended up getting dedicated outgoing lines to make calls and one incoming. We knew that in Seattle, because of the skyscrapers, the cell service was less reliable. The cell systems would become overwhelmed at times with that many people in proximity. I knew we needed landlines.

Denis Moynihan: The IMC was a room with four hundred people in it at its height. I joined the least popular working group with Celia, which was the mainstream media working group. We were doing PR for about a thousand Direct Action Network participants, the various affinity groups. My role was to help get favorable press coverage for the protests. It was far too chaotic to do even a reasonable job but we did.

Jello Biafra: I knew there was going to be a big protest up there, and I wasn't sure whether my presence would really help. Then I started seeing that line from my Gulf War piece—"Don't hate the media, become the media"—on people's leather jackets. So it was a no-brainer to bring that back at the time of the Seattle protests.

Kim Thayil: Jello Biafra, he wanted to come to town to participate in the protest. I'd met Jello a number of times at shows in Seattle and had a friendly acquaintance. He was friends of Krist Novoselic from Nirvana and they'd had some exchanges about getting a band together to play at the protests.

Jello Biafra: Krist called me because he was trying to get a protest show together. He'd been asking Pearl Jam and some others who'd done different activist gigs in the past and nobody was biting. So he said, "Look, why don't we just start our own band for this event?" We got Kim Thayil from Soundgarden, who sadly had broken up by then—he and Krist were two unemployed rock megamillionaires wandering, looking for some action. *Laughs.* And they got a real good, solid drummer, a woman named Gina Mainwal.

Kim Thayil: I did not know the significance of the WTO. I mean, it had been in the news leading up to the events. When they started discussing the number of organized groups that were going to protest, I thought, "Well, what is the significance of the WTO?"

Jello Biafra: Kim Thayil was a little more cautious about the whole thing, and in some ways more politically conservative than me or Krist, but definitely down with playing the show.

Kim Thayil: I was going into it to support my friends, to be involved and, the same time, learn about what was going on. I was really surprised that in this case, there was an organization that had attracted the interest of so many very political groups. I said, "Yeah, let's do this."

Jello Biafra: So, the No WTO Combo was conceived and formed.

Kim Thayil: That was Jello's name for the band, the No WTO Combo. There was a little bit of discussion and debate about that but Jello really pushed hard for No WTO Combo. Okay, that's great.

Charles R. Cross: Seattle punk rockers love a riot. Before the WTO, there had been twenty-five years of tension between the Seattle musicians and the authorities. Musicians organized in response to different laws that had been passed in Seattle that were not friendly to music, such as noise ordinances, anti-postering, the Teen Dance Ordinance. The Teen Dance Ordinance was a set of rules so that if people danced, there were separate police and fire regulations—essentially a city effort to not allow concerts, or to heavily control them. It was easier to get Seattle musicians or artists in an uproar over the Teen Dance

Ordinance or over the anti-postering law. The WTO, itself, was such a fluid and unusual thing. It began to stand for many things. But whether or not punk rockers even knew what the WTO was about, they were certainly willing to be pissed-off. I think the history of punk rock rioting in Seattle gave the WTO riots more fuel than they would have had on their own.

*   *   *

Mike Dolan: By the end of summer, I was on the cover of the *Wall Street Journal*.

Helene Cooper: Mike is such a canny operator. I go around with him and he's meeting with clergy people, he's meeting with all these people who are planning for how they're going to protest this WTO meeting, and I file my story. I remember Mike and I are sitting at the airport, and I was about to leave. It's the end of my reporting trip. The *Journal* has spent all this money flying me out there, so he knows at this point that I'm doing this story because I've invested all of this in it— I'm going to write about him, about Mike Dolan and about what he's doing to get ready for Seattle. Then he says to me, "You know there's a group called Ruckus?"

And I was like, "Ruckus?"

He's like, "Yeah. You think *I'm* about to fuck this shit up? Well, just wait for Ruckus."

And I was like, "Why didn't you tell me before?"

He was like, "Because I knew if I told you before you wouldn't write about me, you'd write about Ruckus."

Patrick Collins: One day when I was at drill, I was reading the newspaper and I saw an article about anarchists. They were going through a training camp in anticipation of this thing called WTO. I had no freaking idea what WTO was at the time.

So I raised that to my battalion command. I said, "Hey, I think we may have an issue here, because if it gets as ugly as people are talking about, I got to believe that there's going to be a riot." We sent that up to our state headquarters and they said, "No, we don't think anything's going to happen. If you guys want to put an annex into your plan for dealing with Y2K, fine." Kind of stupid, because WTO occurred before Y2K, but they told us to put an annex in our Y2K emergency plan.

I'm an infantry officer by training, and I believe in plan, plan, plan. The plan is worth a damn but the concept of planning is priceless—thinking through things that might happen. So we had a detailed plan for how we were going to respond if we got called on.

Helene Cooper: I did my Mike Dolan story, put him on the front page, and I told my boss, "The Ruckus people are the people I have to catch. I mean, first of all their name is Ruckus and when I looked them up, they think Greenpeace is tame." So Dolan put me in touch with John Sellers.

Sellers came to Washington to meet with me and totally looked at me like, "She's this reporter for the *Wall Street Journal*. She's the enemy."

We decided to meet for lunch and I was looking at him like, "He's going to be some vegan, left-wing tree-hugger whatever." So I picked this restaurant, Georgia Brown's, a very southern place. I ordered pork chops just to get on his nerves.

He was like, "Yeah, I'll have pork chops too."

I was kind of like, "Oh wait, he's kind of normal." He still looked at me as representing the corporate oligarchy but he's as smart as Dolan is. He's like, "If the *Wall Street Journal* wants to do a story on us, if they write a good story, that's going to be awesome and if they write a shitty story, it's the *Wall Street Journal*, so it's a no-lose situation for me."

John Sellers: We did an advanced action camp just north of Seattle. It was an amazing confluence of activists that were doing some of the most cutting-edge blockages and direct action in the Pacific Northwest at the time. Folks came from around the world. There were folks from Reclaim the Streets in England who came out. It was a great who's-who. We called the camp "Globalize This!" We had the *Wall Street Journal* camping out with us.

Helene Cooper: The deal I made with him was he had to give me the exclusive. He couldn't give it to the *Financial Times*. By now the *FT* had seen my Mike Dolan story and they wanted in, and they had found out about Ruckus somehow. I was like, "No, you can't give it to the *Financial Times*. I have to be the one who embeds in your training camp. If you talk to the *Financial Times*, you're going to lose the *Wall Street Journal*, so pick who you want."

Mike Dolan: I took my tent and I took all my camping gear and all my shit and I go out there and I'm going to be in the woods with these liberal, vegans—that's exactly what they were. *Laughs.* And Helene Cooper showed up. She was all over that story like a gator on a poodle that whole summer.

There was another guy who was with the *Financial Times*, who really wanted to interview me, but Helene had the exclusive on the camp because she was tight with Sellers. I told her about the other reporter and she goes, "Don't you understand? He's trying to be able to come all the way here so he can file from here!" She said, "Don't let him do that. Make him meet at some coffee shop somewhere—just don't let him file his story from the camp. If he does, I don't have the scoop." The *FT* still sent their reporter out there, and I wouldn't let him into the camp. *Laughs.*

Dana Schuerholtz: The camp was at Pragtree Farm, which was part of the Evergreen Land Trust. A group of us had received stewardship and were trying to fix up the place. We built composting toilets, fixed up old structures, and put up circus tents for workshops.

The camp brought activists together to learn about direct action and how to create a culture of resistance, bringing in the arts, music, and puppets, political theater, and grassroots movements. We brought together two-hundred-plus activists from all over this country, Canada, Mexico, and Europe.

Nadine Bloch: We designated certain fields for camping, we opened up a field kitchen. There was a team of people who did everything from cooking, to being health and safety people, to managing runs to the airport or the train or the bus to pick people up, or to pick up beer or whatever was needed in certain circumstances.

Han Shan: The camp was a little crunchy, little hippie, a lot of tents pitched around a forest clearing. Everyone would come and have some slop on their plate for breakfast and cowboy coffee and then move into workshops.

We'd start with nonviolence training 101. So, get up in the morning and you'd watch a slide show and do stuff that, frankly, I feel like you might do in a corporate retreat nowadays, just to help build teamwork and understanding. Then the second half of the day would be the more tactical.

Dana Schuerholz: It was all scheduled out. There was a lot of networking and planning. We had huge maps of downtown Seattle. We were doing ropes courses in the trees, creating giant banners, building lockboxes.

Lisa Fithian: With lockboxes, you have a tube made out of stainless steel or PVC pipe. There's a pin that's welded down through the middle of the tube. When people are going to lockdown, they wear a chain around their wrist with a carabiner. They put their arm in the tube and open the carabiner and hook it onto the pin. There's no way the police can pull them out because they're latched. Some people would take those tubes and wrap them in chicken wire and duct tape, because if you add a lot of stuff like that, it can make the tube harder to cut through.

John Sellers: It's a conduit. There is no way for anyone to pull your arm out of there without breaking your wrist but if you need to unclip for an emergency, you can get out. No one can take you out without cutting the thing apart. Earth First! would bury a whole car in a road and fill it with concrete and then have people lock themselves in that way, put their arm down into it, and clip into place so that logging trucks couldn't come along and lift them out. They'd have to unbury a whole car and do it without breaking people's arms.

The nice thing is that if everybody's wearing one lockbox that they are already clipped into on their right hand, they can all have a carabiner on their left hand too, so it doesn't matter who they bump into, they can plug into one another. We called it a "human molecule" because you could break off fifteen people to encircle a fire engine, something like that. It is infinitely configurable if everybody is dressed correctly. It's the most effective, low-cost way to sustain a human presence somewhere and lock people safely together.

I remember law enforcement, they heard that the lockboxes were called "sleeping dragons" and they really took to that term because they thought it sounded scary and menacing. Whenever possible they wanted to scare people and make them think we were a bunch of terrorists.

Lisa Fithian: In direct action, you always have to be mindful of some people thinking that militancy is driven by how hard-core you might be. I really try and urge people to take the judgment out. Different people can take different levels of risks. No thing is more hard-core than any other. What you have to do is think through what you're doing. Try and do it well because people are at risk. People can get hurt either through pain compliance holds, or how the cops try and extract them, or because the cops are pissed and they rough them up. This is not a game, this shit. Which is actually a lot of what we did in our trainings—help people understand this is not a game. This is real-life stuff. They'll kill us. They have killed people. We have to be smart.

Dana Schuerholz: At the camp, people would sign up for blocks of training to learn about, for example, making a tripod to sit in that police could not get you out of without breaking your body.

Han Shan: We used thirty-foot aluminum poles to create these tripods to block an intersection. You put an activist up in the crux of the tripod and it's very difficult to get them out unless you have, say, a crane. What you're doing is you're putting that activist in danger. They're thirty feet up in the air in a precarious situation. The tripod is stable but only if you don't mess with it. You can't move a vehicle through an intersection, for instance, without getting the tripod out of the way. And you can't do that without carefully deconstructing it. Usually, you've got to get the activist to come down.

Dana Schuerholz: There was a lunch break where everyone would eat and then go back and do more workshops into the evening.

John Sellers: I remember we brought one hundred drums out and did an activist drum training together.

Dana Schuerholz: Different trainings and multiple workshops would happen at the same time. There was role-playing, someone playing a cop, someone playing an activist, someone playing a provocateur, the whole range so you can practice and be ready for different scenarios. People learned to put their bodies on the line symbolically or take nonviolent civil disobedience courses of action. If people make mistakes, get violent, get hurt, it puts everyone else in the affinity group at greater risk. The idea is to understand the gravity of making the choice to do civil disobedience nonviolently. I don't think anybody in their right mind takes that lightly.

The role-playing dates back to the Student Nonviolent Coordinating Committee and all of the civil rights stuff. Rosa Parks had done nonviolent civil disobedience trainings before she ever got on that bus and wouldn't move.

Han Shan: Ruckus had a curriculum that we developed over years that got tighter and better and had an arc through the week. We'd talk about the context of Martin Luther King and Gandhi and the civil rights movement. For some people we helped connect the dots between, say, Rosa Parks and the Highlander School. She didn't just randomly get on the bus and get arrested because she was just too tired to move that day. She got on a couple buses and she didn't get arrested the first two times, and the third one finally worked. It was a strategic, purposeful commission of civil disobedience. We contextualize these things and, for some young activists, it was an "aha moment." They'd never understood that.

We would show civil rights marches and point out how well-dressed people were, not because we were trying to institute a dress code, but because we were thinking about these things. We would talk to people about, "All right, what's your message? Your outfit that you're wearing, is that part of your message?" I took my earrings out for some of the press conferences and sometimes I'd dress nice because I would be able to slip through police lines. I would wear a button-down shirt and a windbreaker and slacks. I have literally walked right up to the police line because I was wearing khakis and a blue button-down shirt and said, "Excuse me." And the cops just separated their arms and let me walk.

On one hand it shows we should take advantage of that more often on our side. But also it was clearly me employing a certain level of privilege, looking enough like what police feel comfortable seeing to think that I was of no threat to them.

In the civil rights movement, people were wearing a tie to their demonstrations because they wanted to present as respectable, recognizing they may have resented the fact that people wouldn't deem them respectable without fucking putting on a goddamn tie. But fuck, you have to say, "I'm going to allow my message to move through as unimpeded as possible."

Nadine Bloch: Some people would learn climbing techniques so you could go up and down a tree or a structure in an urban setting. We would teach people how to silkscreen or stencil or think about what's the best way to make banners that won't rip or that you can deploy easily.

Han Shan: For ninety-five percent of people at the camp, it was about challenging them and showing them that they could do something that they didn't think they could do. It was like, "Watch somebody overcome an obstacle, watch someone face adversity and a fear that they might have, about heights or whatever it might be—watch someone think they couldn't do something then watch them overcome that." They feel powerful. That gives them juice to go into the next day and makes them excited about their potential.

Kevin Danaher: Once you're in a protest and you're threatened with police violence or arrest, it's very emotional. You get all worked up. If we do some playacting ahead of time, people get a chance for their bodies to develop some muscle memory and knowledge of what that feels like, and they'll be more calm in the situation.

Dana Schuerholz: There would be dinner and sometimes planning meetings to figure out a spokescouncil and communication among the different affinity groups.

Han Shan: Obviously throughout, there's bonding that happens when you're taken out of your comfort zone and everyone's sleeping in tents and having long days and eating hippie gruel around the campfire and telling war stories about campaigns they've been involved in. That team building, that collective allyship that you're fostering in those environments is amazing, and something that is the special sauce that you sprinkle on. It was very intentional, but you don't design it, except that you put a bunch of people together and you put them in an uncomfortable environment. You force them all to find their way.

John Sellers: It was just a really cool collection of people who were committing themselves to try to shut down the WTO. Everyone who came to the camp had to commit to spending two months after the camp getting an affinity group or action team ready to come back to Seattle in November.

Celia Alario: I remembered that when we left the camp, the charge was that everybody needed to find fifty people to go to Seattle.

*   *   *

Ed Joiner: We knew we had to rachet up our preparation.

Jim Pugel: I had convinced Chief Joiner that we needed to hit the ground running with 220 Seattle police officers. I had 60 state troopers at my disposal and 110 crowd-control officers from the sheriff department. And we started training all these officers.

Ed Joiner: We basically put every officer in the department through riot control training, all 1,200 of our own officers and quite a number from Bellevue, Kirkland, Renton, and some other nearby locations that would be the first to come to our assistance if we needed it. We trained them with that in mind so they had at least the basic understanding of what their responsibilities would be if things did really get serious. The intent was to use those outlying departments as best we could to fill in for the officers that we had assigned to the venues themselves. We didn't really want to have a lot of other officers from other departments thrown into that situation for a number of reasons. I felt much more comfortable with our own officers because we had direct control over them. You don't always have that same kind of control of other agencies.

Jim Pugel: We brought in outside trainers from Los Angeles County who had dealt with the Rodney King riots.

Maud Daudon: The police went into these big warehouses for crowd-control training and people threw things at them and they had to deal with a lot of things that they weren't used to dealing with from pro-testers. Thank god they did it so they were somewhat prepared that way.

Ron Griffin: My officers hated the fact that I took them up to the North Bend fire training academy. We'd go into an airplane simulator and deploy gas in there. Then I would make them take their gas masks off and get exposed to gas. The military guys had done that before but a lot of them hadn't. They bitched and moaned and complained—oh my god. "There's got to be a lawsuit here someplace." *Laughs.* "You're mistreating us." Every bit of training I did myself, and it's not a fun event. But I did that because I knew that, likely, you're going to get exposed to gas and you need to know that you can fight through it.

Maud Daudon: As we got closer, we did ask for additional resources to be brought in from the federal level. We asked the White House spe-cifically, could they provide some support. That was not forthcoming, unfortunately. So I think we really suffered. We didn't have enough manpower and money.

Pat Davis: One thing that we had to make clear was that Seattle Host was not in control of the streets. And the police came right into one of our meetings and said, "You have nothing to do with what goes on outside."

We said, "Good, we're glad about that." So that was definitely a separation there.

Maud Daudon: There was something like thirty-eight agencies that participated in the planning process—from federal to state to local.

Vivian Phillips, communications director for Mayor Paul Schell: We would do what's called tabletop trainings, these reenactments, where you go through these scenarios about what might happen and how things play out from a public safety perspective. There was this necessity for the city to prepare from a public safety standpoint for any kind of terrorist incident.

Jim Pugel: Secret Service came in along with the FBI and in these tabletop exercises their entire focus was international terrorism. People coming in, maybe blowing stuff up, people coming in clandestine and going after the president or the heads of all these other nation-states. Never was there really any mention of any labor-related movement and certainly not much on the Direct Action Network.

Laurie Brown: We were in a new world. We had the internet. We didn't have smartphones yet, but people could mobilize using technology. We were clearly dealing with young people who were using consensus for decision-making. We had never dealt with that before.

Charles Mandigo: FBI headquarters did a threat assessment and we shared that with the SPD. That threat assessment was on the question of whether or not there was going to be a threat of terrorism incidents. The FBI came to the conclusion that there was a low threat of national terrorism events.

Maud Daudon: That was the major concern, terrorism. We would pipe up and say, "There looks like there's going to be mass demonstrations," but the rest of the agencies were not as concerned about that as local folks were.

Han Shan: It wasn't just the Seattle police but the feds, and there were talks about terrorism and frightening things. Obviously, we did our best to say, "If there's concerns about that, it doesn't have anything to do with us. We're as concerned as anybody about any of those reports that might be true. We don't want to see anyone get hurt."

Charles Mandigo: The report we provided did go into prior WTO-type meetings that had happened in other countries and we determined there was significant risk of civil disobedience and protests and getting into some of the acts that were done in other places. Like this guy out of France—I forget who he was, José something.

José Bové, member of Confédération Paysanne: I will explain, please forgive my bad English: I was a member of the French Union of Small Farmers, which is called Confédération Paysanne, and we understood very early that agriculture was going inside of this agreement on free trade and that it would completely change, at the international level, the place of the farmers. It would put most of the big companies in the position of changing the rules for the farmers and the consumers all over the world. It was really a fight for food sovereignty against the big companies which were making their business in the countries in the South. This was for us, really the beginning of the fight.

Most people didn't know anything about the WTO. This was some language that was completely strange for them. If you discuss with anybody in the United States and in Europe or African countries, nobody knew what this was about. This was our first job to make it clear for the people that this is going to change not only international rules but their way of life and for us their way of eating, which was, of course, an important thing for everybody in the world.

In the beginning of the 1990s we founded a new international movement of farmers from all the continents. That was a very important movement because for the first time at an international level, farmers were having the same strategy to fight the big companies and WTO.

In France especially we had the capacity to show to the people what was happening. Just after the beginning of WTO, Europe refused to let the exportation from the United States of beef treated with hormones and this was a big fight we had in Europe since the beginning of the '80s and we win this fight at the French level and then at the European level—it was forbidden to produce beef treated with hormones for health reasons. Then the United States decided to attack Europe because they were refusing the importations. The United States said, "We don't care about health reasons. We only talk about free trade, and you're not allowed inside of the WTO to take health reasons to stop the trade from one country to another."

In 1997, WTO decided with the United States, Europe is not allowed to block these importations. That was a big fight and, at the end, WTO turned to the United States and said because Europe doesn't want to respect the rules of WTO, we give you the opportunity to put a hundred percent tax on agricultural products coming in from Europe. Of course nobody will buy these products coming on the United States market because the price would be doubled. It's not possible for the people to buy those products. Products from Europe were chosen by the United States and one of those products—very symbolic in French culture—was the Roquefort cheese. That's why after that we had two months of demonstrations at the local level, people in our area in the south of France knew very well what was happening. At the national level or the international level, nobody knew about it.

I was at that moment a farmer, making this Roquefort cheese. And I was also a member of the farmers' alliance and we decided to struggle against this decision. We decided on the twelfth of August '99 to make a symbolic demonstration against a fast-food McDonald's which was being built in the small city of Millau, less than twenty kilometers from my farm. On this day, we made a big demonstration with four hundred people, families, music, and so on, a very direct, nonviolent action and we decided to dismantle this McDonald's. The building of the McDonald's was not yet finished and so I dismantled it with my tractor.

The government and the justice decided to bring us, five people, in jail as organizers of this movement. Four of them could leave the prison after four days and they had to pay a bail to get out of jail. But for me they refused because I had been sentenced already for different actions protesting GMOs and so I had to stay in jail while many protests were beginning.

. After fifteen days, they asked me to pay a bail to get out. But it was very unusual to put the leaders of unions in jail for a pacifist demonstration. So I refused to pay the bail, saying that for me I was not in a bad American movie where you can get out of jail if you pay a bail. I stayed in jail saying I refused to pay the bail.

That increased the movement and a lot of people were sending money to pay the bail but I still, with the support of the farmers' union, refused to get out. At the end, these farmers from Texas sent me the money to get out of jail. Their letter said, "What you did with McDonald's we should have done that twenty or thirty years ago."

So that's how I got out of jail in September '99. And just when I get out from the jail in front of the press, I said, "The next meeting together with more and more people will be in November in Seattle."

Jim Pugel: As time wore on, we got more and more information. One friend was the chief of the Washington State Patrol. She and some other guys I knew on the State Patrol were telling me, "Hey, this is going to be bigger than we thought." We also heard it from the King County Sheriff's Office.

Larry Mayes: SPD was much more political than we were. Dave Reichert is an elected sheriff—he didn't have a political boss. So he was able to, I guess, safely become more vocal. That probably started the dissension between him and the mayor's office.

Dave Reichert: First I served as an appointed sheriff, then I had to run a campaign and I was elected in 1998. So there was an educational process between being an elected and an appointed sheriff. I had a lot of freedom as an elected official in determining how I was going to support and offer services to assist other agencies. As far as the WTO ministerial went, my viewpoint was whatever SPD needed, I was ready to help. But there was a lot of angst among the Seattle City Council, the mayor.

Larry Mayes: My guys came to me again and said this is getting serious. Mayor Schell believes that he can pull this off with a best-case-scenario planning. But our intelligence grew to the point where it was clear that the protesters were recruiting additional anarchists from not only Oregon, but across the United States. Some intel even indicated in Europe. They were beginning to gather equipment, gas canisters, gas masks, hammers, spray paint, communications equipment, all that kind of stuff. It was clear they were coming and they were going to disrupt—and it was public. Newspapers were starting to report on the WTO and the protests and how the numbers were growing. The mayor and Seattle PD were skeptical of some of the intel. I kept thinking, "Sooner or later, they're going to change their mind." I still can't understand why they didn't accept the intelligence information. If not that, why not the public information about how adamant the opposition was to the WTO?

I asked one of our people who was working in the planning group if he had heard any discussion of talking to the governor about the National Guard. His reply was "The only thing that I had heard is that

Paul Schell is adamantly against the National Guard." In no circumstances was he going to have them appearing during the WTO. He was not going to present that to the demonstrators. Keep in mind, it wasn't just Paul Schell. He had a City Council of the same ilk. Some of them were out there supporting marching. So you've got Paul Schell, a very liberal, progressive kind of guy, incredible advocate for the city, and you've got a similar City Council. There was a ton of pressure on the police department to go along with it. The police department is not the boss in these situations. The mayor and the council are.

Ed Joiner: There's a process you have to go through to get the National Guard. First, the mayor has to declare an emergency. That then has to go to the governor and then the governor is the one who authorizes the use of the National Guard. We talked to the National Guard ahead of time to see if they would put their officers or their personnel through training and perhaps have them available on standby and they said, "No." There simply was not enough evidence that it was going to become difficult enough ahead of time to require that.

Gary Locke: The Seattle police really didn't have any intelligence indicating any serious threat of violence or destruction. Whether or not they had conferred with enough people, or other agencies had the intel that was not shared, or the Seattle Police Department did not reach out to these other agencies to thoroughly determine the threat assessments—I'm not sure. Obviously there was a breakdown by some elements within our local agencies. But I wasn't privy to any of that. Never got to my level.

Larry Mayes: When I got that response that Paul Schell didn't want the National Guard, Annette Sandberg, who was the Washington State Patrol chief—she was sharp—I knew she had concerns. So I'm thinking, "Well, maybe she's brought the governor in on this." I certainly would have by then.

Annette Sandberg: It was their city. So it's like, "How much can we impose on them?" Clearly, Chief Stamper and some of the folks from the city of Seattle had a different perspective on what should be allowed. We were never on the same page. To be honest with you, Seattle PD was always kind of out in a different realm. I think people were trying to impress upon them, "Hey, be careful about the way you approach this. It could get out of control." Stamper and I didn't see eye to eye. I don't think we had hardly two words.

Larry Mayes: Reichert and I finally said they're not going to change their mind. We began additional in-house training and preparation. Reichert began talking to other departments in the region, their chiefs, about mutual aid because of our belief that things were going to go to hell in a handbasket. Mutual aid is when something happens out in the field and you've got to pull a lot of your troops in from other agencies. Other departments come in temporarily to back you. We saw it coming, that we were going to have to staff more than we had planned on.

* * *

Helene Cooper: I kept writing these stories and my editors were like, "These stories!" They loved them. But they would make fun of me too: "There goes Helene off again, writing about her little crazy environmentalists training to swarm the WTO."

I remember once I had a quote from somebody, one of those stories that said, "This is going to be like Chicago '68"—or something like that.

Everybody in the newsroom was like, "Ooh! Are they going to call them the Seattle Seven?"

They were all laughing at me, and I was like, "Yeah, whatever. I'm enjoying what I'm doing!"

Mike Dolan: The momentum, the snowball effect, of 1999 in Seattle, was downhill the whole way. It just totally worked out. By the time October comes, the symbiosis, the alchemy, the whole greater than the sum of its parts, was truly an organizing fact. The Direct Action Network gave the reformists cover. The reform critique and the symposia gave the Direct Action Network cover. We gave the delegates on the inside cover. It was mutually supportive.

Ron Judd: My whole foundation for dialogue wherever I go: "I don't want to hear what's in it for me. I want to hear what's in it for *we*, and how do we figure that out?"

Tracy Katelman: It seemed so organic. There was stuff popping up all over. Don and I would go to a lot of meetings representing the groups that we worked with. I certainly wasn't representing all the environmentalists but I was working with a lot of them and I've known a lot of them for decades. I knew a lot of tree-huggers up and down the coast. Obviously, our side was more organic.

Don Kegley: I could see that their way of deciding things was not the union way of deciding things. When a situation came along where we had to make a decision, we split up. Labor was over here, and the environmentalists were over there. We allotted one hour for discussions about the decision to be made and then came back together to see what we had. Labor was always done in four minutes. Who knows how long it took the environmentalists to come to a decision.

Tracy Katelman: God, who knows. *Laughs.* Most of the time I probably left before we reached a decision. I'm a big process person but there is a point. I just want to make a strategy and get it done. Union organizing versus the environmental organizing, the union organizing is like, "Stop the bullshit and let's get to work."

Colin Hines: I've done environmental stuff. It can be very doomy and very finger-waggy. I think it's fine to frighten people but then you've got to give them something to hope for. In all the work I've done, I've tried to concentrate on "Okay, this is the problem. How are we going to get out of it?" I worked on a report called "Time to Replace Globalization." We were doing things like proposing AGAST—A General Agreement on Sustainable Trade. Basically, we rewrote the rules of the WTO in order that you still have some trade and some movement but the end goal is not to be internationally competitive but to rebuild sustainable societies.

Vandana Shiva: We were always told by journalists, "You know what you are against but not what you are for."

And I said, "No, we're against free trade and globalization because we know what we are for. We are for the environment. We are for human rights. We are for democracy."

Celia Alario: We did a lot of media trainings helping to find your personal sound bite, your personal reason, your big why, and then role-playing and practice interviews. My hope was that anybody who was approached by a reporter knew that they didn't have to talk if they didn't want to, and how to tactfully turn down a reporter and send them toward someone else, but also how to speak up if they wanted to.

David Taylor: There were trainings that happened all over the city—satellite spaces around the Convergence Center where we were able to do more mass trainings.

David Solnit: Art and Revolution was working out of the Convergence Center but we also had another warehouse where we were doing mass production of art. That was our main space.

John Sellers: Ruckus had our own action center. We helped raise the money for the Convergence Center but we rented our own warehouse action space north of the city in a pretty anonymous location. We were coordinating actions out of there.

Jim Hightower: The Methodist Church became another important center. They just threw open their doors—including the sanctuary—and said, "Come." And we did. All kinds of meetings and sessions took place there, psychological care. It was right in the center of everything.

Michael Ramos: There were a lot of the events at the First United Methodist Church downtown. And the church community was involved in some very particular ways. Food was served there. It was kind of like a respite area. I recognized the symbolism of having that place as a place of hospitality and from which people were sent out to continue the struggle.

Mike Dolan: I looked at the church's library downstairs. It had a big, long table, books all around. It was a perfect ad hoc radio studio! And

I wanted radio. I mean, it was a really nice setup. The acoustics were good and there was a big oak table that guests could sit around. I realized that I was going to have to wire this room. So I called the IBEW local and I said, "Can somebody throw in a T1 line? I need a really fat wire into that room so the radio producers like Marc Cooper of the *Nation*, Jim Hightower, Amy Goodman can hook up in there." And so, labor donated. The union guys came down and wired that room.

Jim Hightower: Susan DeMarco and I had, at the time, a radio talk show that was sponsored primarily by the UAW, so we were connected to labor. It was a national show and we broadcast in Austin out of a place called Threadgill's—that's where Janis Joplin had her first singing gigs. We had taken the show on the road before, so we had an ability to do that, and we started broadcasting from the basement of that church.

Mike Dolan: They worked out a schedule so that they weren't all broadcasting at the same time. And working with the producers, I fed folks into their shows. This is '99, so it's before streaming, and the fact that they were doing live radio from the basement of the Methodist church was a good coup and a really great way to get that message out live and in the streets.

Hilary McQuie: We had many months to organize this. So by the time we got to November there was eight months worth of yard signs and small meetings and church groups and all of that. All of Seattle knew what the critique was and what was happening with the meeting.

four waters: The Convergence Center felt optimistic. That space was beautiful to me. One day, someone I had grown up with—she had no experience in activism—showed up totally randomly to be part of the protest. Watching the space through her eyes and watching this world through her eyes was such a gift for me. I was coming in with my history of cynicism and experience and she was coming in with none of that. You are putting people through not just a process of education but through a process of empowerment and that empowerment then comes back into that space and gets reinforced with all of the activity. David Solnit was doing his giant puppets, which were just awesome.

A sample of the countless posters, zines, and broad-
sheets that circulated in advance of the protests.

You could have said that this felt like going to war, but that's not what
it felt like. It felt like we were going to sing and dance and tell a story.

*   *   *

Pascal Lamy: I became the European trade commissioner in the fall
of 1999. The Seattle preparations were in large part the beginning of
my tenure. Before Seattle, a small group meeting took place in Switzerland. There was a small group of ministers who tried to frame the
thing and prepare it so that the tarmac would be ready for take off. I

remember full well exiting the conference saying, "Wow, what a mess." I began to think, "This system only works in that messy way." But my culture, the French one, is originally a culture shaped in an organized way. I have to prepare myself that this might be messy.

Maud Daudon: I kept saying to the mayor, "Look, this could be really crazy. I mean you have to know going into this that it could be really crazy."

And he kept stating publicly to the protesters, "We want you to come. We want you to be able to have your say, but we also want you to respect our city."

He did a lot of that ahead of time, in part, because all of us were like, "Ah, it looks big. It looks really big." And Norm Stamper kept saying, "Ed Joiner's in charge of this thing. He's got my complete one hundred percent support. Work with Ed." So I worked with Ed.

Larry Mayes: Joiner was still saying this was going to be a peaceful demonstration. But by November, we had solid intel. We had solid numbers on huge groups. We had information that some of these peaceful groups that Seattle had been negotiating with to march in certain areas, they were going to shut it down. It was clear that was the intent.

Norm Stamper: I kept saying, "Stop oversimplifying who these protesters are." Some are of the leftist-Marxist orientation, some are more clearly environmentalists, some were labor and child labor issues, some were immigration, and on and on. Anything you could think of that was significant and global was represented within these people. All those issues appealed to me as important questions that people need to keep asking themselves repeatedly.

Dave Reichert: Some people will say, "The cops assume that everyone was there to create a problem." But that's not true at all. We knew who the peaceful protesters were and we understood there was a large number there that were peaceful. We also knew that some of the peaceful protesters could come in contact with the anarchists and could be affected by their viewpoints and tactics. So it was our job to try and quell that and separate the bad seed from the rest of the group.

Ron Griffin: I go to a meeting, we're probably three weeks out from the event, and I've got Seattle PD saying, "Ron, we've made a decision that we want your group to work under our policies and procedures." Now, I'm sitting at a big conference. I'm the only one representing the sheriff department—everything I went to I was alone. The Seattle PD was almost twice our size and there'd be a bunch of their people around the conference table. One guy would be in charge of pencils, the other guy would be in charge of the erasers, and the third person was a lieutenant who was in charge of the pencil and eraser guys. *Laughs.* I tell the story that way but I'm actually not far off. I'd go back to my boss, Larry Mayes, and go, "Chief, you're killing me!"

They made that request for me to operate under their policy procedures but I did a lot of stuff where either I had to go back and ask for forgiveness or get the chief's buy-in on it because I got pretty strong at those meetings. I said, "We're coming as we are. I'm not changing all this. So let's figure out how we go from here."

Yalonda Sinde: We were prepared for the police violence that we anticipated would happen. A lot of that was preparing for safety. Making sure there was a place we would meet if there were people who felt unsafe, making sure the training was in place and that we had security, because there's also people who aren't necessarily part of the protest who will blend in and start something to make it look like we did something bad. We were used to that and prepared for it. People come and maybe throw a Molotov cocktail and try to attribute it to your group. A lot of it was preparing for the worst. Making sure we had a plan B if the police blocked us.

David Taylor: Our big breakthrough was using Nextel two-way radios. That was absolutely revolutionary. This was before we had text messages to do tactical. The Ruckus Society folks had a radio dispatch center, and each affinity group had communications networks and we could tactically move people around.

John Sellers: We rented dozens and dozens of Nextels. They had radio functions that we would use on climbs and for different actions.

David Taylor: It was this interesting mix of having some level of centralized tactical communication while, at the same time, being decentralized in our organizing.

John Sellers: Our electronic communications were almost as good as the cops', maybe better in some ways, and that gave us a huge advantage. We had never had that kind of flexibility and communications infrastructure before.

Hilary McQuie: Lisa Fithian was the one that realized that this very classical plan that was hammered out, about surrounding the venues and blockading, it didn't really account for all the thousands of people who we knew were going to show up and not be plugged into an affinity group. Lisa was so instrumental in coming up with a tactical plan to account for those people.

Lisa Fithian: We had at least 3,000 people who were trained and had a common vision of how we were going to shut it down. When you have enough people like that to anchor it on the day of, it now enables all those other people who are coming—but haven't gotten integrated—to get pulled in to what's already happening.

Ron Judd: We put thousands of people up in people's homes. It was amazing how many people opened up to people. We turned to churches, union halls, environmental organizations, whoever had community floor space—I got them to open up the libraries for people to come and stay, have a place to put a sleeping bag down. We were always thinking, how can we make sure that people feel like, "If I buy that ticket, if I get on that plane, if I get in my car, I'm going to have a place to stay." We wanted to try to create an infrastructure where we could guarantee that as much as possible.

That was a great thing about all the work, the amount of collaboration in preparation and creating the infrastructure necessary to manage strategically and tactically what we, in our gut and our heart, said was going to be a lot of people.

Nick Licata: There was concern about homelessness and all these 50,000 people, we didn't want people sleeping on the streets. Do you really think they're all going to be fitting in Holiday Inns? Downtown, at that time, didn't have a lot of hotel rooms so there were going to be people in the streets. I said, "Hey, we don't want people living on the streets. We think that if there are vacant rooms, people should be able to offer to let them stay there. Let's pass a resolution." The council said, "Okay, as long as it's framed that way." I remember one of the cartoons that was done, it had council members putting sweets on the pillows in hotel rooms for the protesters.

Laurie Brown: The county had been preparing meals and jail space and they even created space out at Sand Point, a decommissioned military base with a big warehouse. The agreement had been reached that if people engaged in civil disobedience they would be arrested. Of course, there was no discussion about what people thought "civil disobedience" was and what that looked like.

Ed Joiner: We had strike teams, more than two hundred officers that were equipped with some shields and helmets and the whole bit. The expectation was that we would be able to hold the line, so to speak, with them.

Charles Mandigo: Myself and Dave Reichert, the King County sheriff, had gone to the SPD and said, "Hey, look. You're not ready for this."

SPD's attitude was "Hey, we're ready. We've checked all our boxes. We're doing what we've always done before, we've talked to the protesters, we know what the game plan is—we're ready for this." It was kind of like when you've had successes in the past and you get new information and you don't adjust what you've done in the past based on this new information.

Larry Mayes: More and more people were concerned. I know that Washington State Patrol was concerned. I know that the FBI was concerned. I know the Secret Service was concerned.

Ed Joiner: We've always had pretty good rapport with both the FBI and the Secret Service because a number of events have been held in previous years so we had that basic, fundamental agreement in terms of how we would work together so we did not have any inner conflict between the agencies that way.

Jim Pugel: We worked with the Secret Service. They wanted to shut down the whole city and not let anyone in. We were also talking with the ACLU and others that we had a fairly good relationship with, and all these meetings went on for a long time.

Annette Sandberg: We all kept coming to the meetings and saying, "Hey, this really needs to be a holistic effort. Things can get out of control very, very quickly, just because of the volume of unknown people who are flying into the area. If it were Washingtonians and it was the normal business of some big event that we handle every year, we get it. But this isn't. This is people coming from all over the world."

I never got the impression that Seattle wanted to hear that, particularly the higher-up in the police department. I think people down in the rank and file, they were concerned. But I don't think that it was getting to the upper level.

Norm Stamper: Cops are hardwired for action. But it's important to ask the question "Is this necessary? Really, do you need to break up that intersection? Why?"

"Well, they're blocking traffic."

"So? We know what happens when you clear an intersection of people who are blocking traffic. We've done it with terribly awful strategies. Do you *need* to clear it? If that answer is no, then don't! Just don't!"

Ron Griffin:. I ended up with three different readied platoons. The success of a good command is to surround yourself with good people, smart people, and let them help you with the work. Each platoon had about thirty-five people in it. In that process of preparing, I realized that a platoon could get split. So I said to Larry Mayes, "I need a command person with each of those platoons so that the decision to deploy nonlethal weapons—gas and sting-ball grenades and such— would have the command-level person making that decision on that team." I also equipped our teams with an AR-15 rifle guy. Seattle PD didn't like that. But you're downtown Seattle, you've got high buildings everywhere. You would not be able to take out a high threat with a pistol. I know in the movies, they do it. John Wayne's on a racing horse, and he hits a guy 2,000 yards away with a pistol. In real life? Not the case. So I was coming with AR-15s.

Yalonda Sinde: We weren't unrealistic about the danger of it because when you're talking about toppling corporate power you could be risking your life. People could be injured. People could be killed.

Jim Pugel: We had an arson a couple weeks before the WTO. It was the first time that we had seen the circle with the *A* in it, which were left by the anarchists. Those started showing up.

Annette Sandberg: You don't want to ever say the anarchists are organized, because supposedly they don't, but they appeared to be fairly organized. There was some discussion about how many were coming up, where they were coming from. Before the conference started, they had taken over a vacant building. There was a lot of discussion: "Why are we allowing that to happen? Especially since it's pretty close to the convention center. Is that going to create problems?"

Vivian Phillips: I think the gravity of what was about to take place probably hit me no more than two weeks in advance of the event. There was a meeting with the Direct Action Network and City Council. There were public safety officials, some council members, county representatives, all in attendance. It was at the Seattle Public Library and I remember this back-and-forth around what was being framed as an agreement, that the Direct Action Network was going to, for lack of a better term, be very civil in their disobedience.

What I feel like all of the city officials heard was that there would be no major-scale protests. But that's not what I heard. I heard "Something's about to go down here."

Han Shan: I was on a radio program, along with Dave Reichert and the mayor, which was very strange, and I said, "We're going to shut down the WTO. That's what we're going to do."

Dave Reichert: I was on a radio show, and the mayor appeared before me and he was asked the question "Will it be safe for people to come to the city?"

His answer was "Oh, absolutely. It's going to be a peaceful protest." In fact, he said, "I encourage people to come to Seattle and witness the freedom to express your opinions. The freedom of speech will be magnified and glorified and you'll be able to witness free speech firsthand in a peaceful way throughout the city."

And I'm hoping for that. But I was asked the same question and I said, "Please don't come to Seattle. We do have information that there could be some violence and property destruction and the potential of people rioting. So I would encourage people, if you can, to stay away from downtown Seattle during WTO week."

Well, the mayor was not pleased with my comments. I'm an elected official—and a nonpartisan one at that. People couldn't figure out where I belonged because I kept it pretty straight. Democrats were claiming me as a Democrat and Republicans were claiming me as a Republican. *Laughs.* I was just calling it like I saw it and saying what I knew to be true. But the mayor became very upset with me.

I had discussions with the police chief and said, "We do have information"—again, I couldn't legally get specific about it but—"we do have intelligence that we will have riots. I'm offering my help." The Washington State Patrol chief did the same, offered help.

The mayor and the police chief said, "No, thank you. We won't need more help." In fact, the mayor said, "We don't want your help. This is our city. And if we have a problem, our police department will handle it."

I said, "Well, from what I know, you may need some assistance."

The mayor said, "Stay out of our city."

Jim Pugel: About a week before the actual thing started, we wanted to petition Gary Locke's office to activate the National Guard to do perimeter control around the convention center so that we, the cops, would be the front line facing the demonstrators. We were turned down for two reasons. One, the political viewpoint. How can we call a state of emergency when it hasn't even happened? We can't do that. And number two, the Makah Tribe up on the Olympic Peninsula had been granted the right that summer by the federal courts to do their first whale hunt in one hundred years. The Makah Tribe went out in the Strait of Juan de Fuca and they were hunting whales, and the state spent its entire budget of National Guard troops up on the Olympic Peninsula during the summer, thinking that environmentalists and others were going to storm the Makah tribal reservation. That never happened.

Laurie Brown: I was present at a press conference that happened one week before WTO was supposed to convene. Ruckus Society and Mike Dolan and some other protesters were included.

Han Shan: A week ahead, I stood with Ed Joiner, Paul Schell. Dolan spoke, I spoke. I said, "We are here, we're nonviolent, but we are dedicated to shutting down the WTO. We're opposed to it wholeheartedly—full stop. We're committed to nonviolence but we're going to prevent these meetings from happening, if we can."

Laurie Brown: When the press conference was over, I was really alarmed at what I had heard, which was two different realities. The mayor was saying, "Everyone is going to be heard and no one is going to be hurt." Other people were echoing that. The police department said what they wanted to say about their confidence in this going off smoothly.

The representatives from Direct Action Network and Ruckus were saying loudly and proudly, "We're going to shut this down. Yes, we've enjoyed meeting with you, we appreciate you inviting us here, but we're here to tell you that we're going to shut it down."

No one said anything in response. No words were coming out of their mouths. I was freaked out. Whether or not they had the ability to shut it down, I didn't know, but I knew that they were determined to try. How could the city be prepared if they're not even willing to acknowledge that is the goal of these demonstrators?

They were relying on what Ron Judd was saying. They should have been relying on what Ron Judd was saying for the labor community but they didn't understand the nuance of these other demonstrator groups, these other organizations which didn't consider Ron Judd their leader. They didn't care what Ron Judd promised in terms of sticking to a certain march route and sticking to certain agreements with the police department. It was at that point that I became very alarmed.

After the meeting, I exchanged phone numbers with Han Shan from Ruckus. He knew I had a background in the labor movement and he said, "Just in case, can I get your number? Here's my number." We plugged those numbers into our cell phones.

Face it, anybody who works for the mayor, ultimately your job is to have his back and to make sure that he looks good. I was worried that that wasn't going to be possible. There were so many worries on so many levels.

Vivian Phillips: I noticed how monosyllabic the Direct Action Network was. And I think, unfortunately, the skill for listening is not something that everybody possesses. What happens is people start to make up stuff in their head to fill in the blanks. I think that some of the elected officials felt that their conversation with the Direct Action Network meant that nothing severe was going to happen—just by virtue of talking. And I never really heard that.

Norm Stamper: John Sellers at the Ruckus Society, I think he showed some pretty good leadership. He was alerting us to stuff but he would just come out and say, "Don't think we're going to take your side. We are Ruckus Society and we are, in fact, going to convey our political agenda through these tactics and strategies." That's where he was coming from.

Dana Schuerholz: Shutting down the conference and drawing attention to our causes were our goals. I'm a photographer and had done a lot of gorilla art action at that time where we would do false fronts of newspapers for different issues. A bunch of us, mostly Seattle activists, took on the project of a false front of the *Seattle Post-Intelligencer* just a few days prior to November 30. I used mostly my photographs and we had writers write articles to expose the WTO. "Boeing workers lose their jobs as jobs move overseas"—those kinds of articles. We laid out a spreadsheet the size of the newspaper at the time. It had four pages, the front cover, the back, and the middle two pages. The back page talked about the different planned protests, event times and places. We had it printed in Oregon because we knew if we had it printed locally, word would get out. We had something like 5,000 copies printed, a significant number.

We organized about fifty people to meet at a warehouse the night before Thanksgiving. We wanted to target Thanksgiving dinner, when people would come together for conversations. Whoever looked at this newspaper would have some great talking points, vibrant conversations and debates. That night people got stacks of papers and fanned out throughout the districts of Seattle. We gave everyone quarters to open the newspaper boxes and put the false cover on top of each

The false front for the *Seattle Post-Intelligencer*.

paper. Anyone who bought a paper would read what we had written. It would become obvious once they opened the paper because there was another front page—the real one—but they would have already read the false front. The writers wrote really good articles. We got feedback that some of the Boeing workers who had gotten the paper were shocked.

Not all of the copies got distributed but a lot did. What happened was once the newspaper realized that we had done this, they went around to all the boxes and took them out as fast as they could. The other newspaper in town took a picture of it and published it along with some of the articles. The story rippled far and wide. One of the television news stations in Seattle contacted the Direct Action Network, asking to interview the people who had done this. The *Post-Intelligencer* would have had us arrested so we made a deal to do the interview if I could be disguised and they would change my voice. I was interviewed with a giant puppet head on and they distorted my voice. It was on television. They were broadcasting this giant puppet head talking about why we did this and why it's important.

Larry Mayes: The conference was set to begin on Tuesday, November 30. Over the last weekend beforehand things went pretty well but the atmosphere was changing. We had already staged our requested crowd control personnel, and Ron Griffin was ready to go with our forces. SPD was ready with theirs. During the weekend, delegates began arriving. Protesters began arriving. The anarchists arrived. We still didn't have the National Guard.

Don Kegley: We managed to get tens of thousands of people to Seattle, both environmentalists and all fifty-two unions under the steelworkers' umbrella sent people by the busload, by the trainload, by cars.

Lori Wallach: We had organized to put up 3,500 people in homes. We had a volunteer car pool that had hundreds of vehicles, some of them staffing celebrities because we had musicians and movie stars, Vandana Shiva and Ralph Nader and stars of our movement who needed to get taken to different events.

Colin Hines: I was giving a talk at the London School of Economics against globalization and for a kind of localization, just before Seattle. After the meeting one of the professors said to me, "You're going to Seattle, aren't you?"

I said, "Oh, yeah, of course."

She said, "I can't go. I'm so furious. But I've got this friend of mine that's going and she's really nice but she's quite shy. Would you mind sort of looking after her a bit, demonstrations and all that stuff?"

"Oh," I said, "sure—who is it?"

She said, "Julie Christie."

I had actually met Christie before, when I was doing stuff on nuclear disarmament. She was in some demonstrations so we had a bit of a chat. So I said, "Okay, marvelous."

José Bové: When we decided to go to Seattle, we decided to bring Roquefort—free Roquefort—back in the United States to give for the people. We sent ourselves five hundred kilos of the Roquefort cheese, which arrived a day before us in Seattle, and also we had some Roquefort cheese in our bags. When we arrived in Washington, customs asked us if we had something to declare and I said, "Yes, I have Roquefort cheese." I showed her then the Roquefort cheese but there were so many journalists waiting for us, they say, "Okay, you have Roquefort cheese, you can go on and come inside of the United States." *Laughs.* I don't think they're allowed to do this but maybe we had some good luck.

Kim Thayil: I go to visit Krist, and Jello was staying with him and we were rehearsing at a friend of mine's rehearsal space, also downtown, in anticipation of the events.

Jello Biafra: We did two rehearsals, maybe. I got to hand it to them because I didn't want to just play old songs or covers. I had new songs written that I hadn't done with anybody, that I thought might be really good for this protest. So I showed Krist some tunes. There was also "Let's Lynch the Landlord," one of our Dead Kennedys songs, and we did "Full Metal Jackoff" off the album I did with D.O.A.—a long, dark, and very timely one, which takes a lot out, physically and emotionally.

Celia Alario: We gave people a bunch of little palm cards with the Direct Action media hotline on them—which we were feverishly printing at Kinko's and cutting up—so that if they saw reporters, they would also tell mainstream journalists how to find out about what we were doing.

Mike Dolan: Per Lori Wallach's invitation, this guy Jock Nash was in my headquarters during the final buildup in the last hours before the battle started. He was there on behalf of Roger Milliken, the John Birch Society guy. Look, angst over populism and the left-right coalition—that conversation and those aspects of anti-globalization, anti–corporate rule were presaged in the '90s, leading up to the Battle in Seattle, where that conservative money was manifest. You take some John Birch guy's money and it goes through these funnels like me, and it ends up underwriting the Convergence Center, where David Solnit and all the rest of them set up their operation. I just think that's the funniest way that anti-globalization money has ever funneled—and it made the tent bigger than many of us wanted the tent to be.

Jim Pugel: A couple of days before the WTO, there was an event where a group of these Direct Action folks from out of town took elevators up to a timber company that had a branch in Seattle and they stormed that office and trashed it. The closer we got, there were what we call "pre-incident indicators" or "precursor events" where small groups would do a small arson—in a dumpster, or at Abercrombie & Fitch, at Old Navy. John Sellers and some guys repelled off of the Old Navy with a huge banner.

Han Shan: In the final days before the ministerial began, there was an action that we did along with Global Exchange, where we hung a banner outside the flagship store for Old Navy. It was a sweatshops-oriented message.

Chie Abad: I did a demonstration in front of the clothing retail stores that were involved in the sweatshop lawsuits. People think all the clothes that say "Made in the U.S.A." are made according to American standards, but not in Saipan. The flag that they fly over the buildings are all the Star-Spangled Banner, it's the U.S. totally—like Puerto Rico, same thing—but the working conditions not the same.

Julia Hughes: We felt it was important to have a presence at the ministerial and to message that moving forward with apparel and textiles as a global industry was going well. The fashion industry really had a major victory with the creation of the WTO because it ended the decades-long system of quotas on all imports of textiles and apparel to the United States. Back in the '50s and '60s there had been complaints of imports of textile and apparel products hurting the U.S. domestic industry. So there were the first quotas on imports from countries like Japan, Korea, Hong Kong, Taiwan. A huge web of quotas developed all over the world and that system had a life of its own until the World Trade Organization. With the U.S. hosting the ministerial, the expectation was that there was going to be a chance for more market opening and fewer trade restrictions like the old quotas. I think we all felt very, very positive about it.

Victor Menotti: Our flagship teach-in right before the 30th went on for more than a day. We had workshops and breakout groups. It felt like *movement* energy was there. There were people in the hallways, packed with organizing side meetings and all kinds of activities.

John Nichols: At the teach-in you saw fishermen from Indonesia, you saw union members from Detroit, and you saw farmers from France, and they were all listening to each other and they were trying toward the same goal. In most previous iterations of protests, except for maybe the popular front of the 1930s, people would be going for their own goals. In this case, they were going for a broader goal: upend what the WTO was doing in pursuit of a more humane world.

Ralph Nader: It was almost like nineteenth-century stuff, very hands-on, no virtual this or that. No looking at iPhones while you're listening to a speaker. It was the last of the old-fashioned lectures and rallies.

José Bové: We had five hundred kilos of Roquefort cheese in Seattle and we were there at the first meeting at the big theater. We had very big meetings with lots of people from all over the world and unions from the United States and so I was speaking at this meeting, I take out my Roquefort cheese and I showed it to everybody and say, "This is going to be free now for the people from Seattle!"

Celia Alario: There were some reporters who wanted to shadow people through the week. There was a lot of that. The whole embedded-reporter thing was really hot. I don't know if this was coming out of the first Gulf War or what it was but there was a whole "We want to embed with you" thing. Everybody had their little squad of journalists that they were escorting around.

Jim Brunner: I was a new reporter at the *Seattle Times*. Basically the assignment was, "Go be out in the streets." There was no Twitter or anything; we weren't livestreaming. We were out there and then calling in with notes. We had people everywhere downtown.

Dave Reichert: My chief, Larry Mayes, he understood the intel and the importance of intel and how we were gathering it. With his input, we determined that there is no way SPD was going to be able to handle this crowd on their own if it got out of hand. The sheriff, you know, we can enforce laws throughout the entire county. We had concurrent jurisdiction with the Seattle Police Department. I had the authority to move in, without the mayor's permission, to be honest with you. But I wasn't going to do that.

But I did put about 350 to 400 deputies in the basement of the courthouse the day before. We trained 300, 400 King County deputies for crowd control training. We bought the equipment. They had the helmets and they had the nightsticks, the radio systems, the body protection equipment. We also trained in how to keep our cool and control crowds, move them from one street to another. For 1999, it was pretty advanced training for crowd control. I put all of them in the basement of the courthouse on Sunday, all ready to walk out. Even though I was told, "We don't need your help."

Charles Mandigo: We had significant resources brought in from the FBI headquarters—particularly biotech—in the Seattle FBI building, and actually took over a whole floor. These biotech guys moved in and they set up all their equipment and they had chemical analysis and all kinds of things in place in the event that there were suspicious packages found or the need for biotech to respond or to do analysis.

Jim Pugel: Me and another lieutenant met Han Shan and John Sellers at a Chinese restaurant two nights before.

Han Shan: It was the four of us. It felt like a double date. It was weird, just sitting across from two cops. They probably thought it was as strange as we did, but we're making small talk, trying to be friendly, trying to show that we're not scary—because we are on either side of this thing, on a fundamental level.

I've done a lot of work like this over many years, being a liaison between protesters and police. I want them to humanize us. I want them to understand our commitment to nonviolence. I want them to know that there's an open line of communication. I want them to find it harder to beat the crap out of us because they've talked to us and feel like, "Okay, these aren't just random scary people who've rolled into town to cause chaos with no agenda but, rather, a bunch of people of conscience who are there because we feel compelled to be—for all kinds of good reasons." We didn't want to see anyone get hurt. So I felt like that dinner, we were having a good-faith conversation.

John Sellers: I knew that the police were doing tactical training specifically to prepare for the protesters. They were doing their own war games and I heard that one of the cops who was playing a protester had gotten their arm broken by another cop in their own war games. I was like, "Dude, what the hell? What are you guys preparing for? What's going on? What do you think we're going to do?"

And Pugel said, "Well, we're getting reports that we could potentially lose one to two officers during these protests."

I said, "What do you mean 'lose officers'? Are they going to go to Tacoma and make a wrong turn and get lost? Literally someone has told you that some officers may get killed in these protests? Who is feeding you this information?"

Jim Pugel: We were talking about how to do the mass arrests. How many buses do you think we'll need?

John Sellers: They wanted to know if there were going to be mass arrests. Han Shan and I were kicking each other under the table realizing that they didn't really have a very good idea of how many thousands of people were going to be there, willing to risk arrest.

Jim Pugel: I didn't know this, but underneath the table Sellers was kicking his sidekick. They're thinking to each other, "The cops have no fucking clue." And we didn't.

Han Shan: Here's where Sellers and I tell the story differently—we're still good pals—but at a certain point, it became very clear that they didn't really know what was coming. And I do admit to feeling torn at that time, but I think *I* was kicking *Sellers*, because he was like, "Wait, you guys, you have to understand . . ." I think Sellers was trying to do the more, perhaps, moral thing. He wanted Pugel to understand better what was about to unfold, so that they weren't on their back heels, reacting inappropriately.

I was like, "Holy fuck, they do not understand what it is about to unfold! We have the tactical advantage!" I was basically kicking Sellers to try to get him to shut up. I think I was probably all filled with adrenaline, as we walked out and we said our goodbyes, shook hands, and then I said to Sellers, "Holy shit, dude."

Because they would say something like, "Yeah, we'll have a couple buses for people who want to commit civil disobedience," in this kind of line-crossing, very ritualistic manner, on the morning of November 30th. And I was very well aware that no, we're talking about, 40,000 people, 50,000 people.

Well, in a way we were kind of like Babe Ruth, just pointing to the outfield fence. We're just saying 40,000 people. We don't really *know*. Who knows, right? And we kept upping it because it felt like a lot of people and it felt like they were vastly underestimating. If we were overestimating, fine. But they were talking about police and buses for people I could count on my hands.

We'd done absolutely everything I felt like we could, to just say, "We're an open book." Because we knew that this was historic, we knew that there were going to be a lot of people there, we didn't want to get people hurt.

Suzanne Savoie: All around the city, you saw so many flyers and posters and graffiti. You felt like you were sensing something in the air. There were a lot more people around who you got the sense had come because of the organizing.

Celia Alario: The texture of the air around this thing felt like something special was going to happen.

Lori Wallach: I remember seeing Jim Hightower's hat, resting on a conference table. He was all ready to go, to fight this thing, and it just made me smile.

Jim Hightower: It felt like a very freelance protest—that little-*d* democratic protest.

David Solnit: You can learn from history that there has always been an element of confrontation, whether it's been labor strikes or civil rights sit-ins or the suffrage movement. You need to have a confrontation. We needed to have a massive confrontation, put our bodies on the line, and create a crisis.

MONDAY, NOVEMBER 29

John Sellers: On the 29th, we hung a huge banner over the city from a construction crane. We deployed at zero-dark-thirty, probably two o'clock in the morning. We had Helene Cooper embedded with us. The Seattle Police were at DEFCON 5. They were prowling the city everywhere with patrols.

Helene Cooper: Seattle was probably the best reporting week of my life ever because I knew all the different sides. I knew the Ruckus people, I knew the Lori Wallach people, I knew the Mike Dolan people. I could get to wherever I needed to be. They would go, "Oh, there's Helene!" And they would let me through because they looked at me as theirs.

John Sellers: I got into the banner-hang action at the last minute because one of our climbers came up with an injury and it was two days from go time and there were not a lot of people that we could train to be the replacement climber, so I jumped into that action.

Mike Dolan: For the banner hang, they needed a way to get into that work site so they could get to the crane. I got a call from one of the Ruckus Society guys and he gave me the name of the local working the job—he'd seen a trade logo on a truck at the construction site. He goes, "I need to get in touch with those people." He wanted the union guys on the inside, at that construction site with that big crane, that's what they were going to climb to hang the banner. So I called the labor guy—I happened to have the list of all of them—and I say, "Look, you're going to hear from this guy—I gave him your number—and a particular thing is going to happen. Can you, you know, be nice and facilitate what these guys have in mind? Just work it out somehow."

Don Kegley: John Sellers was always climbing things!

John Sellers: So we get into the construction site and start going up the crane. It wasn't raining yet but it was really dark.

Harold Linde, organizer with the Rainforest Action Network: It seemed like everything that could have gone wrong went wrong.

Celia Alario: I had been calling and calling media. We had worked through every contact we had and beyond. There were all these international reporters, and there were people helping to call Spanish-language media.

Because it was going to happen predawn, the reporters were meeting us at a designated spot and then we transported them to the place to see the banner hang.

We had chosen the parking lot of the flagship REI store for the media meeting spot. When we came around the corner that morning, I could see that the entire REI parking lot was full. There were cars on all the side streets. There were satellite trucks ready to go. It was just so heartening. It was like "Oh my gosh, this is huge."

John Sellers: Four main climbers went out onto the arm of the crane. We had another climber supporting, a guy who climbed up with us to a certain level in the crane tower and then locked himself in place so the cops couldn't climb up after us. We had a whole bunch of scouters. We must have had twenty-five people helping us get onto this construction site and get into the tower and climb. Once we got up to the top of the tower, we traversed out on the arm of the crane. Harold was below us; he was our packhorse. He was carrying this giant banner in a backpack.

Harold Linde: The pack was 100 to 150 pounds, somewhere in there. We had practiced with a day pack and a ground cloth—a little tarp, ten pounds—in this warehouse on the outskirts of Seattle. Then the day of, I put on the backpack for the first time, and I could barely walk. We had to climb up three hundred feet of laddering. We get to—I think they call it a monkey cage. It's a cage around the ladder, something to catch workers if they fall. Well, we hadn't considered that, and both me and the pack wouldn't fit through this cage. Then we figured out: attach a rope to the pack and I would push on it as the people up on the crane pulled, which required far more effort. Every time we got this pack over one of the ladder rungs, something would catch—one of the straps that had been cinched up so that it would fit tight to my body. By the time we finally got to the top, the pack didn't fit me anymore. When I put it on again, the straps had all been loosened and the pack pulled me back. I nearly went over the edge of the crane. Like I

said, we'd only practiced with these day packs on. The way we config-
ured our belaying device was oriented toward a ten-pound day pack,
not a hundred pounds.

John Sellers: Harold kept this hundred-pound pack on when he repelled and he flipped upside down almost immediately with that. I
thought that he was going to fall out of his harness. I repelled down off
the arm of the crane too. We had two people guarding our anchors so
that no one could come along and cut our anchors and drop us.

Harold Linde: I start sliding down this rope and picking up speed,
and I didn't understand exactly what had happened. I'm seeing the
rope going through my belaying device. There's always a safety device, a backup, but that wasn't catching either. It was cold so I had
worn fleece gloves. Well, rope and fleece gloves provide no friction—I
couldn't get a grip. I couldn't stop from sliding down. I'm sliding down
this rope, three hundred feet in the air and completely alone.

Because Ruckus training is so thorough, there was this sense of
"Okay, so I have to think outside." I knew I had to get the gloves
off my hand. I took one glove off with my teeth, the other glove off
with my teeth, and suddenly, I had enough of a grip to stop sliding. I
couldn't do it very long, but it bought a little bit of time, and then I
yelled up. What I remember asking the people still up on the crane
was for them to lower down something to get this pack off my back.
They didn't have anything. It was sort of like "Well, find something!"
They eventually found a carabiner and lowered this carabiner on—I
think it was a parachute cord, so relatively thin but strong enough.
Then the wind picked up so I'm trying to grab this thing as it's flying
through the air—and I'm starting to slip down again—but finally I
got this hook, this carabiner around the pack, and I could take it off.
It gave us space and time to think and then solve these other major
problems.

John Sellers: We ended up hanging the pack from the crane where he
could get to it and pull the banner out of the pack.

Harold Linde: The way the banner hanging works is you don't wrap it
but you fold it into a compact "sausage"—that's what we called it—and

COURTESY OF HAROLD LINDE

Harold Linde struggles atop the crane,
300 feet in the air.

then you wrap masking tape around it, which you can break easily;
it's just enough to keep the banner compact so that it feeds out of the
pack smoothly. When the timing is right, two climbers will pull, easily
breaking the tape. But all that ladder-rung bashing of the pack broke
all the tape. So as I'm feeding the banner out to John, it's not this compact sausage. It's opening up, so it is a giant sail, which then catches the
wind, three hundred feet in the air. You can only read something that's

taut but it was all bunched up, and we didn't have the power to pull it tight enough. One, we're not stable, we're moving, and, two, there's just too much force. We were up there for maybe an hour trying to get this thing taut, and we couldn't. We had the feedback from the ground that nobody could read it. It was bunched up. It was getting light. Police were there. It was all this effort and it was a wash. There was nothing we could do. I definitely said some prayers. The banner—the sail—was catching enough wind that it started to move this giant crane arm, so even if we could get it taut, nobody would be able to see it if that crane ended up swinging around too much. The whole thing would be for naught. I just prayed. And, an interesting point, at RAN and Ruckus and at other places, there were many people who were involved in sort of earth-based spirituality, pagan rituals. Well, there was a circle of pagan witches on the ground below this crane, sending prayers up to us. And, at one moment, divine intervention: the wind just stopped. I don't know, ten seconds, maybe. John and I madly pulled and were able to get it taut enough that it was readable, and then the photos happened.

John Sellers: There was a ton of brainstorming to determine what we wanted to say. We have this chance, so what do we say?

Harold Linde: The original message was something very different. I believe it was "Global village, not global pillage," which is interesting but doesn't have that more primal and symbolic meaning.

COURTESY OF HAROLD LINDE

Harold Linde catches his breath after successfully unfurling the banner.

John Sellers: There was a guy named Jeremy Paster—he's no longer with us. He came up with the idea of an image that had one-way-street arrows pointing in opposite directions. In one direction, "WTO"; in the other direction, "Democracy." It was one of those moments where, as it came out of his mouth, everyone agreed that that was it, that was the one. That's the banner we hung. I thought it looked pretty good, pretty taut.

Celia Alario: We chose that crane because it was convenient but also because we had the Space Needle in the background for context. It needed to have a geographic element. It was a framing action that set the stage from a strategy perspective, from a meta messaging perspective. The idea being, if you get one image above the fold in the newspaper and there isn't even a caption, have you done your job of telling the story of what you're trying to say? If you have a good photographer who has good relationships with the wires, we were living in a world where one image can change the world. The Tiananmen Square image, there's so many images that we had seen over the years. The fists in the air on the Olympic podium. One image can do it.

John Sellers: It was a media feeding frenzy. There was one point when I was still in the harness and I had two phones that I was dealing with. These were the early days of cell phones in action. I had taken my personal phone and I had an interview phone. I was talking to someone on the interview phone. I looked down and the guy who was guarding my anchor was looking up at me and I saw his eyes open wide like crazy. Then I saw my second phone was falling. I didn't have it secured. You're supposed to have everything on a lanyard. You don't unclip anything but my phone was falling and spiraling below me. A cop was looking up and I thought it was going to bonk him on the head, which would have increased charges of reckless endangerment. Luckily it did not hit him. And it's a pretty iconic banner image now because it ended up in history books and silly places that make me feel really old. It was on the front page of the *Wall Street Journal*.

It was one of the proudest actions I've ever done because we knew that with thousands of people coming to get arrested with all the labor marchers behind them and 50,000 people converging on the city, we knew that the message could easily get lost. We were constantly having our message marginalized in the mainstream media by reporters and politicians who kept saying, "These people can't make up their minds what they're for. They're for a million different things. They don't have one clear defining message." I think we did a really good job of framing that action.

Norm Stamper: I loved it. I thought, "Goddamn, that's smart!" That's really good. I began to realize this was going to be a good test of my own self-discipline and leadership maturity.

Han Shan: We always talked about framing actions that would help people understand. On the 30th, there was going to be tens of thousands of people in the streets. No one's going to be able to control the message. We wanted to try to provide some framing, and help people understand what this is all about. Democracy, WTO—that felt like a pretty good frame, and still does.

John Sellers: It was early meme warfare days. That's what I do for a day job now, meme warfare, all day, every day. But it took a lot to hang

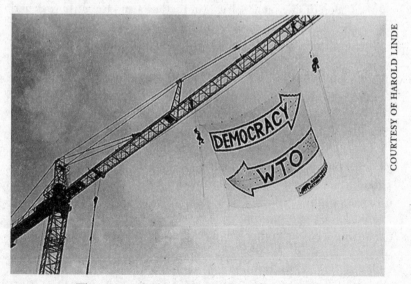

The outstretched banner with Harold Linde (left) and John Sellers (right) still suspended midair.

a "meme" on the WTO back then. *Laughs.* You had to climb a several-hundred-foot crane and rappel down off the arm.

I got arrested when we came down. We had this arrangement with a really cool bail bondswoman. She had my Ruckus credit card number, so I called her from jail and asked her to bail us all out. At that point, the Seattle Police Department was letting people bail out right away because nothing had started yet.

Harold Linde: I had been arrested a couple of times for actions and once in high school for drunken mischief that I instigated. It was kind of an action but with no nobility involved. Nobody was hurt but it was not well thought out. It's such a different experience to get arrested with training and intention and with the fundamental motivation being of service. Being arrested and not resisting, and having a plan, having an intention—being arrested in that context, it's such a powerful experience.

Jello Biafra: A prank a day keeps the dog leash away—I live by that as an artist, activist, and shit-stirrer. That same spirit, it was there in the Yippies, the Diggers, the fun side of the hippies—they scared the shit out of people. The punk spirit is in the beats and the early rock and roll and rhythm and blues, Little Richard on back to Oscar Wilde, among others, Woody Guthrie and maybe even Jesus Christ.

Ed Joiner: Monday was the day before the ministerial began so it was more quiet. We had officers out looking because supposedly the protesters were going to stock up with poles and all kinds of instruments that they could use. So we had officers out looking for any caches like that.

Gary Locke: There were already some rallies expressing concern about trade. I met with some of the leaders that Monday afternoon, Monday night at various receptions. It was all very cordial, very amicable. Even the people on opposite sides of the issues were there and mingling with each other. People were very positive and looking forward to the next day.

Jim Pugel: There was some French farmer who had a protest at Third and Pine, which was in front of McDonald's.

Mike Dolan: We were really glad José Bové was there. This is the French farmer who attached the chain to the McDonald's. He brought in the cheese—against trade law. He wasn't paying any tariff on it. It's his shtick.

Medea Benjamin, cofounder of Global Exchange: We were going to take the McDonald's and turn it into a fine-dining restaurant with the Roquefort cheese that he had brought. We had fancy tablecloths and silverware, nice bread and the cheese. But the McDonald's was boarded up.

José Bové: The McDonald's was completely closed, a piece of wood in the window, so nobody could get inside. I think it was better like that, in the street—this is a bigger place. We had a meeting near a car, a lot of crowds, thousands of people were there looking at what was happening. The aim was to denounce the WTO—not to destroy this restaurant, which was quite protected—and we distributed to all the people Roquefort cheese. People were going away after the demonstration with the Roquefort and on French TV we had very friendly images where people were talking about the Roquefort revolution.

It was something which was quite new for us but I think it was also completely new for the people and the journalists from the United States which couldn't understand in the beginning why French people were there.

Colin Hines: José Bové was impressive in the sense of organizing French farmers, and not just organizing them for more money but organizing them around the adverse effects of globalization—not just on them as French farmers but farmers globally.

Ed Joiner: We had some members of the City Council that were encouraging people to come and protest.

Nick Licata: On the first day I was in the street quite a bit. I was at the forefront of the demonstration along with the other council members who wanted to be there. Being a public official, I wanted to check it out. I went around and saw what was going on but I did not want to get close to the police because I didn't want to be seen as a public official supporting any potential violence.

Laurie Brown: One of the things that was very frustrating to me was that at least a couple of council members were giddy about the demonstrations. I thought, "What are you doing? You're adding to the chaos. Why aren't you doing your jobs? We need to get clear about roles and responsibilities here."

Council members were hanging out at the demonstrations and being gadflies. They would come back to the office and say, "Wow, it's really crazy out there! It's really wild out there!"

I'm like, "Yeah, you have a role here, to get things calmed down and not contribute to it. This is not you reliving your old days as a university student, demonstrating against the Vietnam War." That was a lot of the mood in the beginning until it became not so much fun.

Jim Hightower: DeMarco and I were broadcasting our show every day—midday, two-hour national talk show, set up there in the Methodist Church. It was a low-budget operation, to say the least, but we had enough expertise that we could make the wires work. I knew a lot of people in the progressive movement who were going to be there so I was able to get really interesting people to come in—Leo Gerard, the head of the steelworkers, had been a particularly strong advocate, and Ralph Nader of course.

Michael Ramos: At the Jubilee event on Monday night, we had 15,000 people. Some say 30,000, but I'll say 15,000—at least. We had an interfaith service downtown at First Methodist Church. We were going to form a human chain around the building where the delegates were having caviar, which is, I don't know, eight square blocks—it's huge.

While they're eating caviar, the rest of the world is suffering. We didn't want this trade regime—things like intellectual property rights, theft of seeds, and debt regime—to be imposed on the backs of these people anymore. We had an interfaith event with the head of AFL-CIO, Maxine Waters from L.A., Vandana Shiva, the great Indian activist.

It was pouring rain outside and I had a thousand steelworkers ready to help form the human chain. They were getting antsy, and I had the police on my back inside the building. They were anxious about keeping everything under control with thousands of people outside. I felt the tension in myself.

We formed a human chain with 15,000 people to symbolically break the chain of debt. We had speakers and music and drummers. The drummers came from one of the tribes of the area and they were drumming for quite a while, like ten minutes, and I said to my friend, "I think we're going to have to get done because I don't know how long people are going to hold out," because it was raining. It was one of those Seattle November nights.

My friend said to me something I'll never forget. He said, "They'll be done when they're done." In other words: it's a spiritual matter for them. It was linking them with the people in the bondage of debt and the oppression that they experience around the world. So, they'll be done when they're done.

They went on for quite a while. This is the thing around cultural expression and different people experiencing the meaning of the event, the gravity of the event, in different ways.

We all linked arms, then let go. People inside knew we were there.

Mike Dolan: So on the same night that the Washington Council of Churches was doing the hands-around-the-building thing for Jubilee 2000, we had the People's Gala at the Seattle Center, which—remember—I got for free.

Laurie Brown: We cohosted the People's Gala with Mike Dolan, which meant that we got to help shape the agenda. Elected officials got to be on the agenda. I'm sure Mike felt like that was a win because he got the venue for free but, in my mind, it was a win-win. It was in our joint interests to do it differently than what he had originally wanted to do.

The more progressive council members were fighting over who got to speak. They were trying to get things for the protesters, including housing, camping in the city parks, buses for transportation—all kinds of things.

Pam Schell: The night before the WTO, Paul felt really good about it. He gave a speech saying, "We want people to respect the city, and to have their voices heard, and be kind to each other."

Mike Dolan: I had to be the emcee for it because Michael Moore's plane was late. I had this whole shtick because the WTO had a Michael Moore—that was the name of the director general—and we had a Michael Moore on our side, the filmmaker. That's a fair trade parallel, Michael Moore universes, their Michael and our Michael. *Laughs.* But our Michael Moore's plane was late. Still, it was a fucking great night. Me and Jello Biafra of the Dead Kennedys were backstage and that's where I originally did the two–Michael Moore shtick.

Jello Biafra: Senator Paul Wellstone was there. He's got a beard, he's got wild, curly hair, saying, "We did it! We did it!" I'm thinking, "That's a senator? Damn! I wish we had more people like that." Didn't have a chance to shake hands with him or anything, because then Mike comes up to me and goes, "Jello, Jello. Ken Kesey's not showing up tonight. Could you please go out and say a few words now?"

"Oh, shit. What am I going to say?"

Luckily, I relaxed. The minute I walked on, there was a huge cheer in the whole arena. "Oh my god. They know me! My people, my friends." *Laughs.* I said what was on my mind and tried to rally the troops, so to speak, almost act as a cheerleader—but without those stupid-ass pompoms. I realized this was just the beginning. It got the people pumped. And it got me really pumped to play the show the next day.

Mike Dolan: It was a big party. Jim Hightower, Paul Wellstone just fucking knocked it out of the park. Tom Hayden was there. There were comedians and a dance troupe from England that did this whole weird routine around genetically modified organisms. That was a big issue for the Europeans, GMOs. The whole night was fun.

Jim Hightower: The People's Gala was a big deal because it was the kickoff: "Here we are!" Quite a few politicians did show up. Wellstone certainly, Tom Harkin came, and some people like that. But a number of the Democratic senators were cautious, to say the least. "Well, I don't know if I want to be a part of that or not." Then it turned out to be a big thing and they thought, "I should have gone!"

COURTESY OF THE SEATTLE MUNICIPAL ARCHIVES

Jim Hightower and Kevin Danaher speak at the People's Gala.

Dennis Kucinich, U.S. congressman: As a member of Congress, I was very involved in preparing a congressional delegation to go to Seattle for the WTO. I circulated a letter among members of Congress and had over a hundred members sign it, saying that any agreement between the United States and the WTO had to have workers' rights, human rights, and environmental quality principles. That really was the beginning of a congressional effort to try to bring that triad into every single discussion of trade agreements; it started with the WTO. There were so many members of Congress who were involved that it caused some consternation in the White House because Clinton was just trying to move this through without any challenge from Congress.

John Zerzan: Monday, the day before the more famous day, there were huge crowds. You could just tell something was on the way. It didn't pop off but it was building. So many people in the streets, it was going to go off at some point. The energy, the feel of it—it wanted to go somewhere.

Suzanne Savoie: I remember the night before, having meetings about strategy and getting prepared for first aid and things like that, anticipating that there was going to be police pushback and pepper spray.

Laurie Brown: I was nervous when I went to bed that night. I had worked in emergency management with a number of jobs, and I worked closely with police and fire. I grew up with a lot of traumas as a child so I am hypervigilant and on high alert about things that might be dangerous. I was not nervous for my own safety or the safety of the people I cared about but for the mayor and the city in general.

Dave Reichert: The Seattle cops were already getting to the point where they were exhausted by Monday night.

Ron Griffin: Before Monday evening was over, Seattle PD asked me, "Ron, can you give us a platoon of people for Tuesday morning? We want some help down around the convention center."

I said, "Okay," and one of my captains jumps up on it.

James P. Hoffa: We told everybody, "It's going to get rough. There's going to be tear gas," and a lot of people didn't believe it.

Celia Alario: When you're dealing with direct action logistics in an urban setting, everything can be perfect and then something out of your control can go wrong. I had been in places where the coalition was unprecedented—beautiful banners, incredible artistic placards, celebrities at the podium, everything you could imagine—and then an avocado truck overturns on the freeway and no media can get to your demonstration. *Laughs.* I was holding a space of cautious optimism, attempting this experiment of nonattachment—not at all being able to do it.

There's a feeling sometimes, you can get to a point where almost the texture of the air around you changes, when the moment is a special moment. I think there was a feeling in general around the week particularly because it was very bold. It took a lot of moxie to invite the entire world to Seattle.

TUESDAY, NOVEMBER 30

Laurie Brown: I went to work very early. I had this tiny little office—I think it was a converted closet. I packed a bag and I did not go home until Thursday night. That explains how nervous I was. I could not make myself leave. I thought that I needed to stay there and help in some way. I just knew that it was going to get worse before it got better.

Nina Narelle: I remember waking up at five in the morning, rolling around, feeling like I wanted to vomit, wondering if this was the day that capitalism would win or if anyone would show up. We had no idea, none.

David Solnit: We started at seven a.m. because we wanted to start the blockades and get people in the streets before the nine a.m. opening of the WTO. It was predawn at seven in November in the Pacific Northwest.

Hilary McQuie: They did a police shift change right around seven a.m.—the moment that we were getting into place. So there were no cops out there, relatively no cops out. It was hilarious.

Ron Griffin: Larry Mayes calls me up at—I don't know—around seven in the morning to say, "Ron, have you got the news on?"

"Well, I'm just getting a cup of coffee."

He said, "Well, it's going upside down. Seattle PD is asking for help from everybody."

I said, "Okay. You want us to deploy?"

"Yeah."

I had a Nextel paging system all set up. Today every deputy gets a phone, but back in that day not everybody had pagers. For me to get 150 pagers was not easy. We were burning money on this thing like there's no tomorrow—the amount of money.

Matt Griffin: I remember coming out of the gym that morning at seven and seeing people walk down the street with masks on and the drumbeat. The drumbeat was almost like the kind of drumbeat you expect in the movies when the team has gone to war. I went, "Oh my god, today's going to be different."

Dana Schuerholz: I wanted to just be a photographer and document the event. I wasn't going to protest because there were a lot of protesters. I thought that I could be more useful if I got a press pass. I had the Geneva pass. Those were harder to get. Months ahead you had to go through a protocol, which I had done. At the time I was working with Impact Visuals, a New York–based co-op of documentary photographers. My whole plan for the week was to not be an activist in the sense of protesting but to document history.

John Sellers: On the map that we divided up, the pieces of pie all radiated out from the convention center. There were twelve spokes going out from there, creating thirteen pieces of pie. The affinity groups assigned to each piece of pie were in charge of getting their part of the blockade locked down. We were establishing a perimeter.

Some of the pie pieces were in really public squares like in the downtown shopping area and along the waterfront. We had hundreds and hundreds of people out there forming blockades. Some of the blockades around the backside of the convention center, we didn't

DANA SCHUERHOLZ

Protesters use lockboxes to block an intersection.

have anywhere near as many people, so we used more devices, more lockboxes and things like that that could really lock down an area with fewer people.

Norm Stamper: Some of our guys were saying, "It's going to be too cold and too wet. They are not going to want to be out there." But it wouldn't have mattered if there was two feet of snow on the ground, they would still be out there protesting. The thing that got me more than anything else on a personal level is that I know that I probably would have been down on the streets with the protesters because of my political views. It was a huge challenge.

Kevin Danaher: The idea was to encircle the facility so that delegates couldn't get from the hotels into the convention center or the Paramount Theatre, where they were doing the opening ceremony. Everybody was trained in nonviolence. You're not supposed to hurt anyone, just wrap arms and form blockades and don't let anybody through. The lines were sometimes ten people thick. And each affinity group got to decide how their blockade went down. Most people know about the lockboxes but there were a lot of different approaches.

Harold Linde: As I recall, the first Harry Potter books had come out. Somebody who was there, one of their interventions was a banner of sorts—a helium-filled kind of blimp. It was maybe ten feet high. They walked around the streets, and the message on the banner was "Wake up Muggles."

Dana Schuerholz: One of the affinity groups, the Red Noses, were a bunch of people that I knew from Seattle, good friends. Their tactic was humor. They wanted to engage with the delegates—stop them, block them, not let them through, but they wanted a hook so that the delegates wouldn't be angry and confrontational. They wanted good dialogue. They came up with this idea to all wear red noses just to take the edge off. It sort of worked. One delegate from the Netherlands put on the red nose at one point and they had a really great conversation. There was a human connection. A lot of the delegates were mad but some thought it was pretty amazing that there were so many people who had things to say.

The Red Noses share very different
interactions with WTO delegates.

David Solnit: Clusters of affinity groups could either deploy independently or join one of two marches. I took on the role of helping to coordinate one of them. It was a way of bringing large numbers of people in from two different directions. We had one from the water and one from the hills.

Kevin Danaher: Medea and I were down by the waterfront. It was one of those days where the rain was coming in horizontally—

miserable, cold, wet. We were trying to get people revved up to go but the weather was so awful that people were cowering. This guy from Scotland who had two pieces of wool across his chest, but bare shoulders and arms, he got up on a dumpster and started yelling, "You think this is bad weather? This is nothing! This is like spring-time!" He made this whole speech and got everybody feeling guilty about being such wimps. We got fired up. We had a banner in front and there were a whole bunch of musicians. Everybody started play-ing music; we all got loud and started marching. As we were going, I looked back at the crowd and realized, "Oh my god, we have thou-sands of people here!"

Medea Benjamin: At first it was really great. It just kept getting bigger and bigger—it was very joyous. We couldn't believe that what we had dreamed about for so many months was actually happening.

Jim Pugel: All these groups had pre-staged throughout the area within half a mile circumference of the convention center. They got the sig-nal to go and they all started marching from all angles. We were just screwed.

David Solnit: I was with the Steinbrueck Park march, coming from the water. When we took off marching it was raining pretty heavily. The puppets were getting soggy. The cops were confiscating tripods, twenty-foot tripods that people had set up as blockade items. They had disguised them as twenty-foot cardboard carrots. The cops start-ing grabbing those so we tried to get the message out to people to not bring them.

Skip Spitzer: I organized an affinity group and our plan was just to sit and link arms, which is what most people do. First, we were there with impunity. Then you could see the cops' arrival and waves of tactics.

Jim Pugel: We decided we'd have two platoons—one lieutenant, four sergeants, and thirty officers—those would be soft uniforms up front. There's a philosophy if you send people with riot gear out initially, it can escalate the crowd. So our plan was to present first with the soft officers. Then we'd also have platoons of hardened officers. It was the first protest—in the United States, at least—that we got shin guards, knee guards, elbow guards, chest guards. This was because of information we heard about similar events in Europe, where protesters would shoot wrist rockets, slingshots, throw debris—really anything that's available out there in the environment.

Skip Spitzer: It's getting more and more intense. We were part of a cluster that ended up being in the back of the building, which was the first place that they tried to restore access.

Pam Schell: I had a luncheon at the University Village with my girlfriends. The protests weren't big enough in my mind yet, so I thought, "Oh, I'll just drive in and see what's going on." I drove into town and realized that people were still entering town and marching. Garbage cans had been lit on fire. This woman yelled at me, "You bitch, get out of here!" I got out of there. Went home and started watching it on television.

Celia Alario: Each affinity group had a designated media representative. When an affinity group was ready, I would get a phone call and we would take down the details of what was happening and put it into a template of a press release and then start to put the word out.

Dave Reichert: When we finally got a request for assistance from SPD, I opened up a garage door in the county building where I had all of my guys waiting. It was a large garage door that opened right into the street, at the corner of Third and James Street. So I marched them right out onto Third Avenue. They marched down the street and we started to move people.

Skip Spitzer: They did various things to try to break up our blockade. First, being menacing. Then a line of police officers ran towards us. Our line stayed firm. Then they ran horses at us and the line stayed firm.

Lisa Fithian: We made two public assembly sites in the morning for everybody that wasn't part of the Direct Action structure, for the purpose of putting them into what we were calling "flying squads," which was a formation that was first done by the autoworkers back in the '30s and '40s when they were doing plant strikes. If there was any trouble with a certain affinity group, or a certain slice of the pie, squads would fly in to do support. Also it gave us an advantage because the police knew the public assembly sites. So they were there, which created more space for all those affinity groups to move with the police focus more on us.

Mike Dolan: Hilary was leading one of these flying squad's march to the perimeter. All the banners that they were holding and the objects supporting the puppets, those were actually hardware that they could break down and use at the intersections—the pipes that the people were using to lock themselves and things like that.

So Hilary's leading this—Hilary's a pagan, remember, she's a witch, she's got magical powers, she does.

Hilary McQuie: There's a strong pagan political contingent in California that's been very tight with direct action movements, bringing a kind of magical sensibility into activism. In fact, a bunch of my friends, their idea was to work a spell of finding WTO delegates at a bar—buy a round of drinks and make them all toast to various things. "Here's to democracy! Here's to the end of corporate rule!" *Laughs.* Really, direct action is an act of theater so it's a good place to work a spell if you can.

Mike Dolan: So Hilary gets to the police line and they're going, "Hey, you can't come through here with all that. We're worried about weapons."

And Hilary does one of the sort of Jedi mind trick things with the cop. She goes, "There's nothing wrong here. This is okay."

The cop was just like, "Okay, let them through." *Laughs.*

She somehow, at that moment, mesmerized—hypnotized!—a cop into letting them through. So she gets through and, as soon as they get to the line, they disassemble the puppets and the banners and all the rest, making more hardware available to the affinity groups.

Kevin Danaher: As we were moving towards the convention center, I looked up on the hill where the junior college was and there was a massive wave of bodies coming down from Capitol Hill. It was at that moment that I realized that we had enough people there to actually prevent the delegates from getting to the convention center.

Jim Pugel: Out of nowhere, thirty people came from all angles at Sixth and Pine and they had something like an Ikea-quality stage with all these parts. They had prefabricated it, told all these people where to come and it was like halftime at the Super Bowl—they put the stage up like that. We're just like, "Wow! That's amazing! Just incredible!"

John Sellers: Those seven or eight pieces of pie that were much more public, thousands of people poured into those areas. They were doing big street art and all kinds of things. They created a human barrier, just a wall of people in those intersections.

Around the backside, there were fewer people in a more tactical paramilitary kind of deployment using lockboxes and mechanical devices that would allow them to sustain their presence there. There were thirteen different actions that were happening simultaneously, thirteen well-conceived, effective, brilliant blockades all at the same time or it would not have worked.

The police had seriously miscalculated. They had really underestimated the numbers and our resolve. They had the convention center surrounded by parked buses. It wasn't very difficult for us to walk up to their hardened perimeter and lock ourselves around it and create a cluster fuck in the middle of the city that effectively shut the meeting down.

Ron Griffin: We had Precincts 2, 3, and 4 involved. Precinct 3 command was already down in the middle of it. The crowd came around the corner and just overtook the place. I mean, it was terrible. Larry Mayes tells me, "They're screaming for help. Can you activate your people?"

And I said, "Okay, where do you want us to go?"

"Get to the county garage. We'll get metro buses to take them there."

I'm jumping into my uniform and getting all my stuff together. And I said, "What code response do you want?"

There's Code 1, which is driving normal. Code 2 is flashing your lights and beeping your sound a little bit. Code 3 is all-out lights and

sirens—you're running hard. So he says, "Code 2." *Long pause.* No sooner do I get that out "Code 2," he calls back and says, "Make it Code 3." *Tears up and pauses again.* Most people are blessed that they don't have this emotional piece, and you're a lot better off without it. It's tough. The problem with Code 3 is now I've got eighty-plus people driving individual cars hard. The hard driving is a problem in law enforcement anyway. I mean, this is facetious but there's the old response to "Why did you become a cop?"

"So I could carry a gun and drive fast"—that kind of thing. There's a little bit of truth to that.

One of the first things I did, I came on the radio. Everybody knew that I was the overall commander. I said, "Okay, folks, I want everybody to back off driving 110 miles an hour. You're no good to me if you don't bring it down." *Tears up and takes a long pause.* Eventually everybody gets down there.

Dave Reichert: I had a radio with me. I would go to those places where the cops were having a little bit of a struggle. And sometimes that would help calm things down. Or at least it gave them confidence to say, "Look, the sheriff's got my back."

Laurie Brown: I was with a group of mayor's office staff in the conference room. We were all alarmed because the chief, Norm Stamper, was really nowhere to be found. He was not engaged. He didn't report to us but he reported to the deputy mayor and to the mayor—and he was missing in action. It's not that we didn't have confidence in Jim Pugel, who was a captain at the time, and there was Chief Ed Joiner—but the parent was missing. Where was Dad? The police chief was missing.

Norm Stamper: This is hard for me to relive; I let my people down and I feel terrible. I let my people down, the police department. There is a way to lead and a way not to lead. I was not informed. I was not prepared.

Pam Schell: Stamper was like a neighborhood policeman. He liked to have block watches, do it all from the ground up. Paul said, "Are you going to lead on this event?"

He said, "No," he wasn't going to lead.

Then Paul really turned to Joiner and Pugel and a couple of others. I know that Paul really liked Pugel.

Laurie Brown: We sat there in the mayor's conference room and watched people peacefully sitting in intersections with their arms linked singing some kind of hippie song. A police vehicle came up and started physically touching the demonstrators, nudging them as they were sitting there. The demonstrators were like, "Oh hell no, no, no. This can't be something that police leadership is condoning. This can't be happening!"

We called Paul and said, "Are you watching the news? Does the chief know what's going on? If he doesn't, he needs to understand what's going on."

Norm Stamper: I was probably in the office for two to three hours max that week. I really do believe that police executives belong on the streets so that they can see it and feel it. I was out, going to each of the precincts where there was any kind of activity. I was talking with the cops and talking with the protesters.

Laurie Brown: It's not our place to tell the police how to do their jobs, particularly at our level, but it had gotten to the point where it didn't feel like anybody was in charge or that there was any kind of strategy. It was just officers doing whatever occurred to them in the moment.

Vivian Phillips: It was just this incredible confluence—pardon my French—of major fuckups.

David Solnit: Delegates were being told to stay in their hotels because it wasn't safe to go out. We learned that the authorities were freaking out that the ministerial had been delayed.

Vicente Paolo Yu, fellow at Friends of the Earth: In 1999, as a WTO delegate, I was a very young lawyer, almost fresh from passing the bar. I was working closely with the Philippine government and some of the other Asian governments. I was focusing on interacting with official government delegates from Asia to get a practical feel of what they were thinking.

When we got there, the protests had already started. I remember trying to make my way into the conference center, all dressed up in a suit and coat and tie and the official badge. We had protesters booing all of us who were looking all official and trying to get in.

Maud Daudon: I went with the mayor to what was supposed to be the opening of the WTO. We had his security detail with us. We're on Capitol Hill coming down to the convention center and, as we descended, I could hear the roar of crowds in the street. I just thought, "Oh, boy." There was no way to get anywhere close to the convention center because everything was blocked with protesters. Eventually the mayor got out and went onto the street.

Norm Stamper: I saw Paul Schell at an intersection. He was actually bending over and patting a constituent right there. I heard him talking to himself. He said, "It will pass, it'll pass."

Pam Schell: He never locked himself in. I mean, he never kept his telephone number out of the phone book! And he never asked for extra protection for anything. He always had this sense that he didn't really need it.

Maud Daudon: We finally got there by walking through the crowd. I was behind the mayor and people were sort of jostling us and we finally got through it all and the mayor was greeting everybody—"How's it going? Glad you're in our city, be kind to our city"—that kind of stuff.

We got to the convention center and the security detail got the mayor and I together and said, "That is not a Seattle crowd. These are not our people. They are jostling us. They are pushing. They are aggressive in ways we haven't experienced. This is going to be a really tough day."

We were overwhelmed pretty much instantly. It went from zero to 150 miles an hour. We opened the Emergency Operations Center. Ed was there all week.

Ed Joiner: I really never left. You couldn't be out in the field and, at the same time, do the things that you needed to do from the command position.

Jim Pugel: Ed Joiner was in the EOC, the Emergency Operations Center, in the old Public Safety Building. That's where the head of the State Patrol, head of the Secret Service, FBI, all those guys were. We really didn't have a command post. I was on the street and I had good lieutenants, midlevel commanders. I had one adjunct sergeant and I would meticulously go from point to point, trying to address the really problematic areas. I was always moving around.

Larry Mayes: There wasn't a peaceful dialogue between the delegates and the protesters. The protesters were not friendly toward them. They began shoving, pushing, and they impeded the delegates' ability to go anywhere. They couldn't get into the building for the opening ceremonies. Many of them just stayed in their rooms. That was an extremely dangerous situation.

Jim Brunner: It was partly peaceful but people were locking their arms together and physically preventing delegates from getting in.

Pascal Lamy: The preparations in Seattle were messy and Seattle was a mess. That's my synthesized memory. It was a mess on all grounds. The preparation on the authority of then–United States trade representative Charlene Barshefsky—she was a good friend but it was a mess. What happened around the conference was a mess. I was lucky enough to cross three states of governance: the solid state in France, the liquid state in Europe, and the gaseous state in global issues. Seattle was my entry from solid and liquid to gaseous and for some time I probably thought that I had to get accustomed to the fact that it's gaseous. It was way too gaseous.

Julie Hughes: In a normal ministerial, there are a million meetings going on, everyone's meeting with everybody else, business group to business group, and business groups to government organizations, all of that information sharing. But all of that was disrupted. The meetings weren't happening at all. No one could get to the convention center. We didn't all have a smartphone where we were able to be in constant contact with everybody else.

Tetteh Hormeku: Once we got in there, all we were met with was chaos because the official start was affected by all these protests. I found many, many, many African delegations, wandering around, getting lost.

Colin Hines: I was having a chat with Mike Dolan in a big grand hotel foyer. We were talking about what was coming. And he said, "Who are you going with today? What are you up to?"

I said, "Well, don't make a big fuss about this but I'm actually going to be spending some time with Julie Christie."

Now, Mike's not exactly a retiring flower. So of course, at the top of his voice he goes, "Julie Christie?!"

Everyone around him is looking, and I'm saying, "Mike, shut up!"

"I'm sorry, I'm sorry—I'm just a huge fan."

I said, "Yes, we all are, Mike, but keep quiet." So off he goes and off I go and meet Julie and we go to the labor march.

Annette Sandberg: As the thing began to just deteriorate, it became apparent that some of us were going to have to intervene. When things started getting out of control, I called my statewide dispatch and said, "Put everybody up to the next level of alert." That meant certain troopers got called from off-duty. They were told to stay in a certain location and wait. Because I anticipated, at that point, there's no way that the city could take it back. They just didn't have enough officers.

Maud Daudon: We were in touch with the state, with the governor, to get some help. We activated all of our reserves very quickly across the region. It was quite a bit of a shock, to say the least.

Gary Locke: I got a call from my chief of staff indicating that there were problems in downtown Seattle, and we might need to call out the National Guard. Things were getting out of control.

Celia Alario: At the Independent Media Center you've got people coming in or calling in who are doing audio, print, or video, describing what's happening so that the people inside the center, of which there are many, many, many—the place is packed, every surface that you could be working at is just full of people—so that they have an understanding about what's happening.

The other thing that's going on is the corporate media has helicopters, has people on top of buildings or poised in various places. So watching live TV is providing a vantage and an understanding of what's going on in the streets. We were monitoring televisions and feeding information to affinity groups. There's a whole bunch of information that's moving; people are starting to piece together what's happening.

COURTESY OF SEATTLE MUNICIPAL ARCHIVES

Protesters marching from the
labor rally on their way to the ministerial.

Jim Brunner: It was all hands on deck for this. I'm out there on the streets. We had dozens and dozens—a hundred or something—people out there, filing notes. We were all scrambling.

Mike Dolan: There was the labor march, Ron Judd and nearly 30,000 of his closest friends. They had a rally at one of the stadiums and then they were going to march into Seattle where the Direct Action Network just so happened to be deployed.

Kevin Danaher: The labor march was a big deal. They ended their rally and marched out. The official policy was that they were just going to march by us and not participate in the blockade.

Mike Dolan: Ron Judd told me, confidentially, "Mike, here's what's going to happen. When we get there, when we get right up to the convention center, we're going to sit down. Don't tell anybody."

I said, "Ron, that's awesome. Great. Sit down. By all means. Wow, that'll be massive."

There was going to be this direct action and then the cavalry was going to come in. So that was the plan, and not many people knew it. Certainly the city, the cops, nobody knew they were going to sit down. I was personally really looking forward to it.

Michael Ramos: From the Memorial Stadium down to the convention center was about a mile walk. I think we had 25,000, 30,000 people there. So this was 25,000, 30,000 of what became 50,000 people.

James P. Hoffa: It was raining and the Teamsters had yellow slickers with the Teamster logo on it and you could see our yellow slickers for as far as you could go. We rallied along with all the other unions that were there. We had Paul Wellstone, we had Sherrod Brown from Ohio. They spoke and I spoke, and I remember we had a flatbed truck. We got them up on the flatbed truck with a bullhorn and we rallied everybody. I said, "We're going to march and we're going to show who we are and what we stand for!" People were so excited about going out there with their yellow slickers, marching on the avenues.

Don Kegley: George Becker, the head of the steelworkers union, was up onstage and the whole stadium looked like it was just full of steelworkers. There were thousands and thousands of them. Then we heard this noise in the distance from up on the hill. I went over to the stage and said to George, "Here comes mine!" He looked up and all he could see for thirty blocks were environmentalists. They just poured down from the hill into the streets. It was mind-blowing, it really was. It was the most unbelievable thing I had ever seen in my life. I never felt so proud.

People were pouring into Seattle from everywhere. The head of the AFL-CIO, John Sweeney, was there. All the heads of the unions were there, all the presidents, all the district managers, the truckers, the miners, Richard Trumka, all these people were there. The AFL-CIO sent everybody they could find. The longshoremen shut down ports from California all the way to Seattle and sent the people to Seattle. People came from Europe! The Europeans knew what was happening with the WTO.

Tracy Katelman: I was thinking about the French farmers who were there.

José Bové: With the farmworkers from California we were there, a delegation of farmers from all the world were there in the march with the workers from the United States. We had the delegation of farmers in the front line.

I think it was very symbolic of the issues of the meeting of WTO to have this very strong link between the union workers and the union farmers. It was the first time that we had this kind of link between farmers and workers. Because traditionally, for the workers, farmers looked like people who were individualists. The fact that we were there and that we made a lot of noise about WTO with our Roquefort and so on, everybody understood that the link was there, and a new age was beginning. Struggling against globalization.

It was clearly the big companies were against the local food and the choice of the people for health and food sovereignty. People understood, and we had a lot of journalists from all over the world which came to meet us.

Vandana Shiva: I gave a big speech to the Teamsters. They had a big rally in the stadium and then we all started marching together.

Ralph Nader: We marched arm in arm down the incline toward the water. It was very festive. People were selling food from food carts. There were some people strumming guitars.

David Solnit: We had the Infernal Noise Brigade, which was a marching band.

Kevin Danaher: We had steelworkers. We had Buddhists. We had pig farmers from Oklahoma.

Celia Alario: There were quite a lot of regional, state, and national elected leaders who showed up. Some of them were inside the proceedings but many of them were on the streets. They knew that their power to govern was being usurped by this mysterious tribunal of businessmen who was going to decide how they could and couldn't run their town. So, of course they were going to show up with their constituents.

Puppetry loomed large over the protests.

Dennis Kucinich: I was marching with the Teamsters and the machinists. I was out there with President Hoffa and leading environmentalists who were all combined in their efforts to protect workers' rights, environmental quality, and human rights in any trade negotiations. This was an extraordinary coalition that came together that showed the power that happens when groups that may not naturally align suddenly do so. It had a catalytic effect.

John Nichols: The protests immediately blocked traffic throughout all of downtown Seattle. I was there with Tom Hayden and as soon as he saw what they were doing, he sat right down with them at this intersection where we were standing. He wasn't locked in with them, per se, but he sat right down with them. He was saying what you're doing is really important here. I remember saying to somebody, "You know who this guy is?"

A young woman said, "No."

I said, "Did you ever hear of the Chicago Seven and the protests in 1968 at the Democratic National Convention?" Tom was so genuinely excited to be there and to show solidarity.

I think people who were protesting realized, "Wow, we could really have an impact here. This could be bigger than maybe we even thought, not just a protest, but something that might actually alter the pattern of what's going on." The police also recognized that. They recognized that they were up against something much bigger than what they had expected. Everybody sort of ramped up at that point.

Laurie Brown: My ex-husband was marching with his union; my son was marching with his union. I called them to say that there were a bunch of folks at the Emergency Command Center who had made the decision to use tear gas. "You need to get out of there and get home or at least get out of there." They did.

Pam Schell: There was our niece, Amy, who was protesting the taking of albacore tuna in nets. She was in costume. It was everybody wanting to have a say.

Charles Mandigo: Activating the National Guard became a dispute between the mayor and Annette Sandberg because, as head of the

Washington State Patrol, Annette Sandberg is the initial contact point for mobilizing the National Guard. And she said to the mayor, "If you want the National Guard, you have to declare a state of emergency in Seattle before I can recommend to the governor to mobilize the National Guard."

The mayor was taking the position, "I don't want to declare a state of emergency because politically this would be disastrous." There was not only responding to the crisis but also a lot of politics mixed into the whole thing.

Vivian Phillips: There were these conference calls that happened between the city, the county, and the state. A state of emergency is the only thing that can then trigger the presence of the National Guard. So there are all these conversations about "Well, we don't want to be too heavy-handed, but we need to restore order." And at the same time, all of the national media's eyes are all on Seattle. It was the pager generation, so every news outlet in the world, not just the country, is blowing up my pager. "We want a statement. We want a statement. We want a statement."

Dave Reichert: The mayor had instructed, through the chief, that Seattle was not to make arrests yet. My instructions to my guys were to arrest anybody who was committing a crime, not to coddle them and give people warnings. If they were destroying property, assaulting people, assaulting officers—make the arrest. We had metro buses set up to temporarily hold people. We were all prepared and so we started to make arrests.

I got a phone call from the mayor's office and they said, "This is our city. We don't want arrests made."

I said, "Look, you've asked for my help. My deputies are not going to be in that situation and not arrest people for breaking the law. You want our help? The condition is we're going to be arresting people."

Denis Moynihan: The police didn't try to arrest. They tried to disperse. That was a bad move probably on the part of the police. They probably could have disentangled people and arrested them, and it would've been over.

Dave Reichert: State Patrol asked me, "Are you making arrests?"

I said, "Yes."

They had the same policy.

Eventually, Seattle police officers were also allowed to make arrests. Our strategy was to arrest those people who were the most egregious in breaking the law.

Vivian Phillips: Let me put this in context, because I am black: For a little bit of time, they were looking at different options for dealing with protesters and I had this moment where I thought if these people were black, the response would be a lot different. There would be fire hoses turned on people. That had been my experience. I'm a child of the civil rights era. So I had some real issues. But I also have an enormous amount of compassion. I understand you don't want to mix chaos with violence. That's not the way to go. The older I get, the more I understand that, but at that particular point in time, I was having some issues.

Laurie Brown: I don't know what was happening with the higher-ups in the Emergency Operations Center but I do know that no one wanted the governor's office to get involved. The optics were bad. It would muddy things up in terms of who was calling the shots and who was in charge. I think people politically were concerned that it would make Paul look like he failed or needed to be bailed out.

Gary Locke: I called the mayor and said, "Hey, do you need some help? What can we, at the state level, do? Get back to me as soon as you can." I never heard back from the mayor. I never heard back from the mayor or anyone from his office.

Laurie Brown: There were five or six of us that were huddling and trying to get information from the mayor and the Emergency Operations Center about what was going on. We were just on pins and needles. We needed to make sure that our leaders, Paul and Maud, knew what was happening.

Maud Daudon: I was all over the place. I mainly tried to be wherever I needed to be to try to get a sense of what was going on. I spent quite a bit of time with Ed Joiner in the Emergency Operations Center. I also spent quite a bit of time in the office of the mayor just trying to calm down the staff and trying to keep people informed about what was going on. I was in touch with all the White House people pretty regularly about what was going on.

Colin Hines: Julie Christie and I are making our way through the crowd. Now, I've been on a lot of marches and I am a physical coward. So I've got a very keen sense when things might be turning not quite as chipper as they were at the beginning. And on the march, you could see, particularly from the police, that the atmosphere was not so great. So I said to Julie, "Why don't we pop into a café?" We went in and she had another friend of hers there and the three of us were chatting.

Vandana Shiva: I was walking down the streets and there were these young kids with the pipes holding their arms, blocking the squares, not letting the traffic go. I walked up to them, and I said, "Where did you get this idea?"

They smiled at me and said, "Gandhi."

I said, "Gandhi? In Seattle?" And they said they'd been doing training camps on nonviolence and civil disobedience for months.

Kevin Danaher: Medea and I had passes to get into the conference because Global Exchange was registered with the United Nations as an official NGO.

Medea Benjamin: But we didn't know whether that would actually get us inside. The hardest part was getting through the protest lockdown. At first, people didn't want to let us through. We didn't want to call attention to ourselves from the police either, so we quietly said to the protesters, "We're on your side."

Kevin Danaher: We said, "Look, we are not delegates to the WTO. We are protesters too. We want to get inside and fuck shit up!"

Someone said, "Yes, I know him! He came to our campus. Let them through!" So, we got in. In my coat pocket I had a roll of stickers that had the WTO sign with the international cross-out symbol on it and it said, "End corporate rule." I was going to go inside and stick these all over phone booths and bathrooms.

Medea and I got inside and as we were going through the police check-in, I had to put all of my stuff on the table to be x-rayed. Here was this big roll of stickers that have the WTO with the cross-out symbol and I was thinking, "Oh my god, they're going to nail me." But the stickers passed right through. They didn't notice them. They gave us back our stuff. We got inside and I started putting these stickers all over the place.

Medea noticed that after a while there were hardly any delegates that had managed to get through. There were thousands of seats and only one or two hundred people got in.

Medea Benjamin: It was only about one-quarter full because so many people couldn't get in, including the speakers who were supposed to lead the opening session. There were clusters of people talking to each other, everybody giving their experiences of how hard it was to get in.

Kevin Danaher: The media were all there and the microphones were set up at a podium out on the middle of the stage. When Medea saw that they were starting to pack up the translation equipment, she said, "Hey, we've got to get up on that stage and get to those microphones."

Medea Benjamin: I saw the mic was free. My whole focus was how to get on the stage and get to the mic. Someone had gone up and said something on it, so I knew it was live. I was laser-focused on getting onstage. I thought it would be so cool if the protesters themselves were the opening act. I used the technique of getting closer and closer by waving to people like they were my friends. Finally, we got really close and just went onto the stage.

Kevin Danaher: My little five-foot wife was going up onto the stage full of cops with guns. I couldn't say, "Oh, go ahead, honey, I'll just stay here. You've got it." We went up on the stage together. The plan was that she was going to go over to the microphones and introduce me. I had a statement from the crowd about democracy in global negotiations and how farmers have to be represented. She walked past the podium with all the microphones. I was like, what the hell is she doing? This gives you a sense of her personality: She walked over to the side where Mike Moore—the head of the WTO—was sitting with some other State Department officials. She said to him, "Hey, when are you going to get this show on the road? What's happening?" Just as a little insult to them. She came back to the microphones and introduced me.

Medea Benjamin: I got up and started talking into the mic, saying, "We're sorry for the inconvenience but the opening of this conference has been shut down thanks to these protesters. We want to read you the manifesto of what the protesters are calling for."

In the beginning we looked like we were part of the whole program and that gave us a little more time to talk. We pulled out our demands and started reading them.

Kevin Danaher: I started reading this statement. I got about halfway through the statement and one of my arms gets jacked up behind my back and then my other arm. I was thinking to myself that I was a redwood tree, my roots were in the ground. I wasn't going anywhere. I was finishing the statement when these cops dragged us out.

As they were taking us out, we were yelling about free speech and democracy. There were two cops holding Medea, one on each arm, and there were two cops holding me. As they were dragging Medea in front of me, she flopped down and stuck her feet out and tipped over one of the metal detectors and it crashed. Sparks were flying, wires were popping out, I was laughing. One of the cops actually said to me, "What are you laughing at?"

I said, "That's my wife, man. I've got to live with that. You only have to deal with her for ten minutes."

One of the cops laughed but the other cop said, "That's not funny."

Me, the cops threw out. Medea, they detained because she had done some damage.

Medea Benjamin: Kevin walked out nicely but I was not so nice, dragged by these big security guards. I put my legs out to stop them from getting me out the door and the metal detector machine came crashing down. *Laughs.* They held me, contemplating whether to arrest me or not.

Kevin Danaher: I ran back to the intersection where Global Exchange was based and there was a Teamsters truck with a great sound system. They had parked it right in the intersection. I got up on the mic and said, "Hey, we were just inside, and we disrupted the opening ceremony! Medea got arrested."

I looked into the crowd and saw Medea coming through the crowd. I was like, "What the hell is going on?"

Medea Benjamin: They were holding me in a trailer. I said that I had to go to the bathroom. Because there was no bathroom in the trailer, they had to take me out to go to the bathroom. They didn't want to get into a big thing with a bunch of protesters, so they let me go.

Kevin Danaher: She started screaming, "I've got to pee!" They had to find a woman cop to take her to the bathroom. They brought her back and she said, "I'm having my period! I need a tampon!" They had to deal with that. Finally, they just threw her out, she was so much of a pain in the ass! They just threw her out! This has always been her strategy: persistence.

Vivian Phillips: You've got police officers all over the city trying to hold lines. It was cold. It was rainy. Protesters were squirting pee out of squirt guns, onto the police. Officers were getting sick. It was just chaos, absolute chaos.

Annette Sandberg: I had commanders who were in the field who were reporting the amount of damage. Police officers were on the run. We had put fences up and officers were behind them. A group toppled the fence and officers were scrambling to get out of the way.

I think what turned it around, I was talking to the State Department because the president was supposed to be flying in. Madeleine Albright was trying to get over to the convention center and couldn't get over. I'm reporting all this to the governor. And at that point the governor said, "I'm going to come see you. We're going to get the mayor and the police chief over."

Charles Mandigo: The mayor and Annette Sandberg got into a dispute as to who is going to have operational control over the Washington State officers that were responding. The mayor wanted control over them. Annette Sandberg, she's not a very big person, but she stood up to the mayor, who was a pretty good-sized guy, and said, "Look, if you think you're going to have operational control over my people, forget about it."

Anette Sandberg: I was the first female state patrol chief in the nation. I've had my share of uphill battles. I'm used to dealing with—I wouldn't call them bullies but people who want to puff their chest and say, "Hey, get out of my area." I learned early in my career not to be afraid to stand up for what you believe. And I had great conviction. I started as a trooper in Seattle. I know what the city was like. It was a city I absolutely loved.

When the mayor wanted to politicize some of these things, I'd say, "Listen, I get that. But here's the reality. Let's look at what's happening here. You can't allow this to continue."

Part of it is: Let's bring the facts. If they want to ignore the facts then, okay, but I'm going to keep pushing the facts. What I try to say is, "Here's what I've seen. Here's what the problem is and here's the solution I'm going to offer." Because, as a leader, you have to have a solution.

I had already started ramping up troopers to come in and help—not to take over the city, just to help clear the protest, give it a chance to calm down, let SPD regroup. But they had to regroup in a way that meant they could take control. I wasn't shy about speaking my mind: "I've been to meetings for the last year. I understand what's going on and here's a solution. We better do something quick because this is devolving. It is getting out of control very quickly."

Charles Mandigo: Annette, she appeared to be the one sane person there as far as saying, "Okay, this is what needs to be done and this is how we're going to do it." Some other people seemed to be somewhat influenced by the politics of the situation, as opposed to reality.

Laurie Brown: It was a mess about who was in charge. I learned that that's typical when there are a number of different agencies. The governor's office got directly involved. I don't know who was calling the shots or who felt like they had authority.

Gary Locke: I rushed to the satellite governor's office that we have in the downtown area and was able to turn on the newscast and see the violence on the streets which was just a few blocks away from where I was. I also saw television coverage of the planned, permitted, organized rally that was moving from the Seattle Center, not far from the heart of downtown where all the violence was occurring. The anarchists were in the heart of downtown. The rally was supposed to end at the heart of downtown. I felt that this was a recipe for disaster to have peaceful, law-abiding, permitted protesters at the parade mingling with the violent protesters. There was no way that we would know who was who and I really felt that this could get out of control. Many of the permitted protesters could be hurt in the violence. So I called the city and said, "You should talk to the people and try to turn the lawful protest around. Don't have them come into the very, very heart of the city. Have them stop short of the downtown area." That didn't happen.

Annette Sandberg: When the governor showed up, I said, "Here's what I've done. Here's how many officers I have on standby. Here's how many I can get from western Washington. Here's how many can come from eastern Washington. And here's how quickly I can get it done."

We had staging places over in Bellevue where we were going to have officers show up and then bring them into the city in large groups. The governor was hearing that there's problems from the White House and the State Department, and I think the governor, rightfully so, wanted to make sure that he was doing what he could do. Basically he went to the mayor and said, "Okay, what are we going to do? We've got to get this back under control."

Gary Locke: I don't know what was going on in the mayor's office. At some point I moved from the satellite office to the Emergency Command Center. Maud Daudon, she did come down and stay there, so I was working with her. I was there fielding phone calls from Janet Reno and the White House.

Maud Daudon: There was a lot of pressure from the White House and no resources. It was really a frustrating thing.

Vivian Phillips: City employees took a lot of the brunt of what was going on. Everybody had to be locked down in the building. So they couldn't get home to their families. They had to be subjected to that. Not to mention all of the civil servants in the fire department, the police department, all of these people, they left their families behind in order to secure our city.

Ron Griffin: I had two radios. The Seattle PD could talk directly to me and I had a phone for talking to my troops. I'm listening to what Seattle is saying and they are screaming. I mean, just screaming. When you have your largest agency yelling for help like that . . .

John Sellers: We had incredible radio geeks set up in a tall hotel, monitoring all the cops' frequencies. We had a really good idea of all the security state's transmissions. This was before they could really hide from us in super-encrypted ways. They were just too lazy or hadn't adopted that kind of technology. We knew a lot about what they were saying to one another.

Nina Narelle: There were a few people who had really good lines of sight over the city and they were coordinating and dispatching. There was a network of people who had two-way radios, those big five-pound, brick-sized radios. If there was a breach in the barricade, we could tell the dispatch that we needed people to come right away.

Han Shan: I had three phones, and a Nextel. It was just ridiculous. I was trying to coordinate tactical stuff—send people here, hold this intersection. But at that point, it was written—done. I probably yelled some shit into a walkie-talkie without holding down the button, and I thought I was a genius. *Laughs.* "Yeah, send everyone over to fucking Union and Pine!" Like I'm Douglas MacArthur out there.

Kevin Danaher: You could mobilize the flying squads to certain areas. "We need another flying squad at the intersection of Thirteenth and K. Get over there right now!"

Jim Pugel: This was kind of a harbinger of how protest changed in the late '90s. This was the first event that was coordinated with the assistance of the early internet and handheld radios. We were never able to prove it but the Direct Action Network had a mobile radio station in a car. They also used bicycle messengers like the Pony Express.

Lisa Fithian: I've learned over the years that you need some levels of centralization or coordination, but you also want the culture to be that every group bloom as you may, so that you have this kind of cacophony of resistance. It's not all central but it's everybody bringing their creativity, their artistic selves, whatever, to the fore. And it was brilliant and beautiful and wild, and nobody had ever seen anything quite like it.

Norm Stamper: A few protesters would get together, hook up one-to-one, and you could not pick them up off the street and put them in a transport vehicle. These were people who were taking a seat in key intersections that were necessary. You can't block intersections even if you have a permit to parade.

I wanted people to be able to gather and protest. I felt the same way about some of the issues, but I had to recognize that what I felt as an individual police executive was much less important. I knew what I had to do, but goddammit—

Jim Pugel: The first time I gave the okay for pepper spray was about eleven in the morning at Sixth and Union. A crowd was trying to crash the front door of the Sheraton hotel. A bunch of delegates were staying at the Sheraton, right across from NikeTown. My guy said, "Hey, we're being overrun."

I said, "Soak 'em." You know, "Bring 'em down."

Pepper spray is for individuals. It's usually in a canister—something like the compressed air you use for cleaning a computer. It's finger-activated like a trigger and you shoot at individuals, to repel. It doesn't work good on a crowd. Tear gas works well on a crowd.

Tear gas, you have a can that has a pyrotechnic activator inside and you pull a pin. You toss it and it catches fire and it starts putting out smoke. That's for what we call "area denial"—keeping a group of people away from an area.

Maud Daudon: The police started using tear gas. They'd been trained. They had to pursue their own protocols but I remember just feeling like, "Oh no, oh no, oh no! No, no, no, no, no, no!" The use of tear gas, immediately it went right like a pang to the heart.

Jim Pugel: We also used sting balls. It was the first protest in the U.S. where we tried pepper balls. You know paintball guns? This company had converted one and had made pepper spray inside of the balls that usually hold paint. It was a test item. We used those on individuals who were coming forward and throwing environmental debris at the cops.

Ed Joiner: Pepper spray is far more effective than tear gas. Tear gas makes your eyes water. It's uncomfortable, makes it harder to breathe, but if you're determined, tear gas is really not very effective. When the department got approval to use pepper spray a few years earlier, we guaranteed that every officer who carried it would have been directly exposed to it. If they had it, they could, on the stand, say, "I know exactly how it works and how it feels."

Pepper spray is extremely effective but it has to get into the eyes or the nose or the mouth or something like that. If you hit him on the shirt or a pair of pants, there's not that direct contact and so it minimizes the effect. I can tell you because I've had it. It can be extremely effective but if you've got damp masks on, or cover your eyes with a wet cloth, you can minimize it. It didn't work as well as I would've liked but it was about the only option we had.

My personal choice, which we couldn't do—it's not done in the United States to my knowledge—I would have big water hoses. That's what they use in Europe. When you have water coming from a spray, those sprays are really strong, and you're drenched and it's cold, you want to go home. The interest in continuing to protest doesn't make a whole lot of sense when you're trying to keep from freezing to death. It can be very effective and you're minimizing the injuries. But I think it's one of those things that doesn't look good on film.

Charles Mandigo: I called Annette Sandberg and said, "This is out of control." The word was Stamper was somewhere wandering around on the streets and not to be found in the situation. He had left overall responsibility to one of his captains.

Laurie Brown: It felt to many in the mayor's office that Norm abdicated responsibility. I was crossing the street at one point and our police officers in riot gear were marching down the street. I was shocked when I looked to my side and saw Norm in riot gear marching right along with the officers. Not in charge but as if he was just one of a hundred or so officers who were following the orders of someone else who had authority. I was stunned—and scared for the city. I felt like a kid who realized there was great danger and the parents weren't home. Including Maud.

Norm Stamper: I got gassed twice, big-time gassed twice. That had to do with shifting winds and the method of administration of the gas that was used. I turned the corner one time and some of my officers were wearing face masks and the horses were wearing shields.

Ron Griffin: By now our guys have deployed gas and all that. We're downtown and a lieutenant, he comes up to me and I said, "What do you want us to do?"

He says, "Use whatever force you need to use, you know, other than lethal. We've got to push these people back."

Skip Spitzer: A tear gas canister was fired from some kind of launcher. It hit me in the back, caused an injury. Just as I was starting to have some conscious process around the tear gas hitting me, next thing I know there was pepper spray hitting me. Then I was feeling that. I remember having one sensation leading to another and not really having time to react. At some point, you're just locked in. None of those tactics were enough to actually break our blockade.

Han Shan: The violence against nonviolent blockading, civil disobedience demonstrators happened without any breaking glass, any violence—any provocation. Someone said, "Clear out the blockade." I don't know who, I don't know whether it was Stamper, or the Secret Service because Clinton was arriving, but police started pepper spraying and firing projectiles and pulling masks off of people who were sitting with their arms linked just to clear intersections—long, long, long before any vandalism started happening. There's this bullshit narrative of cause and effect—"Oh, the Black Bloc got violent and the police had to respond."

Norm Stamper: It got bad, bad, bad. I never wanted to give up on the idea that police can be good, that they can exercise important and essential social controls through laws that are defensible, but that wasn't happening. It just wasn't. A lot of tear gas thrown and projected on the demonstrators, mostly to clear intersections. Did we really need to do that? In every case? We may have had legal justification, even procedural justification, but how about efficacy? How about whether or not that would backfire?

Nadine Bloch: The police had tried to blockade certain locations with buses and dump trucks and of course when the crowd meets these things, they're just things to climb. People get up and start preaching and jumping and taking over.

Protesters climb on top of buses that
the city intended as blockades.

Celia Alario: Seattle had taken some of their light-rail trains and put them out on the tracks in various places. So there were empty trains that were not running, on tracks. I was trying to figure out how to get around one of these trains, and I realized there was a certain spot where the two train cars met and I could get through. I came through into this scene: Medea Benjamin is there, and the Teamsters have brought the semi that's got their logo, and they're sitting there hanging around, serving donuts and coffee, which is what they are prone to do—god bless them. There were probably three dozen people in these incredibly beautiful, elaborate, turtle costumes, hard-shell cardboard, with a little head and a body, and their little raincoats underneath them.

Vicente Paolo Yu: The shrimp-turtle case was one of the first decided by the new WTO appellate body. It was a case where they interpreted this famous Article 20, a "general exceptions" clause in the WTO's governing rules. The U.S. had a regulation that said, more or less, "You have to use fishing nets with certain characteristics that would either be effective in not accidentally catching turtles or allow turtles to escape." The U.S. was sued by some Latin American and Asian countries about these nets and won the case because it was able to justify the net requirements under Article 20. But the way the appellate body ruled meant that it was still giving priority to making sure that whatever measure you put in place for environmental protection would not constitute a trade restriction. In essence, the WTO said that the country imposing such a measure most likely will not be able to meet the requirements laid down in Article 20. Only something like three out of forty-four cases have succeeded since the early turtle case.

Celia Alario: These turtles are milling around and Medea is so on it. She asked the Teamsters if someone had a ladder, which of course they did, because Teamsters have everything you could ever want for every protest—not just donuts. And Medea got them to slap a ladder up against those trains, and said to the turtles, "Get up the ladder," and up the ladder go all the turtles, and they're fanning out. So now you've got this silhouette. Then Medea says to the guy who was the head of the local chapter of the Teamsters, "You got any music?" So they have their big thumping sound system, and he takes a request. Some-body asks for "Respect" by Aretha Franklin. All the turtles were on top of the train, dancing, and right beyond them, the giant logo of the Teamsters on their semitruck, and all the Teamsters in their gear with their signs, dancing around. The Teamsters and the turtles, together forever, born in that moment of all of this.

James P. Hoffa: It wasn't planned, the Teamsters and turtles, it just happened.

John Sellers: The Teamsters had one of the best sound trucks I've ever heard in my life. The street party was epic and loud. There were liter-ally Teamsters and turtles dancing in the streets of Seattle.

Don Kegley: Signs that said "Teamsters and Turtles" blew away the trucking industry. They could not fucking believe that! They were just going crazy!

Colin Hines: I'm a great lover of Rodgers and Hammerstein musicals. *Oklahoma!*'s got this wonderful song, "Territory folks should stick to-gether, / Territory folks should all be pals. / Cowboys dance with the farmer's daughters . . ." This was Teamsters and turtles. They made quite a good slogan about Teamsters and turtles to link labor and the environment. That was a very interesting linkage. A lot of labor people still see the environment as a threat to jobs. That's changing now with the whole green-jobs shift but certainly in the run-up to Seattle, and probably the decade after that, often it was "You're my enemy. The environmentalists can put me out of work." Whereas, in Seattle these people worked together and got on very well.

Suzanne Savoie: I remember getting downtown and seeing the whole city with throngs of people everywhere, thousands and thou-sands of people everywhere, and seeing all the different types of people, from the marching bands and the steelworkers and people locked down, or people just doing peaceful protest, people singing "The Star-Spangled Banner" with American flags and lots of differ-ent groups.

Jello Biafra: There were so many people in the street you couldn't move after a while. I felt really, really pumped. I'd never been in a protest that size in my life. We had to rehearse too. So I was on the street early but then had to, you know, stretch, work out, and get my voice in gear—go down and get these songs rocking.

Yalona Sinde: Everybody had their roles. We had our media team and we had the people that made sure that there was water and snacks along the march for people who needed to keep their blood sugar regulated. We took care of each other and made sure there were enough video cameras on-site, we wanted to record everything. We weren't using phones to record yet. People actually had camcorders.

Celia Alario: There were hundreds of citizen journalists, community journalists who had been out with their cameras and their uncle's old everything from Hi8 to Betamax and VHS-C.

Ron Griffin: My kids were in school. My oldest was like fourteen. My youngest was seven or eight. The school knew their father's involvement and they stopped school and got in front of a TV and were watching it.

Nick Licata: The police and the authorities were prepared for sit-ins but they weren't prepared for people handcuffing themselves in circles so you couldn't arrest individuals. The demonstrators didn't resist but if you go deadweight and you're connected to other people? That's what happened. That worked to stop the WTO from meeting.

Julia Hughes: Unlike all of the other ministerials that we've been to, this one deteriorated so quickly that you couldn't get around the city; you had to change your route because of the tear gas and the riots on one street versus where you were supposed to be at that time. It's just so inexplicable how this could have happened, particularly in Seattle, a city that thrives on trade. Those of us from the business community who were there didn't understand how the hell it could fall apart so badly. How could they screw up so badly when you have the president coming?

Pascal Lamy: We landed in Seattle with very little hope that any consensus would be made on any of the pressing topics, which were many. As if this was not enough, the team that prepared the conference for the U.S. side obviously had not properly coordinated with the White House.

David Solnit: We could see the delegates that were not being allowed through and the ones who had the boldness to try to break through. At a certain point, there was an announcement over the bullhorns that the ministerial opening had been delayed. That really bolstered everybody as we were dealing with tear gas and pepper spray.

Anette Sandberg: I was in constant communication with the governor about what was going on. We had the traffic cameras that we were looking at. Keep in mind, this is before cameras were really big. We didn't have very many. But DOT had a few traffic cameras that were mostly intended for I-5. I knew a couple of them were in strategic locations, like Denny Way. We asked DOT to give us those feeds and then we would ask them to move the camera for us—because they still had control of the cameras. It was valuable because it gave us the ability to see where groups were coming from. Sometimes on the radio there's so much noise in the background, you can't really hear what the officers are saying. Keep in mind, the technology was old. We were using any bit of intelligence that we could, to find out what was going on, on the ground. Those traffic cameras were extremely valuable. We tried to use them the best that we could.

Pascal Lamy: It was not a big concern for us what was happening outside, the circus. It did not really influence things except that it was noisy and a lot of people were unhappy.

Noam Chomsky: Of course, anyone on the inside is going to say, "Oh, we never pay attention to protests no matter what they are," but they do. It makes a difference. Kind of interesting when you get documentary evidence—take a look at the Pentagon Papers. After the Tet Offensive in January '68, Johnson wanted to send a couple hundred thousand more troops. The Joint Chiefs of Staff were opposed because they said they would need them for civil disorder control in the United States if the war was escalated. Women, young people, others would just blow up, which is what happened with Nixon's invasion of Cambodia the next year. So, they pay attention. They can't be oblivious to what the public is doing. In fact, they all know that their hold on power is very tenuous. If people ever decide to take their power away from them, it's gone. All policies have to combine ways of trying to pacify the public while pursuing the efforts that you're carrying out. That's a common feature of class war. Of course, somebody on the inside of the WTO is going to say, "We didn't pay attention"—naturally.

John Nichols: I can't begin to emphasize enough the confidence of the WTO. In the early stages of their leadership, they were absolutely certain—they were basically going through a dance. "Yeah, there are some protesters outside but we're going to be in here with our bottled water, our shiny tables, and our comfortable seats. And we're going to sort this thing out. May have some minor differences but, at the end of the week, we will put out a declaration or an agreement and the WTO will go from a very powerful place with regards to global trade to a definitional place." That was the leap that really was proposed at this point, locking in the authority of the WTO to effectively override the nation-states, to override environmental, labor, and other interests, in the interest of free trade.

Julia Hughes: It sounds Pollyannaish now but we were really excited about moving toward opening more trade and trading with more rules. But it became clear that it wasn't going to be a smooth path going forward.

Gary Locke: I got a call from Madeleine Albright. She used some very X-rated words and said, "What kind of a city do you have here?"— expletive deleted, expletive deleted. She said she was a prisoner in her hotel room. She could not get into the convention center to hold the proceedings.

Charles Mandigo: There were so many things going on at once. Frontline SPD officers are running out of tear gas so calls are going out frantically to surrounding law enforcement districts, as well as prisons, saying, "Hey, have you got tear gas? We need tear gas. Bring it in." They're making phone calls for reinforcements and mutual assistance to come in.

John Zerzan: There was a call for an anarchist get-together around late morning. Some of the punker types barely get up by eleven a.m. so it didn't exactly start on time. For obvious reasons, people were not too vocal about what exactly they planned on doing. People knew enough to wear masks and keep moving. They gathered, then it just took off. I wasn't necessarily expecting all that much. In fact, I wasn't even wearing a mask for a while. Somebody handed me one and I put it on. I thought, "Time to wake up." Things are happening here that are kind of amazing, these giant windows just coming down like waterfalls, the glass.

Mike Dolan: The Black Bloc started smashing shit, which made the cops react even more. When they first started breaking windows it was the middle of the day and it continued all afternoon. They did a Starbucks. They were moving around and breaking shit. Everything had been peaceful up to that point. Everything was going swimmingly and then these fuckers from Olympia or Eugene or wherever started breaking shit.

Dennis Kucinich: Part of the sideshow at the WTO were protesters who were anarchists, who were determined to create disruption and violence, and who were baiting the police into aggressive reaction. As a result of that, the streets were filled with tear gas.

Celia Alario: I encountered some of the Black Bloc, twelve or fifteen of John Zerzan's devotees from Eugene in black, hooded sweatshirts and bandanas, and they're getting ready to start smashy-smashy. I start this whole conversation with them: "Look, I've read my Subcomandante Marcos. I understand why the mask. I'm trying to be with you here for a minute but it makes me uncomfortable. Actually, it makes me nervous. I'm scared. I can't see your face."

A couple of them pulled down their masks so I could see their face, and they start, rather eloquently, going on and on, they have a grave analysis about capitalism, and the WTO, and all of that. Then they make a pivot that's hard for me to follow, on why these corporate targets need to be called out. They're starting to run, so I jog a little bit with them.

The first thing I saw them smash was actually a small family-owned jewelry store. They didn't take anything but they smashed the windows and they'd run on.

Annette Sandberg: Watching the traffic cameras, we were watching environmental groups that were dressed like butterflies and flowers and stuff like that. They were walking down and all of a sudden, these people that were clad in black and completely masked started attacking them.

Suzanne Savoie: I was part of the Black Bloc contingency. I think the WTO protests were kind of a manifestation of rage for a lot of people. When you feel like your voice is silenced and you feel like all the traditional ways of making change are just not working. Believe me, I had done a lot of traditional activism up until that point. There was definitely an opportunity there to express that rage in a very physical way. I've been thinking about it in comparison to the January 6th riots. Just thinking, "Well, how could somebody objectively think of the two differently?" But people who came to the WTO protest, if they brought a hammer, it was to destroy a window. It wasn't to hurt a person. It wasn't to create violence against people. In fact, what we were there for was to oppose the violence against oppressed people across the world. The property of those corporations was the target— not people—going after the physical manifestation of that company that's right there in front of you.

Corporations are really hard entities to influence and to get access to and to have any sway over. So when there's a big protest and there's a physical entity representing that corporation, there's an opportunity to break windows or do some property destruction to show that we're physically trying to tear down this power structure—not by violently hurting people but by trying to do symbolic actions. Breaking a window isn't going to bring a corporation down. But it's a symbolic action that's saying, "We are trying to break down the power structure that causes social injustice and environmental injustice across the world."

four waters: The Black Bloc was the group that caused property destruction. They put on a hood and take direct action. There couldn't have been more than thirty-five or forty people out of tens of thousands of people.

Dana Schuerholz: The media didn't cover the Red Noses. They covered kids smashing a window. That then became what the protest was known for when, in fact, many amazing things were happening. People doing more traditional nonviolent civil disobedience was ninety-nine percent of what was going on.

David Solnit: The Black Bloc was a narrative that parts of the media adopted to scare people away and diminish the people power and mass participation narratives. It didn't help with the shutdown.

Jim Brunner: The protests happened on a couple of fronts. There was the "global protest." What does it mean? Are they having an impact on this trade regime? And then there was "What's happening in downtown Seattle with a lot of chaos going on?"

It was like, "You've got a deadline. You've to make a quick snap decision and you've got to write." I think people could make their own judgments about whether the focus on vandalism was overblown. Sometimes a lot of it has to do with how you place the images, what's the lead image. On TV, of course, the images carry everything, but it's not surprising to me that the vandalism would be the kind of thing that would be viewed as super-newsworthy. I don't think it was wrong to report all that. I was certainly very cognizant of the fact that most of the people there protesting were not the black-clad anarchists and they were down there to talk about a message that, at the time, was kind of new. The strength of the protests was something new.

Kevin Danaher: Some of the people who broke windows, they were not involved in the early organizing. They came in like the remora.

They were riding us to do their window-breaking shit and then they were gone and you never saw them again. There were questions about who they were. We couldn't see. They could have been cops.

Ralph Nader: If they weren't provocateurs paid by outsiders, which happens all the time, including with the FBI, they were radicals who had no sense of long-range strategy. They just wanted to smash windows.

David Solnit: There is a history of agent provocateurs, people who fight cops or break things. Often people are hired to do that because it can hurt movements. It's a chess game. Movements have to have the ability to think about how to counter that image and build power, push back on the authorities, and bring the changes that we need for our communities.

Our goals with the shutdown were if you need to move objects or decorate the city with art, that's fine, but don't break things, just shut down the institution, which is more powerful. There was a political disagreement with the Black Bloc.

Kevin Danaher: We tried to explain to them that if they break windows at Starbucks, insurance would cover the damage but people could get hurt by flying glass. They were scaring the employees who were not the enemy. Those of us who had studied the World Trade Organization didn't want to cede ground to people who thought breaking windows would bring down capitalism. But the media went to the broken windows.

Medea Benjamin: The Black Bloc was really intimidating and forcing people to agree to their tactics when it wasn't even their space. They hadn't worked with us to create the event. We had worked hard and created coalitions, all kinds of people, but they just showed up. Then they wanted everybody to respect their right to manifest their frustration in their own way. I felt that it was like coming to someone else's party and destroying what others had built, turning everything upside down. It was tough in terms of the coalition itself.

Nina Narelle: I'm not really interested in the question "Is property destruction violence?" Who cares? Police murder is violence, I know that. Let's talk about that. That is clear. Did it feel amazing to see people smashing windows all over the place? Yes, it felt fucking great! All of the rage, anger, and sadness that I felt about the ways in which I saw people being oppressed and the ways in which I saw the earth being destroyed.

I also really respect and acknowledge that when the most fringe radical part of a movement can go out in public and express rage without murdering or harming people, it galvanizes people. It gets people's attention. It inspires.

Jim Flynn: I don't feel bad for Nike or Starbucks or McDonald's. Fuck them! They can afford it. Insurance will pay for it. Property damage is not violent. It might look violent but when the dust settles nobody gets hurt. It's just property damage. It is disturbing that people equate property damage with violence to living beings. Certainly arguments could be made that some people get more upset about property damage than they do police brutality. That's so backwards and fucked-up!

Ron Griffin: One of the protesters climbed the Nike building in downtown Seattle. He's kicking the Nike sign off the side of the building with a—wait for it—a Nike shoe.

John Zerzan: All the cops were at the convention center, so there wasn't much of a battle. There was nobody to fight except your nasty corporate landmarks to go after.

Jim Hightower: Corporations were being demonized for something that they were getting written up for in *Fortune* and *BusinessWeek* as the heroes of the capitalist system. The protests had the advantage of having corporate logos, so the enemy was real—right there. It was in people's minds. It wasn't some esoteric—well, it was the esoteric bureaucracy of the trade councils but it was easily presented as, say, General Electric.

Wasn't it Jack Welch who said that he wished he could put his corporation on barges so they could go from country to country, wherever the cheapest labor was? I just think they were so narcissistic, thinking they were doing god's work with expanding trade and making money. They didn't think anybody would pay attention.

Vandana Shiva: The WTO made the state a corporate state. Then the corporate state, in the face of popular protests on a very wide scale, it has to become a *military* corporate state. The first time we saw it was in Seattle.

David Solnit: The rain lightened. A lot of the clusters had already shut down parts of the city. We brought masses of people in to back them up and some more people blockaded from there. We had hundreds of people, many of whom had never had any contact with us, seeing what we were doing and that we were linking arms and physically repelling all the delegates.

There were many young activists who had been to the teach-ins and had educated themselves in different ways. They were engaging in heated debates with governmental and corporate delegates from all over the world about why we were not letting delegates in. A lot of people in three-piece suits would try to throw themselves at our line or push themselves through. One actually pulled a handgun out on us. Largely we were successful. We controlled the streets. Very few people were able to get through.

Pam Schell: An assistant to a diplomat held a gun up in the air. It was really dangerous, and things just got worse and worse.

Larry Mayes: I don't know what SPD's protocols were on checking delegates for weapons. They had large staffs that came with them. That's a recipe for disaster right there. SPD crowd control lost that whole area.

Jim Pugel: At one point, it was really tenuous. The Secret Service told us that if any of these protesters get into the convention center, people will be shot. We had something like one hundred nations represented, some high-level delegates, and they all had their security and weren't going to put up with a bunch of people.

Nina Narelle: We had to network in on the radios with street medics because so many people were getting injured by being hit in the face with rubber bullets or chemical burns to the face from pepper spray or beat up by the police. We were unprepared for that level of state violence—naïvely, in retrospect.

Vandana Shiva: It was merciless, the way the violence took place and was engineered. I could see the police do it with my own eyes.

Kevin Danaher: The police actually screwed themselves because they did things like beating people, shooting people with rubber bullets. We had it set up so that when frontline people got attacked and had to retreat, there was another phalanx, the old Roman army system of having another group come right in and replace them.

David Taylor: To some extent, a lot of people expected to go sit down and get arrested in the first twenty minutes. I was surprised we had the sustained tactical success we had in the mass direct action, as far as actually being able to prevent the flow of delegates, to really overwhelm the infrastructure. Then the marches came through, and the expectation had been that when the marches all got downtown, the direct action stuff would be over. But that is not how it ended up.

Mike Dolan: The whole Sellers crew was still hanging banners. They had gotten up in some elevator shaft and some banners were coming down on buildings. I mean, it was looking good. The lockdown is going on, the fucking Black Bloc is starting to rampage, there's tear gas, there's a lot of skirmishing going on, and then—here comes the cavalry!—the labor movement, with banners and jackets and flying their colors and all the rest. I said, "Hooray! The calvary is coming over the hill! Here they come! It's the labor march! God bless them."

But the people with vests who were in charge of managing the crowd, they said, "We're turning it around." And I saw them turn. I knew their route and suddenly they turned. Some of the cavalry was peeling off, like in retreat. John Sweeney, he went back. And some of the other labor leaders, they went back.

When they made the decision to turn it around, I was shouting, "What the fuck? Where are you going?"

One of the guys came over and said, "Yeah, we're turning it around and they're going back to the Seattle Center, where they started."

I said, "That's really a bad idea."

Ralph Nader: Organized labor wanted to be present but they went down the street a bit and didn't do shit.

Dan Seligman: We turned out people but our instructions were to not participate in any civil disobedience. We don't do violations of law. Nor did the AFL-CIO. So we were parallel in the approach we took. Neither of us were involved in the lockdown part of the protest that actually shut down the whole convention center.

Ron Judd: I was at the tip of the spear on that march. There's no DNA in me that's going to suggest to somebody that they shouldn't keep moving forward. My calculation was "How do we make sure that we have room for those that want to continue protesting and how do we protect those that did not come down prepared for that?"

We'd invited a lot of parents and kids down. There was a lot of shit happening and we did not want to put kids in the middle of it. People got to select, and our peacekeepers talked their way down the blocks letting folks know what was happening so that when they got to that point they could choose. The families and many others went back to the stadium. Part of the conversation was policy differences and tactical differences but a big part of it—I can tell you because I was on the front line talking to all the general presidents—a big part of it was making sure that their families, their spouses, their kids, their grandkids that we invited from the community were safe.

Dan Seligman: I know that there was a lot of back-and-forth with Sweeney about peeling off but they'd made a commitment to the Seattle police.

Don Kegley: We were not all on one street. We were on seven or eight streets, and we started hearing that the police had stopped John Sweeney and the people with him. Of course, they weren't willing to start a battle. But on the other streets where there were more union guys like me—the environmentalists, the Teamsters, the turtles, and all those great folks—we heard that the police were trying to break up the march so that we didn't get to the hotel. A few people from the other streets came over and said, "The cops have got the AFL-CIO head and people with him stopped." Everybody looked at me like, "What are we going to do?" Then I started hearing some other people say, "Hell no! We're not turning around! It ain't happening! We are not quitting!" The cops had put up roadblocks but we just pushed through all the barricades. People ran the message back that we were not stopping. We were going all the way.

Jim Pugel: You have to remember during that time the United Steelworkers had been on strike for eighteen months. The company was definitely trying to break the union. They were pissed.

Don Kegley: I actually had a lawyer walking with me the entire time because they didn't want me to go to jail because I was involved in some of the lawsuits over the lockout. They tacked my lawyer onto my coat sleeve and said, "Don't let him out of your sight and don't let him do anything crazy!"

John Zerzan: The union field was striking. They were trying to get into it. They wanted part of the action, and the bosses were not having that. They were terrified at the thought of those people joining in because then it would be more than a bunch of anarchists. It would be pretty serious. Some of those union guys, they wanted the whole thing. Unions don't play.

Kevin Danaher: Myself and a whole bunch of other people were saying to them, "Come on, join us! We're shutting them down!" There was a breakaway group of trade unionists that came over.

Nadine Bloch: I was trying to convince labor unions not to leave us in the dirt but to come downtown and support. We were in a moment of real potential there.

Mike Dolan: Some of the rank and file realized what was going on. They were like, "I didn't come this far to miss this piece. Here's where the action is!" God bless the rank and file because that added to our numbers on the street. Suddenly in the crowd on the street there were the anarchists, the protesters, the turtles, and now all the labor people. The cops had never seen anything like it.

Of course, I knew most of the cop leadership and they were like, "What the fuck?"

I said, "Well, I warned you!"

We owned downtown Seattle. We had it. It was the cops who were pissing in alleyways because they couldn't get out. They were locked up. We had the police surrounded, not the other way around.

Ed Joiner: The old shit hit the fan as soon as the labor march was coming down. Once it became apparent they were not all going to abide by the initial agreement, we knew we were in for a very difficult situation because we simply didn't have the resources to cover that whole area given the number of protesters we were dealing with.

Larry Mayes: SPD was completely overwhelmed. Now everything's gone to hell in a handbasket. Even Paul Schell knows it.

Jim Pugel: A group of the labor organizers kept coming north on Pike, where they were supposed to make a U-turn. It was just pandemonium. We called out for mutual aid. I remember calling Ed Joiner and said, "We're going to need more state troopers here."

Three hours later I saw a state trooper I knew from Spokane. Going the speed limit, that's at least a four-hour drive. He made it to Seattle in three hours.

Vicente Paolo Yu: I was able to get inside the conference hall and speak to some of the other delegates and I think that everyone was realizing it was all really much more complex than any of us were thinking.

Pascal Lamy: The police were totally unable to control everything. There was a local-versus-state-versus-federal issue, the coordination of which totally escaped the participants in the conference, including myself. I'm not a specialist on how street police operate in the U.S. but it was a mess.

Larry Mayes: The anarchists moved into the downtown area with the vandalism, the fires. This was during the Christmas shopping season. There were open stores down there. There were people shopping. There were people working in these stores.

Hilary McQuie: People get so bent out of shape in the United States if a car gets burned. It's like if you're in France, I mean, that's just due diligence.

Medea Benjamin: Property is so critical to the whole economic architecture of our country. We put way too much emphasis on property, on a glass window where these stores probably have plenty of insurance that will pay for it, or graffiti where someone has to clean it up. It's not a big deal and yet it is seen as a big deal. In this country, there is this undue reverence for private property that you don't find in many places around the world. Look what the Yellow Jackets got away with doing in France—oh my god! We could never do that here. When I'm in protests in Latin America, people have spray cans of paint and as they go along, they spray every building. The police don't do anything. But in our country, this issue of property damage is like, "Whoa." The consequences can be severe, and if people haven't signed up for that, it's not right to put them in a position where they are in the middle of that.

One of the big issues was that a lot of people we had with us were undocumented and the vandalism was putting them in jeopardy. There are times when people want to put themselves at risk of arrest and times when they can't afford to do that. We should distinguish those opportunities.

Maud Daudon: Seeing the breaking of windows and destruction going on downtown—to this day, I don't completely understand who those individuals were, what they were up to, but it did feel like there was this small group of people that had come in specifically to just be destructive, and it wasn't about protesting, it wasn't about globalization, it wasn't anything but just sheer destruction. Definitely it changed the tone.

Han Shan: Initially the police and the Black Bloc weren't in the same location—things happened blocks away from each other. The Black Bloc was moving the way they liked to move, which was staying *away*. They weren't engaging with police. They were staying as far away from police as they could.

John Zerzan: It wasn't planned this way but the people that block-aded the convention center and prevented the delegates from coming in and stopped the WTO—that's where all the attention was, all those rings of protesters hunkering down and getting sprayed and hit. That was incredible. In other words, you could say that the two things worked together, not consciously, but in fact.

John Sellers: The cops weren't trying to arrest Black Bloc. They loved Black Bloc. They could have arrested them at any time when they were smashing Starbucks and McDonald's but it gave them an excuse to kick the shit out of everybody else.

James P. Hoffa: They tear-gassed us. They had rubber bullets they shot at us. They did everything they could because after a while it started to get pretty rough. The police were trying to restrain us from

Clearing pepper spray from the eyes of one protester.

exercising our First Amendment rights. We wanted to demonstrate, we wanted to show them who we were, so we had a lot of tussles. I think that's what a good demonstration is about. We were peaceful demonstrators but we would not be restrained.

Lisa Fithian: They started deploying concussion grenades, those huge, loud flash-bangs. That definitely was one of my traumas coming out of Seattle; loud bangs do this. I think they did that to scare more labor from coming. I think labor all of a sudden was hearing these loud bangs. They're like, "We're the fuck out. We're not going to take our people into that."

Skip Spitzer: They moved on to concussion grenades and unleashed so much tear gas that you were in a thick, opaque cloud and just couldn't breathe.

Kevin Danaher: A guy was standing right next to me in the line when we got attacked. He got hit with a rubber bullet just below his lower lip and it opened his face up where you could see the roots of his teeth.

Don Kegley: We were outside the conference center. We had them trapped. We were in the streets and had most of the streets shut down. They pushed but we pushed back a lot harder than they thought would ever happen.

Yalonda Sinde: With the tear gas, some people had to go out in stretchers. I was able to back up in time and not really get hit as bad as some people did. It was really scary. I could see people passed out on the ground gasping for air and people helping them up and trying to move them farther away because once it really hits you, you just fall down. It was chaos, people everywhere, screaming. Some people started fighting back, started throwing stuff at the police and it was really tough.

Skip Spitzer: People were getting hurt, so I spent time just trying to be helpful and I realized how much my own body hurt—I had a big welt from the tear gas canister that hit me.

four waters: I was down by Pike Place Market. The entire square was filled with smoke. People were being shot with rubber bullets all around me. We were all carrying water that was filled with things that would make your eyes stop burning if you had been tear-gassed. We had extra bandanas on.

It's really hard if you haven't been in that situation to know what it feels like. It's terrifying being tear-gassed. You can't see. You can't breathe. Part of you is trying to figure out where a safe space is for you. Part of you is looking around to see who else is injured and figuring out how to get people out who are having a harder time. But you can't see—you don't know how to get out.

It wasn't just us. That's the thing that's haywire: they gassed all of downtown. Anyone shopping, or anyone who worked in any of the shops, any of the street vendors, the press, they gassed and shot rubber bullets indiscriminately.

Vivian Phillips: The Emergency Operations Center was beneath a fire station on Fourth Avenue. It was safe and guarded but it was right below ground where the protests were actually happening. I remember popping upstairs and looking outside and I'm going, "Holy shit!"

It was upwards of twenty people in the EOC at any given time. You have representatives from public works, utilities, electricity, fire, police, and a number of public information officers from all of the departments, all of the major city departments. The fire chief, police chief, they were in and out. The mayor is coming in and out.

Larry Mayes: Dave Reichert and I are called down to the Operation Center. Everybody's there. Paul Schell, Norm Stamper, several SPD chiefs, Secret Service, FBI, State Patrol. All these people are there and there's chaos out on the street. Hell, there was just as much chaos in this room. This is the Operations Center. This is where you're calling the shots. We had a big table. The maps of the city are all spread out on it, we're all sitting at this table. Norm Stamper and Paul Schell, along with a couple of SPD assistant chiefs, are trying to figure out how to move the delegates. This went on for a while—it was embarrassing, it was awkward. Reichert leaned over to me and said, "This is going nowhere. The way you get a safe route for the delegates anywhere is to take the goddamn streets back." He says, "Listen, I'm the sheriff, the elected sheriff, of King County." And he said, "I'm done. We've got to get more cops in here."

We both got up from the table. I went over to one of the SPD chiefs and said, "Listen. Dave is going to start calling in other departments, other resources, to the extent that we can. I need to know who you have designated as the coordinator for the staging area and dispersing these troops that are going to be arriving.

He looked at me and said, "I'll get you somebody."

I said, "Get me somebody? You don't have anybody assigned to this role?"

Annette Sandberg at State Patrol started helping. We activated more mutual aid coming in and set up staging down at the Kingdome.

Ed Joiner: We had the news stations on so we could see from that end what was going on but I was primarily scrambling to see how we could come up with more resources. It became clear that there was no possible way that we could get enough resources in to maintain security of all the venues without doing something drastic.

Charles Mandigo: I talked to Janet Reno, just kind of telling her what my observations were at that time. Then I got a phone call from the assistant to Janet Reno saying the attorney general wanted to speak to the governor. Well, I was having trouble getting the governor's attention. And so finally, I said, here is Annette Sandburg's cell phone number. You call that number and Annette Sandberg has the direct ear of the governor.

Gary Locke: During the rest of the day I was in communication with the White House. The White House was essentially calling to say, "Was this safe?" President Clinton was expected to arrive. They wanted to know if it would it be safe for him to come to Seattle.

Ron Judd: It was insane! Absolutely insane. They dropped the ball by not really paying attention and then overreacted. Because that's exactly what happened.

With the mindset of the protester, there's this energy that suddenly gets whipped up and you can quickly lose control of a protest that has good intentions. When that energy starts shifting, it's like a maddening. It draws that energy and others get caught up in it. That's what happened. And the cops weren't ready. When they did get ready it was like a 911 call.

Jim Pugel: Annette Sandberg called me and said, "The State Department said, 'You have to clear this street at all costs'"—she gave a couple of intersections that were most critical—"'because Madeleine Albright has to get out of her hotel and into the convention center.'"

I said, "What do you mean 'at all costs'?"

She said, "Whatever it takes, clear it."

I said, "Okay, well, will Albright indemnify me against any lawsuit later on?"

There was a pause and Annette said, "Let me check."

Annette and I'd been sued in the past in federal court, over actions some of my officers had taken on past protests, so I knew what you're allowed to do and what you could lose a lawsuit over.

She checked with head of security for the U.S. Department of State and came back and said, "No, they won't indemnify you."

I said, "Man, we're going to have to, I mean, literally break heads. We can't do that."

But they kept saying, "You've got to clear the intersections!" State Department, Secret Service, FBI—they all have their role and that's to protect their primary protectee. They don't care about the impact on anything else.

Annette Sandberg: Gary Locke is a take-charge kind of person. He wasn't going to take over the city but when things got out of control and he's got the White House and the State Department calling, he's going to help step in and correct it. He was really a voice of reason. I think the mayor was a little bit in denial, to be honest with you—and I'm not a political person.

The governor got the feds screaming at him so he tried to bring some reason to all the parties. He said, essentially, "Hey, we can't go as extreme as maybe the feds want us to. And we can't be this lax. We've got to cut it in the middle, and we still have to make sure that this conference occurs. We have to make sure people don't get hurt and we have to bring the city back under control."

Gary Locke: I said, "What an indictment it would be if a president of the United States did not feel safe enough to enter an American city. What an incredible stain on America."

Dave Reichert: Gary Locke and Paul Schell are at the command center, Norm Stamper and Annette Sandberg are there, and so is the State Department and FBI. Now, I hadn't been invited but I just happened to be there anyway, and I sat down at the table with everyone else. Of course, the mayor shoots me a dirty look. But I sat down. I'm listening to the conversation, I decided I was going to keep my mouth shut until a question was asked to the mayor by the State Department with the Secret Service standing right next to them: "Mayor, what we need to know right now is can you tell me today that you can keep the city safe? Because you've got the most powerful man in the world coming to your city. Can you keep Seattle safe for the president of the United States of America?"

The mayor pauses and looks down. He's not saying anything. Then he looks over at Stamper and says, "Chief, what do you think?"

The chief kind of pauses a minute and he says, "Well, I think we need to evaluate the current status and how many officers. We've got to take some factors into consideration." And then he stopped talking.

I was sitting next to him and I tapped him on the shoulder. I said, "Can I talk to you for a minute?" So we left the meeting and went into a private room. I said, "We can't do this. The answer to the question is 'Yes!' So 'we don't know if we can keep the president safe' is not the right answer."

He says, "Well, let's go back in and we'll listen to this just a little bit more, and we'll get some more information."

I'm shaking my head going, "What a bunch of crap."

The meeting broke up and I asked Chief Sandberg to meet with me. We went into a room, just the two of us, and I said, "We've got to take control here. This is totally getting out of hand." Charlie Mandigo, later he and I talked about the same thing. We've got to make the city safe for the president of the United States. There's just no question about it. They both agreed.

Charles Mandigo: Janet Reno had had somebody working for her, kind of checking things out. He had called me and he says, "Hey, on the q.t., I just wanted to let you know that Janet Reno was so concerned about everything going on that she had called the Pentagon, making an inquiry as to what it would take to activate the military to come in." A little bit later somebody from the Pentagon called her back and asked some clarification questions because they were in the process of mobilizing. Janet Reno had to explain, "No, no. I was only asking what it would take *if* we did ask. I wasn't asking for mobilization!" It was a misunderstanding apparently. Fortunately, somebody called back for clarification.

Julia Hughes: There was a point in time when the U.S. delegation was locked down because of the protests outside. Me and some of my colleagues, we happened to have a briefing scheduled with them so we actually were in lockdown with the delegation. They weren't really happy about that. Textile policy was not Trade Representative Barshefsky's favorite part of her job, let me put it that way. *Laughs.* Everyone tried to get away from the businesspeople because we're going to be asking questions: "What the hell's going on? What are you doing about it?" And I don't think they had any more control over it than we did.

That was probably several hours they were stuck with us, the businesspeople they didn't really want to be talking to right then. Some folks tried to sneak out back doors but it seemed like the better thing was to hang out where you were and wait and see what happened.

Ron Judd: It all unraveled because they never quite accepted that we were going to be so successful. They never bought into it. When I first told them, "I think we're going to have easily north of 50,000 maybe to 75,000 people," they coughed up hairballs while laughing. Part of it was that everybody involved was saying, "Well, people love trade here. All these humans are not going to step up to risk their jobs that are based on trade." They never got that this is bigger than one individual job and that we can step out of those individual jobs and understand there's a bigger picture. People are suffering. We have a moral responsibility as human beings to speak up. They never believed it and that's why things deteriorated.

Norm Stamper: I'd say the moment that affected me more than any other was looking in the faces of my officers who were shocked and surprised at the opposition they were facing on the streets. The fact that they didn't get why they were facing opposition was alarming to me.

Jello Biafra: Krist called me and said, "Jello. Dude, don't even come down to sound check. I'm here now and I can't get back out. The police are going crazy. They're gassing people, and there's a pitched battle going on right on the other side of this wall."

Kim Thayil: Since Krist lived there, he was free to walk around downtown. For myself or Gina, who were outside the downtown core, a lot of it was closed off. We couldn't just easily access the area for rehearsals.

Jim Pugel: One thing was just keeping the officers calmed down. I had a set of fake teeth, you know those Bubba Gump teeth at the trick store? Whenever the officers would get real tight in front of a crowd, I'd put them in and my back would be toward the crowd. I'd walk in front of the guys: "Calm down, calm down." Try to chill them out a little bit.

Nick Licata: There was dancing, costumes, turtles, things of that sort. There were children there. They were dressed up in costumes. There was a festive Halloween sort of feel. It was like a celebration of the good earth. Yet if you walked three blocks away there was violence going on, property violence going on. I kept thinking, "This can't exist very long before either the celebration is going to stop, or the breaking of the windows is going to peter out." They both continued for quite a while actually. You know sometimes in war, actual wars, you can say, "Yeah, there was tremendous fighting going on here but, on the other side, the markets were all open." A bifurcation of reality. Well, there's a little bit of that going on.

Colin Hines: So I'm in the café with Julie Christie and I was kind of keeping an eye and ear out to see what was happening outside. I thought, "Well, it seems to be a bit quieter now." We go out and suddenly, bang. We're in the middle of the tear gas. I can see fifty yards down the road, Mike Dolan. Someone was pouring water in his eyes.

Mike Dolan: I'm retreating from tear gas and pepper spray with my eyes ablaze, my face on fire. I'm going slightly downhill, and one of the medics from one of the affinity groups comes up to me. She's part of Solnit's crew and she's just pouring water into my eyes and asking if I'm okay. There were so many of those medics out there, I love that.

So, now I'm a little bit better and at one point I find myself standing in front of this restaurant and Colin Hines comes out. He sees me and he goes, "Michael, look at you. I mean, you're all messed up."

I said, "Yes, Colin, it's bad out here!"

Colin Hines: Mike was much more of a brave, in-the-middle-of-it chap.

Mike Dolan: He said, "Well, let's take you back to the hotel and get you washed up. But first, I want you to meet someone." He points to this woman and says, "This is Julie Christie."

Colin Hines: As the water cleared from his eyes, he saw her. So he said, "Julie Christie! I'm a huge fan of yours."

And she said, "I'm a huge fan of yours, Mike."

Mike Dolan: What the fuck do you say? It was Julie Christie, the actress! *Far from the Madding Crowd*! My original fantasy in the flesh!

Colin Hines: Mike said it was the best tear gas clarification experience ever. *Laughs.* The three of us went back to the hotel. I was hoping to bathe his eyes a bit more.

Mike Dolan: Off we go into Colin Hines's hotel room, which is two blocks away. He pulled out a Double D lager and handed it to me out of the fridge while I was washing up. My phone's blowing up. My walkie-talkie's blowing up. Julie has the TV on. All the news channels are breaking the story and all this shit is going on. She starts crying. Colin was just like, "Hey, you want another beer?"

For me, it was this Walter Mitty moment and I just said, "I've got to get back out there." Julie Christie's crying and Colin Hines has the beer and I've washed up and I get back out on the streets. But I got to meet Julie Christie. That was a tender moment.

Han Shan: My phone is blowing up. Laurie Brown is calling me. Pugel was calling me. I agreed, of course, to be a liaison and to talk to them and be an open line of communication. I tried to communicate, "You can always talk to me and I will always tell you what I see." But I never told any of the people, not Pugel, not Laurie Brown, not anybody else that I am here as a leader of these people. I was a communication conduit. But the city and cops would be like, "Get your people to fall back!"

"No, I can tell them what you're asking and then I'll tell you what they said, but I'm not their leader. It's not how this works."

Larry Mayes: You can negotiate with the Teamsters, the environmentalists, and some of these other groups, prior to an event. But when the event actually happens, the leaders of those groups lose control. A lot of the people involved are good people with good reasons to be protesting, people with concerns that are legitimate. I agreed with some of them. But the leaders lose control and people get caught up in the destructive part of it.

Jim Pugel: In the afternoon, there were small dumpster fires and the Black Bloc was using the peaceful protesters as somewhat of a foil so they could break windows behind a group. In order for us to get through to the Black Bloc, we had to trample over these peaceful protesters that were sitting down. It wasn't coordinated that way but the Black Bloc knew that we weren't going to, you know, beat up all these peaceful protesters. So we cobbled together this other group of police officers and they tried to catch up with the anarchists. They never did.

Dennis Kucinich: The lobby that I was in, people were choking from tear gas. There was a great amount of chaos and it made you wonder if these groups were provocateurs designed to try to slow the growing momentum of labor and environmentalists that were really getting traction in insisting that the United States trade policies had to be based on principles that would protect jobs and wages at home and make sure that we weren't exporting pollution to poor people around the world.

Larry Mayes: The arson and the looting and the property destruction wasn't just the anarchists. There were a lot of street criminals down there, people who wanted in on the looting and joined in. It was a large number of them.

Ed Joiner: There clearly were the instigators for most of the violence. Where the local demonstrators became a real problem for us is that they protected the agitators because we would have people throwing rocks and whatever from the crowd. The agitators would be behind the crowd but you couldn't get to them because the crowd wouldn't let you through. We tried to get into this one particular group and the crowd simply refused to let the horses through. That's a pretty strong statement if you are so determined not to let the police in that you stop a group of mounted patrol officers. The officers can't force their way through because people are going to get hurt by the horses; it's going to be a confrontation you can't have. This dynamic really hamstrung us in terms of the ability to get the people who were really the ones behind a lot of the violence. I don't think the bulk of the protesters came down with the intent to break windows. I think it was the instigators that were doing that but they were being protected by the masses, just the sheer number of people between them and the officers.

Yalonda Sinde: They were just coming to use the opportunity to steal things from Nike and all of the different stores. They would actually throw things at the police and egg the police on. Because they were in the crowd where we were, it looked like, "Oh, see, look at these thugs." The people causing the vandalism, they knew that. That's why they would latch on to us.

To me it was very racist. Like, "Why are you doing this where the people of color are, where the black people are? You want to make it look like we're doing that." It was very strategic where they would do their mess. People caught on that we weren't doing that.

Nick Licata: You had a much smaller core group of—I don't want to use the word *anarchists* in a generic sense because there's all kinds of anarchists but these were violent anarchists, violent in the sense of property damage. They would ignore all the volunteer protest monitors.

Dave Reichert: The mayor did not want to call the National Guard in. Gary Locke made the final decision there and said, "Hey, we need to call on the National Guard."

Larry Mayes: Madeleine Albright, secretary of state, was trapped in a room. Bill Clinton was trying to come in. There's clarity in my mind that it was Secret Service that whispered in Schell's ear: "Mayor, you have no option here. You will do it."

Gary Locke: We informed the mayor. I made the call around one o'clock in the afternoon that we had then mobilized the National Guard.

We need to make sure that people have an opportunity to express their views, to have rallies and marches. In this situation we had members of the clergy and labor who were very concerned about the impact of trade and wanted to express those viewpoints and those concerns— and I shared some of those concerns, I wanted to make very clear that there were peaceful, law-abiding protesters. But there were those who were just hell-bent on violence and perhaps were using the WTO as an opportunity to engage in anarchy and violence. I certainly did not want the objectives, the methods, the views of our legitimate protesters' message diminished and tarnished. Or their actions diminished by what I consider anarchists. Also, I feared for the safety of many of my friends who were in the peaceful protests.

Patrick Collins: Beep, beep, beep, beep, beep—my pager goes off. We start mobilizing guys, bringing them in from their civilian jobs. Then we got a second order: "No, send them back home to get their Class B uniform instead of their combat uniform because it'll be less threatening."

Of course we're like, "What harebrained idiot came up with that one?"

An hour later: "Hey, change of mission. No, just have the guys come in with the combat uniforms."

So we did this back-and-forth thing.

Ed Joiner: When you have a protest and it starts to get unruly, pretty soon a protest becomes a mob. When you have a mob there is no control. They don't do reasonable things. They do extraordinary things. The dynamics are easily influenced by a few. I don't think the number of the Black Bloc was more than fifty or seventy-five people. That's probably high. They had no interest whatsoever in keeping things peaceful. Their intent was to incite the crowd—and it worked.

John Zerzan: A friend of mine was having a conversation with one of the peaceful people who said, "These people who cause the ruckus, they're stealing our place in the limelight." They had floats and parades, the peaceful stuff. "They're preventing us from getting our due attention."

The friend of mine said, "What makes you think you would have gotten attention?" Those types of things are a dime a dozen. You can have a nice event that doesn't cause any big deal or the other event which does.

Suzanne Savoie: I'm very much in support of using all the different tools in the toolbox; there's value in all sorts of activism. I was very much in support of everything that happened that day. I wouldn't say that I thought that everybody should be breaking windows. I felt like it was a stronger movement because of the diversity and because of the willingness for people to work together.

Gary Locke: At one point, the sheriff and I went down to the waterfront where there was a county helicopter available, and we went up into the air and surveyed the situation and looked over the entire downtown area and could see that there were so many intersections that were being blockaded by the violent protesters and just incredible scenes of things out of control.

Jello Biafra: Somebody threw a newspaper vending machine through a window of Starbucks. Look, I love the sound of breaking glass. But wrong idea, wrong place.

Not only did that give the police the excuse they were waiting for, to attack the protesters, but it also became the coverage in corporate news, both TV and print. From that point onward, it was an anarchist riot. The nurses union no longer mattered, or pilots union, the Teamsters, the AFL-CIO and organized labor and teachers, everything else, they weren't there anymore. It was an anarchy riot and that's all they showed on the news.

You have to pick the right time to do it. During a peaceful protest that, up until then, was being covered as a peaceful protest? No, don't do that. You see somebody else about to throw something through a window, lock your arms and stop them. No violence, no violence, no violence.

Denis Moynihan: Frankly, I don't care if someone smashes a Starbucks window. I know that it's a huge company that has plenty of insurance. I just don't think it's particularly effective. There's other forms of property destruction that have much more enduring effects.

Ron Griffin: I think Jim Pugel would tell you that, "Oh yeah, we only had X number of violent protesters." I would probably disagree with the number that Jim would give. Jim is more forgiving on those issues than I am. Because if you go down there to be a peaceful protester but, when the bad behavior starts, you step in front of law enforcement in some way to help prevent them from getting to the bad person, you're part of it now. There was a lot of that. The media will say, "Oh, yeah, there was only about one hundred bad people." Bullshit—no sale.

Yalonda Sinde: We had our own security. They walk on the edges and look around for someone who might even have a gun. They look around for things and they call the police. They're not armed, just unarmed security guards watching. They had megaphones so if something popped off, they could alert us. It's America, so we have to be prepared if someone wants to start shooting.

Jim Pugel: By then, we've got officers from all the smaller jurisdictions—Auburn, Tukwila, Port of Seattle. The hard thing there is that when you bring outside jurisdictions into your jurisdiction, you own it. So we, the Seattle Police Department, own it. These outside jurisdictions can come, have fun, and split. We valued their help, loved their help, but there were a few in each group that went off the reservation. They did some bad things and those were publicized.

John Sellers: The cops started using pepper spray directly on people's eyes. A bunch of women just got fucking brutalized because they were using lockboxes. The police state really started losing it over them.

David Solnit: The police brought out giant fire extinguisher canisters of pepper spray, spraying our blockade lines and people who were

STEVE KAISER

Law enforcement releases pepper spray.

locked down. I got on the bullhorn and said, "We're not armed. We're not violent. People are locked down and cannot move. Do not use chemical weapons on us," which they then proceeded to do.

At that point it was about taking care of each other and also not backing down. To everyone's credit, people spent the rest of the day dealing with tear gas, rubber bullets, and pepper spray but not backing down. We moved people out who got injured. There was a wide range of arsenal and projectiles that they were shooting from canisters and riffles.

Vivian Phillips: I remember at one point, we exhausted the supply of tear gas. It was kind of like, "Okay. What's going to happen now?"

Jim Pugel: I'd been promised that we had plenty of tear gas and pepper spray but we didn't. They have small quantities in the local uniform stores so we had detectives go in unmarked cars and buy them all out and get them down to us. Then it got to the point where the FBI brought in a small private jet and flew to wherever they manufacture the stuff in Colorado. They literally jetted down there, filled up, and flew back with the stuff.

Charles Mandigo: We had our airplane there and we made two flights to get CS—tear gas—and flew it in. The problem then was the logistics of getting the CS to the officers on the street. Some of these officers, they basically were sheltered in. The protesters were basically holding them in place. Some officers were out there ten, twelve hours on their own.

Don Kegley: Police from different cities were there. They were scared. You could see the fear in their eyes, and they had guns and other arsenal. They were dead serious but they were scared too.

Han Shan: I remember talking with Laurie Brown. She was pretty freaked out. I talked to Pugel some. I was pretty upset about the police actions and I didn't have any real power other than perhaps moral power, just in that I'm talking to these folks and I'm saying, "What the fuck? Why? You're attacking nonviolent people?"

Denis Moynihan: They actually tried to break into the IMC. All of these armor-clad guys. One of them, they were pushing to get in and there were about four or five of us, six of us, pushing the door shut. It was just a commercial glass door. They were pushing in from the street. We were keeping the doors shut, but one guy managed to slip in a weapon that I had never seen before: a hose. Tear gas delivered through a garden-size hose, and it flooded the fifteen feet around the door. Just intense. But we managed to keep them out and lock the door.

Hilary McQuie: The culture of Seattle, it's an extremely passive-aggressive culture. People pretend to be super-nice and they're really not. They're just really nonconfrontational. They're not very chatty. They're kind of insular, you know? That's my experience of it. The cops too. They kind of expect this level of civility. They're very white, it's a very whiteness kind of thing. Like, "Oh, you're not being nice"—I think that's Seattle cops. But of course, the Seattle cops weren't running anything after a while. You had all those cops from everywhere else that were coming and fighting people. The Seattle cops, I'm sure they were throwing tear gas but they weren't fighting that hard.

Pam Schell: The police were prepared for some shenanigans, they were used to what they had known before, but they never thought of thousands and thousands of protesters who were coming from other places who had no knowledge of how nice Seattle was.

Ed Joiner: I think the officers were kind of stunned by what they were confronted with. I think it came as a shock and disappointment because I think we all felt that we let the city down and I think my only regret on the whole thing is that I know a lot of officers didn't think we prepared them well enough, that we didn't get enough resources in. They would have been in a better position to deal with it.

Jim Pugel: We had trained several officers and some firefighters in how to cut through those sleeping-dragons sleeves weeks before because we had heard they use those in Europe. So it's not like we weren't prepared but it was just the sheer volume.

Suzanne Savoie: As the afternoon progressed, it just got more brutal. There was a lot of street fights going on, mainly trying to free people because people were getting arrested for really doing nothing.

Mike Dolan: I ran into Tom Hayden in the midst of all this. We had been onstage the night before at the People's Gala. All this shit is going on all around us, tear gas, and I went for it. I said, "Tom, how does this compare to Chicago in '68?"

He said, "The difference, Mike, is that you are winning!"

I said, "Thanks, Tom."

He was the permitting guy of the Chicago Seven. I was the permit guy. I won't lie, it felt good to hear him say that.

Jim Pugel: From about three to about six it was just pandemonium. About four thirty, five it's getting dark. By then, individuals who saw the opportunity had no interest in the protest. They started showing up because they had seen the Black Bloc, the anarchists looting, so they started showing up.

John Zerzan: If people see the stereotypical anarchist damaging things, yes, it can be shocking at first. I don't know how to put it, exactly, but you get over that. Some people are sympathetic—but some people aren't so sure.

Jim Pugel: There's what's called the contagion factor. I actually saw it in person. There's this great book, *The Crowd*, it was written in the late 1800s and it documents how perfectly law-abiding, rule-based people, when they come together in a crowd, they lose their sense of individuality and they become anonymous. When a rule-abiding group of people come together and watch the guillotines, they go crazy with excitement, and afterwards they feel bad. We saw it in the Los Angeles riots. People go loot stores. Two days later, they bring all the stuff back. Because they feel bad. I was seeing this dynamic in Seattle, this crowd behavior. It was kind of scary to see what can happen when this thin veneer of rules goes bad.

Suzanne Savoie: I think that for some people, especially some of the local residents, they were like, "Well, if this is against corporate greed, then I'm going to go in there and take some of that corporate greed." Those were sometimes people just off the streets. They weren't even necessarily part of the protest. But they saw the message and took the opportunity. There were a lot of different things going on and that was what was so powerful about it.

John Zerzan: There was a sense of celebration but there was a sense of really hostile stuff from the more liberal-oriented people. One woman said we should all be arrested. Where was the unity, the common struggle? Man, they just glared at us. They had built their little floats. For what? That doesn't do anything. Let's face it.

Medea Benjamin: I had been involved in anti-sweatshop work and had particularly focused on Nike. In fact, I had recently come back from China and Indonesia, where we met with Nike workers. We did a lot to pressure that company to improve its conditions. We had worked around pay at McDonald's. These were not companies that I liked and yet when I saw that people were breaking windows and looting, I realized, "Uh-oh, this is not what we are about. This is not a look that is good for us." I said, "We've got to form a chain around the Nike store to stop people from looting." I got some people together and we formed a chain. It was surreal because here I had been doing all this work against Nike to try to make its name like mud, including going to the shareholder meeting and bringing Nike workers to the United States to talk about how bad their practices were—doing all kinds of things to make the brand seem like it was synonymous with sweatshops and here I was, protecting the Nike flagship store. It was very surreal.

I remember a *New York Times* journalist coming by and saying, "Why are you protecting the Nike store?"

You talk a lot to journalists, and they pull out whatever they want. My quote that got pulled out was something like, "Why are the police arresting the peaceful protesters instead of the people who are vandalizing the stores?" Boy, that one comment took me years to live down.

John Zerzan: There were certain people, and they would stand in front of places like Starbucks so people couldn't break the windows. They were just annoying. They carried on some good conversations though.

I remember talking to this yellow-jacketed guy asking him, "Do you think symbolic, polite protests ever do anything? Do you?" It was two different scenes. The liberals were horrified. Some even said that we should be arrested like we were the enemy and not the corporations.

Mike Dolan: We were really concerned that the property destruction, all of this breaking of glass, was diluting our message. So Danaher and I are standing in front of the NikeTown with our arms out. That's not something I really want to be remembered for, as the guy who guarded NikeTown during the Battle of Seattle. Nonetheless, we did it. That's when, inconveniently, the cops lobbed a bunch of these tear gas grenades that exploded over our heads. It was a boom and gas would come down on us. So we're fucking gassed and it was very painful. Needless to say, the crowd is dispersing. The good guys, the not-so-good guys, everybody's getting out of there. It sent down a rain of tear gas on top of us. That hurt. That shit was very painful. I was like, "Fuck this! Fuck NikeTown! What am I doing protecting NikeTown?"

Suzanne Savoie: There's been a lot of criticism of people creating property destruction but the police definitely were the most violent aspect of the protest. All the armored gear and the brutal response they had to people just sitting in the streets, spraying pepper spray right into their eyes and pulling them down the road by their hair, really brutal things. The police response was so brutal that it changed the mood. There were a lot of pretty inspiring efforts by different bands that were there to try to create a mood that was more focused on creating a presence rather than creating chaos but the cops were even attacking the bands.

Nina Narelle: The whole experience was pretty traumatizing. Almost all of the experience I remember as splintered fragments of memory that I can't stitch together linearly. I can't totally remember if that was day one or two. I remember it was nighttime and gas was coming off of everyone's clothes and my eyes were burning. I do remember how it felt when I saw the police and how *Matrix*-level-terrified I felt. It was like, "Is this actually happening? Am I actually seeing this?" At one point I was very paranoid that I was going to get spotted because the police were targeting people who had radios. I remember being so flooded with adrenaline. I was really paranoid. I went down a side street and ducked into a coffee shop. I remember going in, my mind just fractured. I started thinking, "I am in a war outside but people inside here are having coffee." Everything was totally normal but everything was deeply not okay outside of that café. I also was thinking that these people might be about to experience chemical weapons. The Terminator might has well have stepped out and said, "I am from the future." I just felt so disoriented.

Jim Flynn: We were running by cafés where people were sipping tea. It was a crazy scene, just absolutely weird and surreal.

four waters: The Black Bloc was what defined us to the public, which was really unfortunate. We did a lot of fun things—people came in costumes, David Solnit had amazing puppets—but the thing that ended up in the news was that the Black Bloc threw bricks through a McDonald's window. I want to say that because I think there is relevance to today's society. This issue with reporters continues because they report on what is sensational and that foments public opinion. It affects what the public thinks the issues are and what the public thinks the participants look like.

Jim Brunner: We spent hours and hours all day and evening, filing notes. Now the equivalent would be like tweets. You're kind of swimming in it. Maybe later you might realize a different context but in the moment there's a lot of reporters feeding in raw material and the editors deciding, blowing up the original plan for coverage of trade issues.

Mike Dolan: We tried to distinguish always, for the press, between violence against people and property destruction. As an NGO guy, I wasn't really allowed to support property destruction, per se. But as soon as the Black Bloc kicked in that Starbucks the press coverage changed. I have to say that, but for that, I'm not sure how much international press we would have gotten. The press, they can't always handle the depth of our analysis and understand the coalition that we built and understand this in the larger terms of neoliberalism versus civil society—that's not a lead for them. "Oh, the Starbucks just got kicked in?" That's a lead.

Ralph Nader: You can't blame the media enough—you cannot blame the media enough. They were ideologically incarcerated.

Pam Schell: They'll get a video that's really sort of exciting, and it gets people upset, and they replay it again and again and again.

Suzanne Savoie: I know the media attention to the protest was increased because of the property destruction, for better or worse. I don't like that dynamic. I don't like the dynamic that you have to do something really sensational to get social justice and globalization issues in the media. But, unfortunately, sometimes when there's not something sensational to cover, the media just doesn't cover it. So, partially, the tactic was to actually grab media attention, and I do feel like we were successful in that.

Helene Cooper: I remember my editors at the *Journal* asking me how big of a deal they should make out of the anarchists. I chose not to write about them because they were a small percentage. The whole Black Bloc? There weren't that many people. I didn't want to paint a portrait of a violent movement because it wasn't a violent movement. But other people did and it's hard because your bosses are constantly coming to you and showing you what your competitors are doing. But you have to focus. They look to you to be the expert on whether this is an angle to go after or whether it's bullshit. With the anarchists part, I was like, "This is bullshit. We're not going to do that." If you've got 40,000 or more protesters here who're into indigenous rights and environmental issues and shutting down the WTO, I think that's the story. Not the Black Bloc.

Matt Griffin: I can remember about six that night we finally made a decision to board up the stores at Pacific Place and we worked with contractors who had a bunch of plywood. I can remember being so disgusted, just sitting there on the sidewalk. Literally sitting on the sidewalk on Fifth Avenue thinking, "How the hell did all this happen?

How did we go from such a great place to just being run over?" We don't want to look like a boarded-up city.

Gary Locke: The White House wanted to know, "Should the president come?" And we assured the safety of the president. We had heard—how can I say this without sounding egotistical? Some people in the White House later on said that they felt that I was the only sane, rational person in control in the situation.

Dave Reichert: We developed a strategy to start moving them out of downtown. We cordoned off certain areas—you know, it's kind of like how you herd cattle. You fence off a street and you move them through the city one block at a time.

Gary Locke: The National Guard arrived and they cordoned off areas, provided a safe perimeter around the convention center, and we created a zone, an area, a few blocks away where people could protest if they wanted to. Then we also used these police vehicles to forcibly nudge the protesters away from downtown Seattle.

Nina Narelle: To see the police roll through in a tank, wearing riot gear was something I would have expected to see in an unstable banana republic.

Patrick Collins: I remember Mayor Schell said, "It'll be a cold day in hell when the National Guard marches in the streets of Seattle." Well, I can tell you, it was cold that day, and those guys had made downtown look like hell.

We got everybody there by Tuesday evening. We had a planning session to confirm what we're doing.

Ron Griffin: We ended up pushing back the crowd. We then owned several blocks of street. Then Jim Pugel and I and others were leaning over the hood of a police car with our maps out going, what do we do now? It just went on like that forever, block by block.

Nadine Bloch: I was in a particularly odd situation because I was running down the street and, at some point, I realized like, "Oh yeah,

I'm pregnant!" I was almost three months pregnant, and I had not told anyone. I knew that under three months, I was pretty sensitive to things like pepper spray and tear gas and I had to make a decision about staying. I was able to eventually retreat to the Convergence Center.

Gary Locke: Our State Patrol and other law enforcement under the supervision of the State Patrol had formed these vehicle chains, so to speak, all these cars side by side—no spacing in between—to really move the protesters out. They were slowly moving up the streets starting from the periphery just to nudge the protesters out from the core of downtown Seattle, so we were doing this in all different directions. Pushing them out in different directions.

Jim Pugel: We got most of the people out and cleared the downtown areas.

Julia Hughes: We did finally get the all-cleared to leave. Walking back to our hotel, there was broken glass and it still smelled like tear gas. There still were security folks blocking certain streets where you couldn't walk down. It was a pretty shocking time actually.

Charles Mandigo: Everything the rest of the day was canceled, probably the right decision. Who knows? There wasn't a good answer as to whether to go forward or not go forward.

Ron Griffin: The first day we went eighteen hours with no food or water. Eighteen hours on your feet, moving. Somebody in the command staff, they were tasked with getting us some food and water and meals. They ended up with half of what we needed. Another guy, a sergeant at the time, he took his personal credit card and went into some store and bought every bagel on the shelf and bottles of water and brought it down to us. That was a lifesaving thing there.

John Zerzan: I didn't stay around. I got out of town because my name was too much in the media. Media creates its own reality. You find things that are sort of true in the media that are not true in real life, like me being "the leader of the anarchists." If I tried to be an anarchist leader, that would be the end of my anarchist days. It just doesn't work that way.

Laurie Brown: Tuesday night, I slept on the floor of my office, which I would not be able to do now, but I slept on the floor. Things were shutting down. The city became a ghost town because business owners didn't feel like they could safely operate. It was very surreal.

Matt Griffin: There was the feeling after so many local people had put our heart and soul into trying to develop downtown, we just got vandalized. I went home that night and thought about what we could do and within a few hours we rallied a group of business owners and the city government, the city finance department, which owned the garage at Pacific Place, and said we all agreed to put in something like twenty thousand bucks, twenty-five thousand bucks each. We raised $100,000. We knew we'd have to launch an effort to get people back downtown and take back our city. It wasn't so much about money. It was that we can't let others overrun our city and destroy the fact that we're trying to build a great place. We wanted to show the merchants that people care about them, that we wanted to help them rebuild.

Laurie Brown: Paul was involved with the governor's office, and they were establishing no-protest zones and curfews. Everybody had to be off the street by a certain time or there would be a sweep and they would all be arrested.

Nick Licata: It was the equivalent of an emergency ordinance, martial law. They took ten blocks of downtown and said you can't be strolling around shopping. There were only three of us who voted against that emergency ordinance—myself, Peter Steinbrueck, and Richard Conlin—and then I remember I was on the street at one point telling people that they could, in fact, walk in certain areas, making sure that they understood they weren't trying to shut everything down.

Maud Daudon: By the evening, we had set up the no-protest zone. It was really to try to say, "We need a buffer." We needed to have the separation between where the delegates were staying and where the protesting was happening, and we were able to get that established. People were not happy with that; they did not want to see barricades in their city. Seattle did not take well to that sort of thing. From our vantage point, it was an absolute necessity because these delegates from all over the world did not travel alone. They had security guards and many were armed. My biggest fear was that one of those security guards was going to haul off and shoot a protester. That was absolutely terrifying to me. We had zero control over any of that stuff.

Ed Joiner: We had to get the authority through the mayor's proclamation of emergency to set up the perimeter. I had shown him exactly what we were going to do, and I showed the same thing to the governor. We then used all our resources to push everyone all the way to Denny Way. Once we had them out, we established the perimeter around all the venues.

John Sellers: The cops actually came past Denny, up to Capitol Hill, and went bananas. They were assaulting people in the streets. They really lost a lot of goodwill of Seattle that night just going crazy.

Kevin Danaher: The first night of protests, the cops went into a neighborhood that is largely students and academics and shot tear gas that went into people's homes and retail stores. It was just retaliation. There was no WTO meeting happening at night. They did it out of frustration. Protesters were throwing water balloons filled with urine off of apartment rooftops onto the police. It was total chaos. It made the police look unnecessarily brutal and stupid.

Lisa Fithian: Around eight or nine we all went back to the Convergence Center and plotted a little bit about what the next day would be.

David Solnit: A battle raged through the evening. We were at 420 Denny in the spokescouncil as the police were pushing hundreds of people right past our space. We lost part of the spokescouncil because some wanted to be in the street.

Han Shan: The police were on a rampage, still. They were on the offense, chasing random people uphill. They seemed to be firing flash-bangs randomly. It felt chaotic and scary and like there was no one in charge.

Nick Licata: Capitol Hill is a highly dense neighborhood. At that time, probably seventy percent renters. A lot of younger people lived there, in their twenties, thirties. I was still living in a collective household with about twenty people, a big mansion on Capitol Hill, so I walked through all this. You have police going into neighborhood streets and they don't know who's protesting and who's leaving a restaurant because everybody looks the same. I wouldn't say they were being hit by police but they're being tear-gassed and they're being chased so it's frightening. Locals didn't like being invaded by the protesters but their anger was towards the people who they felt were the most threatening to them, which were the police.

Hilary McQuie: When the cops are moving up in riot gear with lots of chemical weapons, coming up Capitol Hill, people are fighting them back and throwing things. That's when a bunch of really old-time radicals came out and started fighting with the cops. That was a new thing for me. I hadn't really seen that kind of street fighting with cops with chemical weapons. I wasn't quite sure how to—where I wanted to be. What was my stance? I'm not a fighter. I'm never going to try to fight somebody with weapons. But after that night, I'm much more likely to pick up a shield. That was a change for me.

That night I ended up going out for dinner with John Nichols and Mike Dolan and Ralph Nader and all those guys. They're all being all laughy and jokey. One of them said, "Yeah, there was just the right amount of violence."

And I was just super like, "Fuck you guys!" Like, "These are my people that are getting beaten up and arrested and put at risk. And you guys are acting like they're just foot soldiers in some grand plan." It really kind of pissed me off, even though I love all those guys. But, you know, I felt very emotional and responsible and concerned.

Mike Dolan: There was, to my mind, exactly the right amount of property destruction. Any less, and the international press would not have picked it up. That was a sweet spot.

Jello Biafra: Now that they had established the curfew, we needed to make a decision about whether or not we were going to go on with the show.

Kim Thayil: There was a curfew and people hunkered down. There are blockades, a lot of roads are closed. My girlfriend at the time was like, "Yeah, don't go." It just seemed ridiculous. We had a drum tech who was a friend of mine and he lived in the south end of the city, far out of the downtown. He said, "I'm not coming into downtown." So the show that we were supposed to play was canceled.

But late at night, another venue on the south end of the downtown, Central Saloon, it did have a gathering with some speakers. Krist and Jello were able to access it. I think Jello did some of his spoken word and there was some music going on. Gina and I couldn't get past the police barricades.

Jello Biafra: I was so bummed we didn't get to do the gig that night. There was so much energy in the air! Even inside Krist's little apartment, let alone out in the streets. But we were committed to trying again the next night. It had to happen. The No WTO Combo would prevail.

John Nichols: Throughout the whole ministerial, there were all the official nighttime events, even as things got very intense. There would be these town halls with somebody like Vandana Shiva talking about fundamental issues or Ralph Nader would be on a panel. And, at the same time, there were these activists in the streets. Sometimes they intersected, sometimes they didn't. Sometimes they really were on parallel tracks. For the folks who were protesting, that was an incredibly useful reality. Because people in Seattle saw church groups having events. They saw grassroots people doing important educational work. And then if they saw some folks blocking traffic, they saw it as part of a whole and they didn't necessarily have a negative view. It wasn't just protesters who showed up who they don't know anything about. There had been a lot of education that had occurred in the weeks before the ministerial began—and it just kept going. That's a subtle part of it all.

Nick Licata: Mike Dolan had 2,500 people show up in Benaroya Hall, which the council made sure was open to the public. We turn over this huge, beautiful hall that we recently built for concerts and symphonies to these potential protesters. There was a little trepidation but it worked out fine. But the media barely mentioned it. You have a few people in the street breaking windows with 1,000 people watching. They had 2,500 people in a building a few blocks away who were discussing the WTO in intellectual terms—no coverage whatsoever. Media is worse than a sugar junkie. They're strung out on a quick hit, a visual image. Quite honestly, the audience responds to that.

Vandana Shiva: We had a town hall debate. Me and Ralph Nader on one side and on the other side there was a government guy and a corporate guy and it was a fascinating debate. That night we had a big party. All of us had the confidence that we would shut down WTO. We had the confidence.

Colin Hines: I remember these big meetings, Ralph Nader speaking, there was a general feeling that we sort of cracked it. We really had a solid phalanx of arguments about why globalization is bad—the range of people and interest groups affected, it brought them together.

I remember Julie and I went. She was just so moved and outraged. You know, when you've been in this game for a long time, you're not as sensitized to stuff. Whereas, she being a very brilliant actress, was very sensitive to it all—and in Britain she was always very political.

Charles Mandigo: Later that evening, nine o'clock or so, I got a call from Janet Reno asking my assessment for the next day because Clinton was coming out to address the WTO. I told her, at that point, my belief was that basically things would be okay the next day for three reasons. One, the National Guard was being mobilized and they could get control of access points around the city and around the convention area. Secondly, we had brought in all the CS. The CS makes a lot of difference if you're doing crowd control. Everybody's affected by CS. The third factor was it started to rain again. I said, "Hey, it's raining and the rain is going to keep down the number of people that are going to be out there." If it keeps down the number of people, it doesn't provide the cover for the anarchists to hide their activity. So I said, "I think we're going to be okay."

Dave Reichert: Eventually they got to that point where they said, "Yes, we can make things secure enough that the president can feel safe."

Jim Pugel: I had a cot inside of my office in the West Precinct and I was in bed by about ten because I knew I had to get up at five. We had so many people that I had to develop a new plan for the next day.

Pam Schell: Paul was up late, reading a briefing book. He was working hard at it. *Long pause.* He got so depressed. He was so horrified that despite his best efforts to make this a wonderful meeting in Seattle and be for everybody's benefit, it had fallen apart. He was feeling really badly and I don't know how hidden that was from anybody because everybody was in a state of shock.

David Solnit: There is a great essay called "Black Flag Over Seattle" by Paul deArmond, looking at network theory. His analysis, which I agree with, is that we had better information and were better organized in Seattle than the police. Because we were self-organized in independent decision-making units that had lots of horizontal communication, we were better able than the police to adapt to changes, make quick decisions, and take care of each other. They had bad information and a hierarchical command structure. We were much more fluid. I think decentralization with a high level of coordination is important. It's partly a political thing. We saw the WTO as the ultimate hierarchical, antidemocratic institution where small groups of rich people and corporations would make decisions affecting billions of people. We were trying to create models where we practiced ordinary people having a say in the things that mattered.

Often when people say "decentralization," they mean disbursement. It's actually more organized than a hierarchical system. There are more people who have more information and are invested and understand the decisions whereas with the police, it was only the mayor and the police chief who understood and told what the decisions were. But with us, we had consensus. Everyone said, "We think that's the best solution. We agree to that." We are more bought into our decisions, more informed, and more capable of being really resilient.

Mike Dolan: Really, they shut down the WTO. It happened! That happened. It was genius. Not mine at all. That was the Direct Action Network and it was tactically genius work. I was really impressed.

Lori Wallach: We took a day away. We didn't know if we could succeed in doing that. That's the only time it has worked, the element of surprise worked.

David Solnit: It's interesting that the Direct Action Network was the bad protesters through the eyes of the establishment and, to some degree, labor and fair trade. But because we successfully shut it down, all of a sudden everybody was retroactively in support of us.

Tracy Katelman: That night, we were sitting there with a bunch of folks. This was pretty early on in cell phones but we all had them. I got a call and it was somebody from the AP. He said, "So what do you think?"

I said, "We won! We shut it down!" That story went everywhere.

Don Kegley: Tracy was on the front page of the *Seattle Times* the next morning: "'We've won!'—Tracy Katelman."

Tracy Katelman: They said, "Who are you with?" I said, "The Alliance for Sustainable Jobs and the Environment." It was cool.

Annette Sandberg: I didn't leave until late that night, when Sheriff Reichert and I started clearing the streets, it was probably midnight, one, maybe two a.m. He and I drove around the city just to see how much damage had been done. It was really eerie. It almost felt apocalyptic, in a way. Some of the protesters had turned over dumpsters, lit them on fire, and had broken out windows of all these businesses. We see these fires everywhere and the amount of looting that had occurred in the downtown business core, it was really sad. I was saddened to think, "This is my city. This is where I live. This is where I'm supposed to be protecting and serving. I can't believe this happened here." We were both dumbfounded, just to see the city in such disarray and the damage. It felt like a swarm of locusts had come through and wiped the city out.

WEDNESDAY, DECEMBER 1

Annette Sandberg: When the president flew in, it was in the early morning hours. I remember talking to the State Department and others, and it's like, "Hey, we need to bring them in the back way." Let's not bring him in by I-5. It's going to be too obvious.

Jim Pugel: I remember talking with the special agent in charge of the Secret Service and they actually delayed his airplane. They said, "This is the first time we ever delayed the presidential arrival to a U.S. city. Because we just didn't know if was possible to get him here safely."

Annette Sandberg: Some of my motorcycle units were leading the motorcade and they had their helmets on with a gas mask because when the motorcade went through, it was an area they had just gassed out a bunch of protesters. There was still a lot of tension. And now we're dealing with the president of the United States. It's like, "We have to be very, very careful and sensitive here. This is the commander of the nation, let's make sure we do this right."

Patrick Collins: POTUS was coming into town. So there was an internal security line and then there was an external security line, then an *ex*-external security line. They were worried about POTUS being on the ground in the middle of a riot. And they refused to call off the trip.

James P. Hoffa: Bill Clinton finally flew in. I'll never forget it. The Secret Service put a line of school buses around his hotel so they must have been afraid we were going to get Bill Clinton. *Laughs.* We weren't going to do that. We were just wanting to demonstrate and show America that this is the wrong policy.

Annette Sandberg: As soon as the president's motorcade came in, there was a group of protesters that came up to that area, and we were trying to push them back.

Jim Flynn: The cops had to clear a path for his motorcade. They really stepped up their efforts and showed their militarization at that point. They were chasing us with armored personnel carriers. It was very crowded. There were several lines of cops making sure that thousands of people could only move in one direction. By odd coincidence, suddenly all of my housemates from Eugene were running with me—I didn't go to Seattle with any of them—as we were being chased by an armored personnel carrier down the street near Pike Place Market.

Ed Joiner: As soon as we set up the perimeter of the no-protest zone, they immediately went to court to get that overturned—get a judge to issue an injunction against us. Had that happened, it would have continued to be a mess. But the judge was aware of what was going on and the fact that some of the dignitaries had been assaulted. He turned them down. That allowed us to maintain the no-protest perimeter. We had to be very clear in terms of why we were doing this, street by street. We tied it to the venues themselves and that gave us the justification for putting the zone in place. It made all the difference in the world. If we hadn't had it, if the judge had ruled against us, Wednesday would have probably been worse than Tuesday.

On Wednesday morning, much of downtown was in disarray.

Maud Daudon: All hell would have broken loose if the judge denied the legality of the no-protest zone.

Medea Benjamin: We talked about the vandalism and thought this is exactly what we don't want the press to focus on. So we went out and bought a whole bunch of brooms, gloves, aprons, dustbins and got some people together and went out on the streets early in the morning and started to clean up.

Charles R. Cross: Windows were broken. There was shit everywhere. Protesters got together and cleaned everything up. That was not the city. It was people who cleaned up the mess. That gives you a sense of Seattle.

Medea Benjamin: That's the image that we wanted the press to capture, us trying to show that we respected the residents of Seattle and didn't want to make things difficult for them. That, too, was super-controversial because here we were, cleaning up and acting like we were these upright citizens who don't believe in property destruction.

Matt Griffin: Early the next morning we had maybe fifty or a hundred thousand dollars' worth of damage. That's a big deal. But the *real* question was "Would our tenants have customers?" Morale was horrible.

Jim Hightower: We were appalled by the way the national media was treating it, as a bunch of ne'er-do-wells and people trashing McDonald's. *U.S. News & World Report*: "Hell no, we won't trade." They said that was our slogan. Nobody was against trade. We were against the usurpation of our democratic power—it had everything to do with democracy. They completely missed the story, the seriousness of what was being argued and the moment that was being launched. This was not just something that happened in Seattle. It was the start of a protest that goes on today.

Jim Brunner: Editors were making the choices on what to make the lead story of the day. I do remember one headline that caused head-scratching. It was Christmas season and the headline said something like "Shoppers barred from retail core," and I remember there being blowback to the editors, "That shouldn't be what this is about. There are constitutional questions here. There are questions of crowd tactics. People being allegedly mistreated by the police."

Mike Dolan: The National Guard was on the street on Wednesday. That was fucked.

Nina Narelle: Once the National Guard showed up I thought, "Wow, this is freaky." A state of emergency was in place.

Han Shan: We were going to resist the no-protest zone no matter what. The WTO and other antidemocratic institutions get their way by militarizing some kind of exclusionary zone around them so they can do what they do without the prying eyes of citizen activists. There was a feeling that we needed to stay engaged and not be intimidated whatsoever. People were lit up, people were exhilarated—there was momentum.

David Solnit: We gathered at seven a.m. on Denny, at the edge of the no-protest zone. There were forty or fifty people. We had circulated the start time and everyone knew the plan. We started marching into the no-protest zone and our numbers grew pretty quickly to a couple hundred. At a certain point the police surrounded us. We spent the next few hours outflanking the police. It was stunning.

We lost a huge amount of art. If you have a giant cardboard puppet and the police are chasing you, shooting tear gas at you—and it's raining—sometimes you drop your puppet. But every fifteen to twenty minutes, our numbers would double. We kept a super-quick pace, moving so that the cops couldn't surround us.

John Sellers: I remember getting up the morning of December 1st. Some of us were having a lazy morning because we had been up really late. We were watching the coverage. The city had shut down several square blocks to any kind of protesting. They declared it a "protest-free zone." We knew we had to challenge it. It was bullshit. We didn't do anything wrong the day before. All the violence came from the cops. I remember some people had finished their coffee and they walked out of our apartment. Half an hour later we'd see them on TV. It was surreal—the activist's dream to be that relevant.

Jim Pugel: Wednesday morning there was a news conference. An officer from outside of Seattle had been filmed shooting a beanbag round at a guy up on Broadway the night before. It was way too close to the guy's head. It was against training. Stamper was asked at a news conference, "Is this proper?"

He said, "No, it's not proper." And he took a lot of heat for that.

Norm Stamper: I didn't hire on with the police to join a cult. That's not why I became a cop. I wanted to be a different kind of cop. I wanted to be responsive.

Dave Reichert: There was a press conference held, and I was asked to be in attendance. I was not given a speaking role. But we wanted to show unity. I stood behind the mayor and police chief as they spoke. When you watch the tape you can see, on my face, a moment of disgust. That's when the police chief apologized for the bad behavior of his police officers. All they were doing was moving the crowd and arresting people. There was no abuse of force.

This week was the beginning of when folks started to recognize they can manage to disrupt a city by making unreasonable claims about the conduct of police officers and the politicians would—I'll put it bluntly—piss their pants, thinking, "Oh, shit. What's going to happen to my political career? These cops have run amok." When they really hadn't.

So they made apologies for the police who hadn't done anything yet—other than their job. You can see me roll my eyes. I left after the press conference—I didn't even want to be up there associated with the comments that were being made.

Vivian Phillips: We had a conversation about the media pressure being put on the police department to divulge the exact weapons that were being used. I was vehemently against doing that. We would just be delivering ammunition for the media. Sure, citizens have a right to know. But the city also has a right to expect civility. So where do those two things line up? We decided we wouldn't tell them.

But then I'm sitting in the EOC, watching the press conference, and they have taken all of the weapons and laid them out on a table. And I'm like, "What the hell?"

The thing about Paul was this tendency he had to take the advice of the last person he spoke with. I felt like I was often overruled. That diminished my dedication.

I loved Paul Schell. I was always telling him, "You do not have to fill all of the air. Answer and be done." But Paul was very verbose and he was really emotional. I don't want to say that he loved to hear himself talk, because I don't think that was the motivation. I really feel like he was compassionate about what he thought and felt. But that got in the way. It could just be too much. You're saying too much. You're doing too much. You've got to be quiet sometimes.

It was later that day that I tendered my resignation.

Maud Daudon: Our communications person resigned halfway through the week, so we had nobody in charge of communications. I was trying to fill that role but also keep an eye on the police. You know, it was just chaos. It was not good.

Vivian Phillips: I remember having a very heated conversation on the telephone with Paul. I felt like my own authority had been diminished, that I had been second-guessed. I didn't feel like I could be effective anymore. It took a toll on me. Paul was disappointed. He apologized. He didn't want me to leave but I think he understood.

Pam Schell: I know it caught him off guard, her leaving. He was very upset about that. But she's always been a friend. It didn't ruin the friendship.

Gary Locke: President Clinton was very concerned about what was happening but things had calmed down. Yes, there were protesters, but they were allowed to protest in certain parts very close to the convention center and I made sure that our National Guard troops were there to simply assist local law enforcement. I did not want this to be like another Vietnam War protest. I was involved in some of those protests in college and the National Guard were all armed to the teeth. I remember coming up against a wall of military police officers with their rifles. It was very intense. I did not want that type of image for Seattle.

Victor Menotti: IFG was one of the accredited NGOs. So I could get into the secured ministerial sites. I was kind of playing that role of bringing the demands from the outside to the ministerial meetings inside—"from the streets to the suites" was what we used to say—then bring back actual intelligence about what was going on inside, keeping that communication flowing.

Nadine Bloch: We had a lot of inside activity. There were all kinds of groups mobilizing to show up in Seattle and support the nonalignment of nations, those who were not happy about the WTO for many reasons, groups that were interested in sovereignty issues and protection of the environment.

Lori Wallach: We had a couple international partners who were parts of delegations. We had some sense of what was going on behind the scenes.

Mike Dolan: Lori was going towards the Green Room—that inner sanctum where top-level negotiations take place, where the rich countries are actually making the deals and then they go pitch it to the developing world.

Vicente Paolo Yu: In the Green Room it was focused conversations and the WTO director general would be attending those meetings. The Green Room was the main feature of the political decision-making at the crunch time of the conferences.

Lori Wallach: The Green Room was invitation-only sessions for certain delegates.

Tetteh Hormeku: It was supposed to be one country, one vote. Each member of the WTO is equally entitled, part of any conversations. But for the conversation to actually take place, the WTO Secretariat, working with the powerful countries, established what you call "working groups." That was not the first time it happened. It happens all the time.

Now, I know that working groups, on the face, are sensible. The point, however: these working groups are not formally known to everybody. Who is a member of each working group? Where do they meet? Nobody knows. How long do they meet? Nobody knows. It wasn't an official process. It's only known to the ones in the working group and the WTO Secretariat. So it is usually the powerful countries who found themselves in the Green Room all the time.

In one of the working groups on investment and competition policy, the European chair of that working group proposed a number of delegates to speak. The EU put forward many proposals because they wanted all the new issues to be discussed. They said, "Okay, this is a proposal that we're going to have. Let's talk about it."

Now, a clear majority of the group, including India, Kenya, Zimbabwe, were completely against those ideas and they expressed it quickly—that those things are not supposed to be part of the negotiation, they're not part of the agenda. The chair had everybody talk, talk, talk, talk, and after that he said, "Okay, I've heard all of you speaking and this is my summary: I can see from a clear majority that you really want the decision put forward by the EU." *Laughs.* So the chairperson for the top group had a lot of power to summarize what they wanted to take place.

Pascal Lamy: The media was telling us inside what was happening outside but not much of the outside was being told what was happening inside, which was incomprehensible. The reason why what was happening inside was incomprehensible was that it was very messy. The preparation was messy.

Noam Chomsky: Negotiators are never going to say, "We're doing this because you guys are demonstrating in the streets." But there's going to be indirect effects, partly in just mobilizing, awakening the public to what's happening.

Mike Dolan: Creating the no-protest zone allowed them to arrest people who weren't doing anything other than protesting. There were these moments where people were sitting down in a park with their signs and the cops would come and load them onto buses and take them away. They weren't doing anything. They weren't breaking windows. They were simply there in large crowds—that's what happened to the turtles. Oh my god, it was so sad. I remember standing with John Sellers in front of a cop bus and they're loading activists who'd been dressed as the sea turtles. They're having to take off their shells. The shells were being stacked outside this bus as these guys all go off to the hoosegow. There's twenty empty shells stacked outside of this cop bus as they're all dragged off. Any kind of peaceful marches were now suspect. Everybody was going to get tear-gassed—even peaceful marches, even those are now dodgy.

Jello Biafra: Seattle suddenly put down an edict where they banned gas masks. You could be arrested and put on one of the arrest buses with plastic cuffs and taken off to who knows where, just plunked there in a cell for possession of a gas mask. Totally unconstitutional. They knew that. But they also knew that by the time they let people out, the protests would be over and they were going to go on with their daily lives. Sure, you can sue over that and sure that edict is going to be found unconstitutional, but that is going to take months.

Nick Licata: Of all the people on the City Council, I was probably closest to the protesters, so I was trying to get them to meet the police and talk and it was interesting that they didn't trust each other. That was one of the big things. The police did not trust the protesters and vice versa. There was reluctance on both sides.

Hilary McQuie: The cops called us in for an emergency meeting and the city said, "You need to call it off. You know, you need to stop."

We're like, "We can't stop. We told you we were going to shut it down."

And they said, "Well, we didn't think you were actually going to shut it down. We didn't take it seriously."

four waters: Some of us met with the mayor's office, the sheriff's department, and the police department. This was a learning experience for me. The sheriff said two things. At the time, I didn't believe one and I totally believed the other. It turned out that I was wrong on both.

The sheriff said, "I have lost control of my people." I believed—most of us did—that was him skirting his responsibility from what was happening.

He also said, "But the upside is we're out of ammunition. We've used it all."

The truth was he was absolutely out of control. He didn't have any idea what his people were doing. The other truth was that they *were* out of ammunition but they had gone to the surrounding locations with armories and bought more ammunition, gas, and rubber bullets. They had been out but they went on a shopping trip.

I think the mayor was in a really difficult position. In that meeting, law enforcement said they believed that we were coming there to hurt them. They were pissed. They were angry that they had to deal with this, or they were angry at the dirty hippies—whatever they were angry about, that anger is what came at us.

Mike Dolan: The reason why the mayor and Stamper were so reluctant to put the hammer down was because they had a six-month-long good relationship with who they thought were the leaders. We were very charming and very out there. "We can work together!" And they're all liberals. I mean, this is Seattle. It had been very hard for me to say to them, "You guys have no clue how big this is going to be."

Ed Joiner: There was disappointment from my end because we had a lot of promises from people that were going to be involved in the protests. They understood that they needed to really help out to keep it from becoming a disaster and all of those agreements went out the window as soon as things escalated. No one kept their promises.

Patrick Collins: Because of the POTUS connection, we had more contact with the Secret Service than we did with the Seattle PD. This is the first time I'd ever worked with them, but you could tell they had a uniform. Everybody had a black coat on and one or two guys had tan coats. It's like, "Oh, you're the boss"—that kind of stuff.

Annette Sandberg: I had a class that was going through the State Patrol Academy at the time. They were maybe two weeks from graduating but we brought them up, and they slept and lived in the convention center for the remainder of the week, just to protect the delegates getting in. I had probably eighty percent of State Patrol in the city for the remainder of that week, close to eight hundred state troopers. We were housing them down at the airport in a big warehouse. We bused them in. They were doing twelve-hour shifts.

Dave Reichert: We used the Kingdome to house all of the sheriff officers. There were bunks down there enough for a thousand cops or more. We had a food kitchen set up for them and water—whatever they needed. We set up a schedule, rotating people out in different shifts once we got control of the streets.

Larry Mayes: Those guys out in the field spent hours without food, water, rest, relief. You've got exhausted, frustrated, undertrained, underequipped officers out on the street dealing with thousands of people.

David Solnit: We were marching and stopped at Westlake Center to gather ourselves.

Steve Koehler: I was a local partner with the Rouse Company that developed Westlake Center around '89, '90—about ten years before the WTO. One of the unique parts of Westlake Center is that you had the monorail station right there. And we had a plaza that was designed to be the place where you go to rally for, say, the Seahawks going to the Super Bowl. We've had tree lightings over the years, and it's a common place to start or end a march.

Yalonda Sinde: There were going to be speakers at Westlake but, before we could get to that point, we were stopped. We were teargassed and pushed back. The police were shooting rubber bullets and throwing canisters. I remember seeing the canisters hit the ground and all this smoke. It was chaos. Complete mayhem. People weren't sure where to go. That's where our training came in. Get back, don't risk your health and safety, try to get to the meeting spot.

Jim Pugel: This group made it through the perimeter line at Westlake Center. We gave them orders to disperse. They all sat down within this limited-access zone. Cops were overwhelmed.

Michele Manasse, small business owner: I first felt the potential for danger when protesters were throwing objects against the storefronts at Westlake Center, as well as at surrounding storefronts.

Patrick Collins: At the last position where we were putting in, I was talking to one of my platoon leaders, and all I had on was my parka and my hat. I had none of my riot control kit because I was getting everything in place. Next thing we know, my platoon officer and I look around and we realize there's a few thousand people gathering around us, and they're looking pretty hostile. I'll never forget, he looked at me and said, "Hey, sir, remember that training we did when we talked about you're only as strong as your weakest link?" I nodded. And he goes, "You're it. You have no equipment with you right now."

"Damn, you're right." I ran around the corner to put my helmet on, put my vest on, all that kind of stuff.

There was, I would say, probably a good two or three thousand people gathered around us, trying to get through an intersection. And of course, we couldn't allow them to do that.

Nadine Bloch: The police kettled us in. They just were like, "Oh my god, we just have to get more people off the streets."

John Sellers: I was tackled live on CNN. I remember someone saying that they were watching CNN and saying, "There's the head of the Ruckus Society." Then these giant fucking football players in black Nike gear with cop regalia charged us. I remember turning to people and saying, "Don't run! Don't run!" Then I turned around and five of them tackled me in the street. They took my cell phone, my Nextel, and then started retreating. I got up. My head was bleeding. I was super pissed-off. I started screaming at them, "You're not going to arrest me? You're going to steal my phone?"

Michele Manasse: We have procedures for evacuation at Westlake Center because it's a central location for protests. The staff followed procedures by locking themselves in the store and evacuating through our back doors down into the metro station so that they would not have to exit out into the streets where the chaos was taking place. I felt an immense responsibility for their safety. They were legitimately scared.

Suzanne Savoie: There was a woman selling newspapers and she was asked, "What do you think about the violence?"

She's like, "Oh, it's awful, people's property," or whatever.

Then she was asked, "Well, what do you think about the Boston Tea Party?"

And she said, "Oh, I love it."

There is this historic acceptance for property destruction for social change when people look back at these very American-patriot kind of ideals of history. But when people look at something like the protests in Seattle, they vilify property destruction. It's no different. There's a history of property destruction for social change. I would hope that we could someday get to a point where that isn't something that is needed to bring attention to issues but it is, unfortunately. And there's a clear distinction between breaking windows and physically hurting people. With corporations, the list of violence that they commit around the world, in Third World countries, towards marginalized communities, against the planet, biodiversity, and the environment is such a long list. For them to look at a couple dozen people in Seattle breaking some windows and say that's violence is a hypocrisy to the extreme.

Jello Biafra: The worst type of addiction in this country—it's not fentanyl, it's not alcohol—it's wealth. It's money. Wealth addicts, when you finally make your first few million, how much more do you need at that point, for crying out loud? You can live pretty damn good the rest of your life and not even lift a finger to do any work. With a lot of these people: "Oh my god. I win! I win! Look at all this money! Now I want more. The more I make money, the more I win. I must win. I must win. I must keep winning."

Nick Licata: The council was meeting. We're debating all kinds of things and during breaks I would go out to the streets to see what was going on. There were far fewer people, much more direct action. I think they still tried pulling off some traffic obstruction tactics but the police were responding very strongly now. The atmosphere totally changed on the streets. There was more anger directed towards police than towards the WTO because the police were trying to allow the WTO to meet, the delegates to get to their hotel rooms, so there was greater conflict in the movement of delegates and the movement of traffic and that conflict resulted in physical contact between the vanguard of the protesters and the police.

John Sellers: I know that there are some people who join the police force to do the right things in the world, but it was in the streets of Seattle that I said, "This is a fucking crazy institution that is just

STEVE KAISER

Law enforcement armed with nonlethal firearms.

here to protect power." When we actually challenged the system, they peeled back any façade of "protect and serve." They were there to protect power.

four waters: One of the things that is different between the civil rights protests and the WTO protests is that the people participating in the civil rights protest were, by and large, people who had historically not experienced positive things with law enforcement. They did not go into these experiences thinking that law enforcement was on their side. That wasn't a thing that lived in their bodies. For the WTO protest, a lot of the participants were people who believed going in that law enforcement was created to keep them safe. It's only true if you fall into a particular category. Once you challenge that category, all bets are off. That is a stunning thing to learn. A lot of people struggle with that.

We needed to have people trained on their rights, how to overcome what felt like being physically threatened, how to prepare to be arrested. You don't want to be on heart medication and get into jail and not have your medication. You don't want to get arrested while your kids are in daycare and not be able to pick them up. These are all true stories. You don't want to have parked your car in limited parking. You have to think this all the way through. You also have to know why you're being arrested, which is another difficult thing.

Maud Daudon: There was, I thought, decent communication the entire way through with some of the protesters. They had their moments where they felt like the police were too aggressive or confrontational, and those were times when I would call Ed Joiner and say, "Hey, do you know what's happening? Are you getting a good read from your people on the street?" When it's a public safety emergency you really have to be careful—this is not an area of expertise for me, I've never been trained in any of this stuff. You can ask questions but you really do have to trust the judgment of law enforcement.

Dana Schuerholz: At Westlake I had a press pass that I showed to the cops, and they let me through along with a slew of other press people. The only people who were in that contingent of the press were people with a press pass from Geneva. So I'm taking pictures, we were all elbow-to-elbow photographing these nonviolent protesters who were sitting down and getting dragged off and arrested.

Then someone from Seattle PD recognized me as someone who had been arrested before taking pictures and had my film taken—I had gone to court about it, I had a history. I was literally just taking pictures and I got grabbed. I was saying to the cops, "I'm press. What are you doing? Here is my press pass." They didn't care. I was so mad because I wanted to be out there photographing. I ended up in jail. I was so mad.

Han Shan: I get a call from Pugel in the middle of the fucking intense standoff at Westlake. People on our side are sitting down, linking arms, and the cops on the other side look like fucking storm troopers in their armor. I get a call and I'm like, "What's up?"

He's like, "Over here." He was waving, getting my attention. "No, to your right, to your right." We're only twenty yards from each other. *Laughs.* He asked if I could get a bunch of people to move in a certain direction, something like that. I'm like, "How many times I need to

CAROLYN CASE FOR THE *LOS ANGELES TIMES*

Dana Schuerholz just as she is grabbed and arrested by the Seattle Police Department.

tell you? No, I can't. Am I a decision maker? Sure. I'm deciding for myself. I'm deciding for the people who have empowered me to decide, but am I a dictator? Am I able to tell people to stand down? No. That's just not how this works." We tried again and again to relay that.

I continue to believe it was worth it to have these communication lines open, and there were fruitful conversations that I think probably made people safer in the end—at least help deescalate potential situations that could have gone worse. But it was hard. No matter how many times you say something they just wouldn't necessarily hear it.

Nadine Bloch: We weren't designating a hierarchical decision-maker. We were designating a person to talk and liaise with a hierarchical establishment because that's what *they* needed. It allowed us to be safer and do our work better.

Maud Daudon: I was like, "Norm! Where the hell are you? Ed is doing a magnificent job but where are you?"

He was like, "Come on a ride-along with me." So we'd ride along in the streets and look at what was happening but he wasn't in a visible leadership role at all and, generally, it was hard to find him. Ed was right in the center and Ed was about to retire, which was why I think he had Ed do the job.

Ed Joiner: My target date for retiring had been August of 1999. That was my thirty years. *Laughs.* But I had more experience, I guess, dealing with protest groups than any of the other assistant chiefs so I committed to stay through the end of the year.

David Solnit: On the inside, the poorer countries, like India, were under pressure at home and ended up taking some courage from watching what was happening in the streets and standing up to the U.S. and other rich countries, trying to topple the deal.

Vicente Paolo Yu: You had many comments coming from the developing countries about the Green Room processes; about how they were being shut out of the negotiating process, about how the Quad— the U.S., EU, Japan, and Canada—were managing the process, about bias from the Secretariat. At that time, China was not yet a member of the WTO, so the big developing country groups were being led by the likes of India and Pakistan and the African group. Developing countries had different priorities they wanted to see coming out from Seattle. You had the Quad essentially making decisions and the director general sometimes trying to put brakes on it but oftentimes just acquiescing.

Tetteh Hormeku: The Americans invited Africans together and said, "Hello, we know these are your issues, your worries. We're prepared to help you. We can sign a joint declaration."

The Africans said, "No, no, we won't sign a joint declaration. Let's negotiate."

They were telling us, "Yeah, you know something, Africa, you've got problems. That's why we should work together to increase our agreements."

The Africans said, "No. We want to negotiate our issues."

Then the European Union convened a meeting with the Africans to say, "The Americans are not very helpful to you. But we can help you." So the European Union and the United States, you know, like good cop and bad cop were convening different delegations.

When this didn't work, they became more brutal. For instance, the African government ministers were meeting, trying to hold their own strategy meeting. It was the duty of the WTO Secretariat to find them rooms in the Seattle complex so they could hold a meeting. They struggled for days to have a place. When they finally found a place to hold a meeting, the U.S. switched off the microphones. So they couldn't even talk to each other. When they finally got the microphones working, the interpreters were taken. Africa is a continent with different languages because of our colonial history. Some speak English. Some speak French. Some speak Portuguese. But the interpreters were taken and assigned to other meetings. These are very deliberate tactics by the WTO Secretariat and the host organization, the United States.

Another example of these brutal tactics was when me and a colleague were talking to an African minister about a certain negotiation. I said, "You know what this negotiation is about?"

He said, "Yeah, yeah. I've had negotiations all day. We have been working on the issues and I've been negotiating with the Americans."

I said, "But have you seen this draft paragraph that's been negotiated?"

We showed him the draft letter that was leaked to us. He was shocked. He said, "But this is not what the negotiations were about." The Americans then got him trapped into a discussion all day about the fake declaration when the actual declaration was going around his back.

Julia Hughes: The United States, we are the leaders and we are committed to the rule of law. For our trading partners to agree that they also will follow trade laws, that's a good thing. We talk about dumping or intellectual property rights violations—all of those things were things we, the U.S., were trying to stop. That's part of why we were supporting the WTO as a positive. I was arguing, "This is a good thing." The WTO is a place for dispute settlements. Instead of having a trade war, you could actually find resolution if a country had a policy that others disagreed with. I still think that's a rational approach to go forward.

Victor Menotti: Some of the delegates from African countries or some of the LDCs, the least-developed countries, the ones who are most marginalized from the decision-making process and whose economies are so ravaged by it, their proposals wouldn't show up in the draft text. Their ideas were just being totally ignored and they're being told it will be done this way. So, many developing country delegates were sitting around, sleeping inside the halls because they were totally excluded from these meetings. They were with us, the accredited NGOS, watching the local news of the protests outside. That outside rebellion was certainly inspiring to the folks inside, seeing how unjust this was. And the energy, the psychology of the two—inside, outside— was such a driving factor.

Tetteh Hormeku: We were trying to share, as much as possible, what was happening inside to our colleagues outside. So that they can become more outraged.

David Solnit: The police surrounded us, the entire Westlake Plaza, and made mass arrests.

Steve Koehler: We're up on the twenty-first floor of the office tower at Westlake Center, watching what was happening. Some of the suites at Westlake Center had decks so we were out on a deck, looking down at the street. We had a great vantage point at Fourth and Pine and we could look right down at the Nordstrom facility and see what was going on there.

Larry Mayes: I just remember being out on the street, seeing an armored personnel carrier with SWAT team members hanging off of it, going through cloud after cloud of gas in the middle of downtown. It was surreal. Over and over in my head: "This didn't have to happen."

Lisa Fithian: I got arrested that day.

Chie Abad: I was one of those arrested protesters. They put handcuffs on the hands. We are in the middle of the street protesting. Because during that time, there were people who broke glasses—anarchists. They mixed up with us. So even though we are silent protesters, police thought that we were one of those anarchists but we're not. I feel, "I know that a lot of people are watching me. I'm not scared."

Steve Koehler: I remember watching these parades, the people and all the costumes, and then all of a sudden, this person jumps out of the crowd, goes up and smashes a window, and then jumps back into the peaceful march. "Holy shit! There're some bad guys that are out there. There aren't just peaceful protesters." It was crazy to see it play out and not be able to do anything about it.

Han Shan: I didn't get arrested that day. I was with that crowd when it happened and I got pushed out of the way. I figured out later that it was Pugel or one of the other captains; they didn't arrest me purposefully.

Nadine Bloch: I was arrested with a whole bunch of people. We were put on buses. Not everybody was planning on risking arrest. Since I was pregnant, I did try to leave. I saw a female officer in riot gear, and I thought, "Okay, that's the person to ask." I go up there. "Look,

I'm pregnant. I need to go out." She takes her baton, and she jams against me and pushes me back and makes me stumble backwards. I'm like, "That was not a good idea." *Laughs.* "Perhaps I should have tried someone else." But then it was too late. They herded us onto the buses.

Han Shan: They had started to use some of the kinds of tactics that they had trained with and did not use on the 30th. They would get eight guys: one in the front, three on one side of him, three on the other side, and one in the back. They'd move quickly through protest lines and grab somebody, then turn around and back out. Impressive football fucking stuff—like something you'd draw on a whiteboard. They did these snatches and they'd grab people who they thought were leaders or organizers or who had comms or whatever. Unfortunately, they got really good at it and eventually they did it to me. It happened so quickly, I was near the front lines and suddenly a gang of scary black-clad storm troopers grabbed me, pulled me through the lines, and I was like, "Oh, here it is. It's finally happening—I'm getting arrested."

But after they grabbed me, the guys melted away and it was Pugel standing in front of me and he was like, "Sorry, Han. I was trying to call you, but you just weren't picking up your phone." He didn't arrest me. He just wanted to talk some more.

David Solnit: After they put us on buses they shipped us out.

Chie Abad: All of us got sick during that time on the bus. It's raining during that period and it's so cold. Not much sleep, almost no food to eat. Especially at night. They treated us very badly.

Norm Stamper: We made six-hundred-plus arrests, people who didn't deserve to go to jail. We arrested people who did not deserve a criminal record and who were just doing what demonstrators do—they were assembling. They had the right to assemble, the right to express, which is extremely important to a democracy.

The police mess it up almost every time. Chicago '68. Are you serious? Mayor Richard Daley was a horrible man, I think, unleashing his cops. They called it a police riot. WTO protest: a police riot. We may not have wanted a police riot but it happened.

Han Shan: They were dealing us a brilliant hand. We now had a responsibility to message this, to make sure that people saw how antidemocratic they were being. If we were smart about this, we were going to be able to fold this back into our messaging around the WTO, pointing out that when civil society rises up and says, "We oppose this," they bring in the goons. They round people up and arrest them and hide them away because they can't operate transparently amidst democracy, amidst civil society. They need to operate by essentially getting rid of their opposition. Obviously it's going to be kid gloves compared to the way that it happens in places where you don't have the media watching and you don't have a lot of relatively privileged people being rounded up. But the effect is the same.

four waters: The thing about going to jail is that you lose your control. The odds of you being hurt, the odds of you being in a situation that is uncomfortable or unpleasant, those are pretty good odds. How you respond to those situations has entirely to do with how you are trained. The process of being arrested is aggressive. You can see in the civil rights protests people having soup dumped on them or spit on or hosed and you can think intellectually that it looks vicious, but when it happens to you, it's very different. You can internalize that by asking, "What would happen when you feel physically threatened? What does your body do?" Your body produces hormones. You want to push back. Your body has a visceral response and you have to have the comportment to overcome that response because if you don't, you will escalate the situation.

Jim Pugel: I had a little handheld Sony TV. You could pick up local TV channels. I remember watching Mayor Schell on TV saying, "It's safe to come downtown"—*laughing*—"it's safe to come downtown. Come down and shop."

I'm thinking "No! Don't!"

Things had broken loose again. After the arrests at Westlake, we followed a group through downtown up toward Belltown and arrested another large group of about one hundred. That was the last big arrest of the day.

Maud Daudon: The president was there for, like, twenty-four hours and we had to figure out how to get him safely and securely into the protest area.

Pam Schell: They got a podium for him down at the port and had him make a speech in a very secure place—and then he left town.

Maud Daudon: The amount of actual resources that took away from just trying to keep civility in the street was really something.

John Nichols: Clinton, when he came and spoke, was tempered in his remarks. Not over-the-top but actually acknowledging that there was something to what some of the protesters were saying. And the dynamic shifted.

Kevin Danaher: What happened was the protest on the outside exacerbated conflicts on the inside between Third World countries and rich countries, between trade ministers and environment ministers. The environment ministers were a little open to the realization that corporate plunder was causing really serious problems.

Pascal Lamy: At the last minute, Clinton and his people came with the idea that there should be a much stronger linkage between trade opening and social issues like workers' benefits, which I love as a theme. I'm a Socialist-Democrat. The EU had been trying for many, many years to make the case that social issues were playing the role that environmental issues are playing today. There are good reasons to do that, especially in the U.S., where the social system is much thinner than it is in Europe.

But the way it came from the Clinton side, saying, "I thought I should tell you that we are a progressive administration." The last-minute announcement totally destabilized a number of developing countries that, in principle, had always resisted connecting trade opening and social issues for fear of protectionism. For France, I've always said that we don't want to talk about these things because if we do that, you will eat our competitive advantages in making us raise compensation and creating social assistance. This is not a trade issue.

Dave Reichert: I decided to go along with the county executive and get a firsthand view. Our intelligence unit provided security. I'd already been out on the street with my people but I got in the car anyway. I was sitting in the back seat. Our detective, who was the county executive's security, was driving, and we're getting an idea of some of the destruction, vandalism, that's taken place.

There's a police radio on this car. The comm center announces that they need officers to respond to the Radio Shack on Third Avenue because they have looters that have broken the front window and have entered. No one is responding because they're tied up with tens of thousands of people a few blocks down the street. So I told my detective who was driving, "Take me to the Radio Shack."

He said, "Sheriff, I can't do that. I've got to protect the county executive. I don't want to take him into harm's way."

I said, "You stay in the car. You protect the county executive, but you take me to the Radio Shack. That's an order." I said that because I knew he was not going to do it otherwise.

So he goes around the block, comes to the Radio Shack. Sure enough, the window's broken, four guys inside. I tell the detective to stop the car. He rolls past it about a block and doesn't want to stop. I said, "Stop the damn car! I'm getting out." He stops the car. The child locks are on so I can't get out. I said, "Pop the locks, pop the locks!" So he pops the locks. I jump out.

I'm sprinting down the sidewalk, headed toward Radio Shack. And some guy—and it's just one guy—is screaming, "Hey, the cops are coming! The cops are coming!" But there's only one cop—there's nobody else with me. They peek out of the store, see me, and take off running, carrying stuff and dropping stuff on the way. And I'm in full pursuit.

Now, I'm forty-nine years old. These guys are nineteen years old. There's no way I'm catching them but I am high-stepping it. They ended up running around the block and running into some Seattle cops who grabbed them.

I get back to the car and decide to go over to the Seattle Municipal Building, where the command post was. I walk in and the whole place erupts in applause. There's a standing ovation. They take me over to the TV monitors and the local news is playing me chasing these looters over and over.

The mayor is now fuming. And the officers are really excited because they believe they have somebody on their side. They recognize what they think is somebody who's going to be a leader and bring the team together. I was just doing my job. It's just a cop chasing some crooks. I mean, that's what I felt like. Then all of a sudden, you're a hero.

Larry Mayes: It went viral. The fact that we started taking over the streets and then Reichert becoming the overnight hero, it really upped the ante in the dispute with the mayor and SPD.

Gary Locke: Safe to say, Reichert's congressional election effort later on was helped by images of him patrolling the streets and jumping out of a car and grabbing some protesters who were destroying windows and shoplifting.

Dave Reichert: All of a sudden, I'm the Seattle PD leader because Norman Stamper's not doing anything. Norm and the mayor, the comments they made about the officers beforehand, apologizing for their behavior, is amplified even more because of this action that happened to be captured on TV. So I'm even more disliked by Stamper and the mayor. The mayor was asked by a reporter what he thought about this action. And he goes, "I'm very disappointed and angry that the sheriff's chasing innocent children out on the streets of my city." All of a sudden, he wants to flip it. The kids are just innocent kids and the cop is the bad guy.

Pam Schell: What happened was, the police and all the strategists had said, "There's just too much to do. We can't go and stop looting. We're not going to put our energy into that." Well, Reichert went to catch a looter, which just infuriated Paul because it wasn't his city to make that decision. He never liked and trusted Reichert ever since.

Ron Judd: There were also some comical moments that day, between all the chaos. The police were chasing us and lobbing tear gas and they were trying to herd our group in a particular direction. We're in the middle of the road and the streetlight changes to "don't walk" and people stopped. Now think about that. Only in Seattle would that happen. Tear gas, concussion grenades, rubber bullets, and helicopters up above, shouting instructions through bullhorns and people respecting the stop signs.

Celia Alario: I was there when Victor got extracted, which was one of the scariest things I've ever seen in my entire life. Sellers saw it too. It was one of those things that was so unlike anything I had seen in the United States in years of being involved in peaceful protests and marches, that if you don't have friends who were standing next to you to confirm it, it can seem too crazy to believe.

Victor Menotti: We had a meeting with the CEQ, the Council on Environmental Quality, and someone from the White House who were responding to our criticisms against the U.S. trade representative. They basically told us that they were going to continue pushing everything through despite all the protests. I felt it was the moment to use my privilege of being inside to then go share that directly outside.

First, I went to news cameras. But the news cameras were more interested in the bricks going through the windows than the actual looting going on inside the negotiations. So I just stood on a street corner until a small group finally gathered around me to listen to what was going on inside. Then I saw lines of cops running after something. Then police cars and sirens. It was kind of a flash, it's hard to appreciate. It was like the moment I started talking, it started a wave of these cops starting to move. I thought, "Oh, they're going after someone. Maybe we should step away." They didn't say disperse but they wanted us to disperse because, finally, there was this moment of like, "Oh, I guess *we're* the thing they're breaking up." I'm in the middle of that thing. So I started to run—run to open field, Walter Payton or something like this. Get out of the way. Then I figured, "Okay, I'm dispersed so they should be gone." But they're still chasing my ass, three or four of these guys. So I stopped once I realized they were coming after me. My brother had recently done something and wound up in trouble because he resisted arrest. You don't want to be seen as resisting so I stopped. That's when the robocops jumped me.

David Solnit: Victor came out and gave a briefing to people on the street and got snatched by cops. The guy from the accredited NGO got snatched up just like a direct action activist.

Celia Alario: Victor, he was a policy wonk. He was a nerdy, technical guy. He wasn't the person you would imagine that happening to.

David Solnit: He later got a settlement.

Victor Menotti: There were a number of suits afterwards but I was the lead plaintiff in the ACLU case because they had footage of my absurd arrest. It used to be on YouTube; you could find several camera angles and now you can't even find it. A federal judge ruled it an unconstitutional arrest—several years it took for them to come to a decision.

David Solnit: They brought all the buses to a processing facility out of town called Sand Point. We had preplanned through the spokescouncil to do jail solidarity, meaning we would use what leverage we could to try to make sure that everyone was treated well, nobody was singled out for harsher treatment. Also, to continue our resistance in jail, we were withholding our names and, at different points, not cooperating.

In the Direct Action Network we had a good rotation of people since a bunch of folks were thrown in jail. Tons of people stepped up and continued doing direct action blockades, marches, and actions. Labor was leading marches; the steelworkers had a rally.

David Taylor: I sprained my ankle three weeks before the WTO so I'm on crutches during all of this. After everyone was arrested we had a spokescouncil and decided to march down from the Convergence Center for the steelworkers' rally. We weren't sure whether the steelworkers were going to be mad at us, the Direct Action Network people. Some of them might have thought we were messing up what labor was trying to do with the peaceful marches. But we were welcomed with cheers. I got pulled onstage to give a speech. I had about thirty seconds' notice.

Giving a speech about students and steelworkers and everyone uniting was a pretty mind-blowing experience for me, to see what solidarity looks like, to see how people with different tactics and different outlooks, really, we were on the same page. Steelworkers, they're in the same place with these radical environmentalists and students and kids, all understanding what we were facing as far as the impacts of global capitalism and fighting back against state repression. Being able to see all of us come together at that moment, for me, was pretty transformational.

After the rally, everyone marched back into downtown. The National Guard had taken over the police presence and we were met with a lot of force, a lot of tear gas. It was as dark came on and it was a violent change in tone. It was the thing that I definitely have PTSD from. We were chased five, ten blocks, pinned in on all sides, and then eventually we were surrounded. They sent tear gas into the middle of all of us, down closer toward the Space Needle. It was definitely an escalation in force and tactics. It was the day Clinton was in town, so it seemed clear that the Secret Service had taken over, or the federal government had taken over, and things were met with a much higher level of brutality.

Ron Judd: They were going to raid the Labor Temple. Tear gas was flying and they were trying to sweep people into traps. They were trying to sweep this group of protesters into a trap down in lower Queen Anne and the Labor Temple was on their route. So a couple hundred young kids, scared to death, took shelter in the Labor Temple. They threatened to actually come in with their SWAT teams, arrest everyone, and we drew a line. We put a call out and people started showing up from all over to surround the Labor Temple in a big wall of bodies saying, "Over our dead fucking bodies. If you want to start drawing blood in the streets, this is the line you cross." It was a throw-down moment and of course all the media was reporting it live. Everybody was seeing it and we had folks on the phone doing callouts and more people started arriving. It just goes to show you the power of that energy when it's stirred—you can focus it.

Most of the cops who were there were not from this area. Most of them were in the Ninja Turtle outfits, the armor and all that shit, which made it harder to tell who they were. I was on the phone with the mayor and the deputy mayor and I was talking to the deputy mayor when I got hit by a club in the back of the head and my phone went flying off into the street. I saw stars for an hour. Fortunately, as I was in the middle of getting arrested and hauled off, Pugel noticed it was me and intervened.

They blinked and didn't raid. I'm very happy they blinked because I'm sure things would have gotten really ugly if they'd crossed that line.

Vivian Phillips: That night, Richard McIver, from the City Council, was going to attend a dinner at the Westin hotel. Richard has since passed but he was a friend of mine. He was detained by Seattle police. It was either the Seattle police or the Washington State Patrol.

Annette Sandberg: We had set up a couple of roadblocks. We made it really clear to everybody that if they were trying to get in, particularly to the convention, that they had to show ID and they had to stop at the roadblock and get clearance to go in. I remember a Seattle city councilman who tried to blow the roadblock. They put his hands behind his back, laid him over the car, cuffed him up, and threw him in. Next thing I know, I'm getting a call from my commander: "Hey, we may have a problem."

Dennis Kucinich: The police pulled him out of his car. I saw it, it was right in front of me. They were stopping cars and there was an exchange of not so many words. The policeman lost his patience and pulled the man out of the car and was very aggressive. I saw it, I was right behind him.

Annette Sandberg: Two of my troopers had arrested him and put him in the back of the patrol car because he refused to ID himself. They were worried about a big political blowup. And I said, "Did he show his ID?"

"No, didn't do it."

I said, "Then keep him in the back of the car until we prove who he is."

Dennis Kucinich: It was very confusing and concerning, because the police at that point were highly agitated and very defensive. Frankly, I think there was probably a lot of fear because there were other elements that were trying to create disruption and it was very chaotic.

Annette Sandberg: I had a captain go over there and release him and say, "Listen, here's why you got arrested. This is why you got handcuffed."

Vivian Phillips: As I understand it, he was called the N-word. I think that it really boils down to an assumption about authority and who has it and deserves to have it. The majority of the protesters were white. So that incident for me was more about biases and assumptions around authority and the right to move. It was really an example of, I think, a breach of trust and respect. The bottom line was respect—or lack thereof.

Jello Biafra: We were playing at the Showbox, an old roller-skating rink. Dead Kennedys had played there. Saw Iggy Pop there once in '79.

Kim Thayil: I think the cops were trying to secure the environment for those who were visiting downtown so there was a little bit more head-cracking. What do you do in that situation? I was young, had long hair, and tended to wear all black. I thought for sure I'd just get beaten up and have questions asked later. But I committed to the show so I knew I was going.

Jello Biafra: Michael Franti was playing that night, too, and he made the point: "Look, at a time like this, people need music." We played during the Rodney King riots in another part of town. People needed us. They needed our music. They needed our, basically, mojo.

Kim Thayil: My friend had a shiny blue '65 Mustang and he says, "I'll give you a ride down there. I'd like to go see this."

And I say, "Oh, you're not worried?"

He goes, "No, I got a couple gas masks in the trunk." He's a really smart guy, pharmacist-science guy, into macho things, but also really bookish.

I go, "Are you sure we should be driving around in a weird—sort of a muscle car?" There's something about that. But when we're trying to go past these police blockades the funny thing was, they liked the car. We were able to park on First Avenue, right near the venue, and no cops bothered us.

It was interesting, people's anxiety levels. I was certainly anxious. Some people were just going to the show or the protests. Some people were going out for a martini. It was odd.

There're couples window-shopping on First Avenue, or young folks coming down to see this show. At the same time, I had acquaintances who were maybe ten miles outside of the downtown area who had all their doors locked, and had their gun on the coffee table next to them. "In case any of that stuff comes here, comes my way." It's odd how people appraise the consequences and risks of these types of events.

Jello Biafra performing on December 1, 1999.

The crowd at the Showbox.

Jello Biafra: It wasn't packed to the rafters with crazy, wild people like it would have been the first night but a lot of people did find out.

Kim Thayil: I imagine had there not been the events of the WTO protest, the place would've been packed but it was not. Maybe half capacity—a number were not interested in trying to navigate police barricades and road closures but some did. You saw long hair, a lot of black, and a number of friends came down. On the album, *Live from the Battle in Seattle*, you can hear that the crowd response is enthusiastic and positive but you can also tell that it's sparse.

Jello Biafra: I didn't even know it was being recorded. Krist told me later, "Oh yeah, we got a twenty-four-track of that. I think we should do something with it." There were some flubs during the actual gig, no surprise—because not only had we thrown it all together but look what else was raging the other side of the wall of the venerable venue.

The band I was in for four days, the No WTO Combo, our album came out with two new songs. One was called "New Feudalism" and the other one was called "Electronic Plantation," about the tech economy.

Kim Thayil plays with the
No WTO Combo.

Kim Thayil: I think Jello came out and did—what?—twenty minutes or so of spoken word. That was the plan: some spoken word, some commentary, some stand-up, and then toward the last piece we would come out and start letting our guitars hum and feedback, and then kick into four or five songs. All the songs we played were chosen by Jello. They were instrumental things.

I'm pretty sure Krist and I were drinking. It was just one of those kinds of nerve-racking things. It was a bit sloppy and it was prior to Pro Tools and the technology that we have today. *Laughs.* But we had a good mixing engineer who managed to edit out a few glitches so you could enjoy it at home without us having to suffer ridicule.

Jello Biafra: Krist had a gas mask on while we were playing. Michael Franti was in the dressing room before we went on. He was writing,

Krist Novoselic performs
in a gas mask.

writing, just trying to come up with something, right at the last second. And he walked out and read the most beautiful poem about the day and about the WTO protests. It was the most beautiful poem any human being could have written. I thought right there, "I'm looking at the next Bob Marley." Which he is to a lot of people to this day, for good reason.

Everybody's got to keep everybody else pumped, especially multiday protests, because we're all going to reach points where we're tired, we are discouraged, or in some cases scared as fuck for good reason, depending on whether the police obey their own laws or not.

Lori Wallach: A lot of the stuff that got done at night was figuring out if we needed to change the messaging for posters or for an event. What press materials are we going to need? Who do we need to try to get out of jail? On the inside, which countries are getting the crap beaten out of them? What senator do we know who can call a certain prime minister and tell them not to get bullied by the U.S. negotiators?

four waters: We were operating on very little sleep. I don't think that we slept more than two or three hours a night for any of that time. Often, we were up for twenty-four hours.

Ron Griffin: I had to go home and undress in my garage because I had gas on me. I couldn't take that in the house. I got young children at the time.

Patrick Collins: We were out on the street for, well, from 0600 until about 2200 that night. We went back to the Seattle Armory and at about 2400, my head was just hitting the cement pad I was sleeping on—I had a sleeping bag and a rubber mattress on the cement pad—my head had just hit the ground and my battalion commander comes by, nudges me and says, "Hey, man, we have an emergency. Capitol Hill police precinct is being surrounded. Governor's authorized use of deadly force. He's asked the National Guard to go up there. Grab whichever platoon you want and get up there." So we did.

We woke everyone up, put them onto a bus. We're heading out, I'm in a van, I've got my noncommissioned officer in charge with me. My NCOIC had just left the Second Ranger Battalion at Fort Lewis and had joined the National Guard. As we get into the van he goes, "Sir, do you remember any of that training we went through?"

I go, "Yeah, of course I do."

He goes, "If in doubt, grab with two hands and swing hard."

About that point, we hear someone say something behind us in the van. We thought we were in the van by ourselves. There was a guy in the back there sleeping because the van was more comfortable than the cement floor. He's like, "What's going on?"

We're like, "Hey, man, we're headed off to war. Get out of the fucking vehicle!"

I'll never forget that guy grabbing his shit, he's still in his underwear and T-shirt and socks with his kit in his hand, trying to run inside the armory as we're driving away.

Other than combat tours that I ended up doing post-9/11, I would say it was one of the hairiest things that I had done in a while. It's nighttime, off-and-on rain, off-and-on CS. You're pulling your mask on, mask off, mask on. Up on top of the buildings, there's these flashes. It's reporters but, at night, the reporter's camera flash looks like a gunshot. You're tense. The engineer battalion that was also supposed to be there, they had one platoon—those bastards took off as soon as I showed up. They left me there with a police force. There was probably, I'd say about fifty to a hundred cops, State Patrol mainly. And then I had forty guys in the platoon. All of a sudden, a detail from the Harris County SWAT detachment shows up. They had just come off of presidential security detail, and they were told, "Hey, get up there. Help these guys out." I met with the noncommissioned officer and he said, "Sir, we have a serious problem." He goes, "If you notice, I don't have anything with me that's nonlethal." They have Walther MP5s, coming off of a live security mission with POTUS. He goes, "I don't want to get near those guys out there because it's bad form. I'll make you a deal, you keep those bastards away from me, and I'll take care of anyone from the rooftops if we actually start taking rounds."

So we were out there for a couple of hours and everything blew up. It started when someone with a wrist rocket shot a rock or a marble or something through one of the State Patrol cars. At that point, the incident commander said, "Oh no, that's it. Clear the streets." I got a warning of "get ready" and the time it took me to turn and look toward one of my platoon leaders, I heard flash-bangs going off. I turned my head around and you couldn't see across the street. Everyone took off running. It took, like, thirty seconds to clear that street. A flash-bang is very disorienting—very bright light and a very loud noise, too. There were a whole bunch of them thrown. You combine that with a heavy CS cloud and officers charging at you that look like they're pretty pissed-off with a riot baton in their hand. Unless you're a die-hard true believer, you're not going to stand there. You're going to break contact.

David Solnit: In the wee hours, people were brought to jail in Seattle. There was still a lot of police brutality. They were in crisis by both the numbers of arrests and the fact that we were not giving identifying information and making demands.

We were demanding to meet with our attorneys. We were also demanding to have a spokescouncil meeting in jail to go over our demands and consider their counteroffers. The jail was pretty freaked out. They had never had that many people come as an organized body and not cooperate with the processes.

They thought they could shut us down by mass arrests. It ended up backfiring and the hundreds of people in jail became the crisis.

THURSDAY, DECEMBER 2

Lisa Fithian: We eventually were taken to King County Jail, which is downtown. They took our bus behind the building at two in the morning where nobody could see.

Nadine Bloch: When we were processed, people were not giving their names. I had brought my ID for some reason and hid it in my shoe, so they didn't know who I was. They took us to the dark side of this facility so the media couldn't see what they were doing to us to get us off the bus. I told people that if they started pepper-spraying people, which they were doing—in the face—to get them to get off the bus, I was going to open the exit window and jump out. That was my plan.

Some people were on that bus for fifteen hours. People had to go to the bathroom. It was one of those double buses where they have rubber in the bottom, so we were able to make a place where people could go to the bathroom and let it go out the bottom of the bus.

David Solnit: We said, "We demand to talk to a lawyer. We're not going to get off the bus until we get to speak to our attorney." The cops came on the buses and pepper-sprayed people and violently dragged people out. It was pretty rough for folks, a lot of police brutality. A lot of folks got dragged and screamed at. A lot of cops were straight-up throwing people around.

Lisa Fithian: We all sit down in the aisle, we're kind of holding on to each other. And that's when they extracted us using pepper spray. That was terrifying. The guy in front of me, they fully spray him with pepper spray. It was horrible. He was screaming as they dragged him off. Then I was next. They came with the pepper spray. *Long pause.* I didn't resist. I got off the bus. I had shame about that. That happens a lot in these things. It's like, "What are we willing to take and not take?" We have to know ourselves. Could I have taken that hit of pepper spray? I could have but I didn't want to. If I was locked down to a gate of a place that we were trying to block them from getting in, I would have taken it. But at this point, I've been on the bus fifteen hours. They're going to take me off the bus, one way or another. I'm exhausted and those are chemical agents. I could really get hurt. I'm principled but

I'm not perfect. Once we got inside, I watched the guy in front of me suffer for hours. It was brutal.

four waters: We got up in the morning, looked around, and said, "Okay, we need to do this with the media, we have this many people in jail, we've had these injuries, we have this problem with the neighbors." Law enforcement went completely off their rockers and started tear-gassing neighborhoods that had nothing to do with us at all.

Patrick Collins: Leading into the Christmas holidays, walking down the street wearing a Kevlar helmet, body armor, and nobody on the street, nobody out walking around, you're like, "Fuck, this is kind of a sci-fi movie."

Julia Hughes: Because of all the protests, there were a lot of mounted police on horseback. So walking to the venue, there were a lot of piles of horseshit everywhere. It was like, "This is kind of a metaphor for how the week is going."

John Nichols: I had the WTO credential so I was able to get into the ministerial, and what was going on inside was a real battle between many developing countries that were looking for a better deal. They weren't necessarily looking to get rid of the WTO or to undermine it but they wanted a different arrangement. Then there were the big countries that had always been dominant and their corporate allies who clearly wanted to go forward with the plan that they already had. There was no question that the smaller countries that were seeking to upend things, or at least change the direction of things, needed the protests. Because if the protests weren't dynamic and weren't big and far more effective than protests usually are, then it was unlikely they were going to upend where the WTO was headed.

Lori Wallach: The press center inside the ministerial was open. If they were in the middle of negotiations, the press would have nothing to do—they might be down there filing or whatever. So we'd stand up in a chair and clap a couple times and say, "Impromptu press briefing. Here's what's going on." It wasn't just me, I'd grab my international partners, but I would be the one that would step up in a chair like a bossy American.

Pascal Lamy: The chaos on the streets, it obviously had some influence on the handling of the conference.

Julia Hughes: We had a mission to communicate with representatives from other countries and textile industries from other countries to not be anxious because they were worried. Particularly Bangladesh, for example. They were very concerned. That's part of why we were there, to talk from a business perspective, a positive perspective.

Vicente Paolo Yu: Philippine trade policy at that time was still very much in flux. It had been much more gung ho in terms of free trade and liberalization. It was one of the founding members of the WTO. Then this former actor, Estrada, became president very much in a populist wave. There was a lot of, I think, influence in the early part of his tenure from some of the left-wing groups and so there was a tendency to take a bit more of a critical perspective on the WTO.

Pascal Lamy: I don't want to be un-nice to Charlene Barshefsky the U.S. trade representative but she was not in control. Who was in control? Basically, my response is "nobody," which is one of the reasons why it wasn't working.

Ron Judd: Everybody was tired. I don't know of anybody that slept that week. People were doing catnaps against the wall, on a couch, in the street, depending on where they were. Everybody was tired and we were all running off adrenaline.

Vandana Shiva: I was helping to organize the Agriculture Day. We had the whole day in the church. We went through every element of seed patenting and intellectual property—it was like a teach-in but it was also workshops. It was really a fast-forward way of learning for the young people who had never understood the details of what these international agreements were. We deconstructed the agreements and gave real life responses of farmers—the words *food sovereignty* grew after that.

Jim Hightower: I brought in a farm contingent. I had been associated with Farm Aid over the years, and they were supportive. We were doing a Farm Aid event with a big flatbed truck to speak off of. Some farmers, they were coming and had been active in the Tractorcades in the late '70s. These were people who were practiced agitators and were really the old farm radical tradition in America that most people don't know much about but was very alive, still, in that period. They had carried a bit of this protest about world trade themselves, in the late '70s.

Vandana Shiva: A Texas company called RiceTec had taken the patent on basmati from India. We did an amazing celebration with basmati rice and we had the Raging Grannies—they are these amazing old women, eighties, and they write songs and sing and they were there with us.

David Taylor: By Thursday, I was one of only a couple of people *not* in jail who understood where the money was. The finances weren't a lot. I mean we're talking tens of thousands of dollars. I was just a college kid but I had a lot more authority at that point.

Jim Pugel: We knew the anarchists had commandeered the empty building in the 900 block of Virginia street, one block east of the West Precinct building. There was considerable discussion about going in there Thursday.

David Taylor: The squat was no big deal. There was an affinity group that wanted to go squat. "Fine, here's $100 or $200"—it was something as minimal as that. And if that took up all of the police's energy and space, great, they're staying away from the Convergence Center.

Charles Mandigo: The sheriff's department was ready to do an eviction of the squat. Under the law, the eviction was under the purview of King County Sheriff's Office, not the SPD. But still they notified the mayor's office and the mayor's office said, "You can't do that."

Norm Stamper: We definitely had leftists taking over the property. Our wisdom was that we knew where they were, who they were, they

Protesters gather outside
a building occupied by anarchists.

were all sequestered. Why would we want to take them in handcuffs out of that facility to jail?

We talked the landlord into letting those people stay on his property as squatters basically. He said, "I have no-trespassing signs posted. Come on, work with me, police!" We did not work with him. We prevailed. Our wisdom prevailed.

Annette Sandberg: At one point, the chief wanted to have blankets and pizzas delivered to them, which I think was a concern to the rest of the law enforcement community. Why are you catering to these folks? Why are you even allowing them to take over a building that's not owned by the city? I mean, it would be different if the city owned the building and said, "Go ahead, take it." But it was owned by a private individual.

I remember my SWAT commander and the SPD SWAT commander came to me and wanted me to go over Stamper's head and allow them to go in and raid that building and move those people out. I basically told my SWAT commander, "Listen, this isn't our city. I'd love for you to be able to do that but that's the police chief's job. And he's not going to tell you to do it. I really can't do that."

Dave Reichert: My position was they're destroying the building. They're trespassing. We need to go in, get them out, and put them in jail. But the mayor and the chief decide to buy them pizzas and get them sleeping bags.

Larry Mayes: SPD did cut water and power. But they were allowed to remain there throughout the whole time. That was their headquarters to coordinate, synchronize and run the hit-and-run operations that they were doing down in the business district, infiltrating the other protest groups, throwing rocks, bottles, golf balls—that stuff—at the cops.

Charles Mandigo: All I can think is, "You've got to be kidding me!" Here are these people who just destroyed your city. They're unlawfully occupying this building as their operational headquarters. And now you have your people in there providing them pizza and blankets? It was a crazy situation. You look back and shake your head and say, "What's the sense or logic?"

David Solnit: It would have backfired if they raided. The police intelligence was awful. They didn't understand. They had tried to freak out the rank and file by saying there could be members of Al Qaeda in the crowd—what the military calls "enemy thinking." They had demonized the folks that the cops are supposed to serve and protect.

Laurie Brown: By Thursday, it seemed like it was a miracle that nobody got killed.

Dave Reichert: I was out, standing in one row with my guys. One of my cops got hit in the head with a stick. He stood his ground. He didn't take any action, stared straight ahead. Got smacked in the head, didn't do anything.

Patrick Collins: One of the things about our training, there's no individuality. We would tell people in training, if you feel an urge to scratch your nuts, everyone's going to scratch their nuts at the same time. If the hand moves, everybody's hand is moving. Everything is done in unison, because that intimidates the hell out of people when they're staring at you, especially when you're standing there in body armor. Being pre-9/11, Americans weren't used to seeing the military out on the street, so it's intimidating just by physical presence. Add to that the fact that everybody moves together, there's no smiling, you're not talking with the protesters—there's no need. That's all part of force presence to intimidate people, so they comply with what they're being told.

Now, when you think of a cop, a beat cop especially, their life exists on that interaction with the public. They're out there dealing with the game. That's very different than the military, all standoffish.

So there was a group of people who broke through a section of the perimeter. Maybe about 2,000 of them came through and there were ten, fifteen police officers and about ten soldiers. That's all there was holding this one street. The protesters stopped like they were told, they weren't coming through but I will never forget this one girl. She was screaming, going on and on and on about how we're violating the Constitution, we're stepping on her constitutional rights. And she's looking at one of my soldiers. I am back behind the line trying to control people on all sides. She keeps going on and on. One of my soldiers, he's not saying a word to her, and the cop there is trying to talk to her. Finally, she stops and she goes to the cop, "What's his problem? I mean, don't they know how to speak?"

The cop—I wish I could have bought this guy a beer—the cop goes, "I think he'd just as soon kill you."

The look on her face. I mean, there was a shiver. She backed up off the line.

Larry Mayes: The jail was outside the security zone so a lot of the protesters went down there. By this time, many of them had been gassed. They could no longer get in the area that they felt a constitutional right to be in. They were angry. A lot of them in that group were indicating that if the prisoners weren't released, they were going to breach the front doors of the jail.

Skip Spitzer: I'm guessing there were a couple thousand people who were marching. By the time we marched all the way to the jail the crowd was smaller but it was spirited and there's something tremendously beautiful, people showing up to support others.

Ron Griffin: Let's not forget the reason why they arrived at the King County Jail: because Seattle PD led them there—it was outside the no-protest zone. They were trying to get other pieces of the city freed up—I understand why they did it—but now, because it was a county jail and one hundred percent our problem, it became one hundred percent my problem. Somehow or another, I *own* the problem.

Larry Mayes: There were a lot of bad people in jail. I had already covertly moved the SWAT team into position and nobody was going in there. That was not going to happen. It became a tense situation.

David Solnit: We knew that people started surrounding the jail and were doing a vigil. The jail had hundreds of people inside not cooperating and making demands. We had a spokescouncil with representatives from every cell, both men and women.

Skip Spitzer: I've been in jail more than a handful of times. It's important what people on the outside do.

Laurie Brown: They had mobilized all these people in front of the jail because there were wild rumors that people were being tortured in the jail and physically harmed.

Nadine Bloch: We felt people were being handled inappropriately and they were trying to separate leaders. There were a couple of instances where, for example, they came to get someone out of our cell. We did a puppy pile on top of them to keep them from taking that person away from us. The jail was overloaded, they were totally overstressed.

Denis Moynihan: The jail, the authorities, did what they do well, which was divide. They penalized the general population. There'll be no privileges of any kind, no visitations while these hippies are outside. That created a lot of tension.

Lisa Fithian: We could definitely hear people out on the street. And we knew that we were trying to negotiate, we were trying to get our lawyers to negotiate and have all the charges dropped.

Denis Moynihan: The abuses inside the King County Jail were re-markable and profound. I'd be on the phone with someone in the jail-house, and I could hear screaming in the background. I was actually taking firsthand accounts from people and trying to assemble them and get them to the press. There was a guy who said a deputy had rub-ber gloves on and suffocated him to the point where he was rendered unconscious. People were having their faces smashed into concrete walls. One guy was put into a five-point restraint chair and had some-thing called pepper foam massaged into his eyes. People still weren't giving their names or cooperating. They were trying to get people to break. The amount of violence that the King County deputies visited on the protesters was remarkable and out of sight of the cameras. Peo-ple were being seriously abused on a massive scale, and all the press was talking about is the broken windows.

Maud Daudon: The mayor's office was sending independent people to take a look. Laurie Brown was my right arm during this whole time, and I said, "Hey, you got to find out what's going on in the county jail. I'm hearing all these horrible things about people are mistreated and people were getting beat up."

Ron Griffin: My boss calls me up and says, "Hey Ron, this is what's going to happen: they've been told they've got to negotiate with you about it."
"Well, thanks."

Laurie Brown: People were outside holding vigil. It was peaceful but it was crazy. There was this big vegetarian buffet going on—patchouli oil, pot smoke. I was a hippie. I felt like I was back in my element. *Laughs.* I knew what it was about. They were in a way almost having a celebration but they were there to show their support for the people in the jail and they weren't planning on leaving.

Ron Griffin: Laurie Brown comes up and she introduces herself. We shake hands. John Sellers is there too, and I shake hands with John. I said, "Hey, I got a question for you."

He says, "What's that?" He's very standoffish, doesn't like cops and all that good stuff.

John Sellers: I look like a cop with my big white head and square jaw. Cops have always liked me and, in a lot of actions, I've been the police liaison and the cops were cool with me and were not dickheads. I gave them a lot of rope.

Ron Griffin: Sellers was the guy who, before the WTO events, he and a girlfriend dangled themselves off the Aurora Bridge, to stop shipping traffic. Apparently they were able to get low enough to where a ship could hit them and kill them. So I said, "It's got to be cold when you do something like that. God, I'm cold standing out here. You and your girlfriend were hanging off the bridge! What was it—ten, twelve hours? So what happens when you've got to take a piss?"

John Sellers: That's the first thing everyone always asks. My first big action was climbing the Sears Tower and that's what everybody wanted to get on the cell phone and ask me, "How're you going to go to the bathroom up there?"

The Aurora Bridge action was a beautiful action to block some factory trawlers in the Port of Seattle from going up to Alaska—massive trawlers with the crazy bag nets that you could fit a bunch of 747s in. It was an antifisheries thing with Greenpeace. It was maybe even two days, living on the ropes.

Ron Griffin: Anyhow, I got Sellers to laugh. He's thinking I'm going to do this tough thing—which I did, in the end, because we negotiated pretty hard—but right away, I sort of disarm him and get him laughing. I said, "Well, hat's off to you—that was impressive. I saw you there personally, as I drove by and I'm thinking, 'Jeez. I'd have to take a leak at some time.'"

He said, "Yeah, you piss your pants."

And I said, "Well, now you're going to be colder."

He laughed and said, "Well, you know, that's how it goes."

We went back and forth and that was kind of fun. Brown's standing there looking at me and going, "Holy shit."

We start going through the list of protester concerns. "So, John, what is it you're trying to accomplish with the jail? I understand you think people are being mistreated in there. I guarantee you they're not—but I understand. So how do we do this safely? That crowd can't stay up against those walls of the jail. I've got to take them off of there."

It's funny, I'm so emotional, remembering it now, I can't even get through what I want to say. *Pauses, gathers himself.* But at the time, believe me, I was in the groove.

We stood out in the middle of the street. My car was in the middle of the street. I had my troops out of sight. We're trying not to be over-aggressive. We didn't have the pads and all that on. We were trying to do the soft approach. I've got 150 guys down around the corner but I negotiated right there in the middle of the street by myself.

Laurie Brown: At that point, people from the city were really tired. The police were really tired, and patience was really running thin. They were like, "Oh, for god's sake." I don't think it was purposeful on the demonstrators' part but there were so many people there, they were spilling out into the street. Buses weren't able to go down that street. There was concern about whether emergency vehicles could get down the street.

We began a discussion. I said, "You know that the police are saying that there is a curfew tonight and if you all are still in front of the jail by the time the curfew happens, you will get arrested. There is no more room in the jail. I'm not sure where they will take you. What do we need to do to make sure that that doesn't happen?"

They explained what their demand was, that Katya, their lead lawyer, would be allowed to go into the jail and be allowed to talk to the people who were jailed and verify that they were not being tortured. Some people really believed they were being tortured. If she would be allowed to do that, she would signal to the demonstrators that the people in the jail were safe, that they weren't being tortured, and that everyone should honor the agreement and depart by curfew.

Ron Griffin: I really had no problem giving them what they wanted as far as going in to see their people. The issue is how do we get out of this? The big thing for us in negotiating with the jail commander was he wanted to make sure we don't get overrun. The personnel inside the jail were scared. Larry Mayes and the chief got the SWAT team inside. There was a sky bridge that led across to the jail. They were able to get in through there without anybody really knowing. We were hoping to avoid using them.

Laurie Brown: It was King County property, so the city did not have an official role at that point. They weren't even in charge of deciding whether people were going to be swept up for violating the curfew.

I was on the phone with my counterpart for the county, and she got Ron Simms, the county executive, on the phone. I said, "Here is what they are demanding. The city thinks it should happen. It's up to you guys." So Ron calls the director of the jail because he and Dave Reichert have to get the jailer's blessing for Katya to go into the jail and talk with the jailed demonstrators.

Katya said, "I'm going to encourage people and recommend to them that they leave by curfew but that's going to have to be a group consensus. I'm just the attorney."

Ron Griffin: Laurie and I negotiate a deal where we would allow a representative to go into the jail to see that their people were not being mistreated and they could talk with them and so forth. But after that these people have to disappear. They can't be up close to the jail. Period. They can be out on the sidewalk—they wanted to show a presence and all that—but they can't be up against the doors to the jail.

Laurie Brown: Then Katya came back—she was fierce—she came back and said, "I'm sorry, but we have another demand."

I said, "No, that's not how this works. I can't get them to agree to another demand, no. You should have told me that before I started talking to them."

She said, "We need two people to go in."

I don't know why they requested that, maybe so one could be a witness—I don't know.

Han Shan: I had been operating not just as Ruckus but as a member of the Direct Action Network, and I think the idea was that folks inside wanted a member of the Direct Action Network.

Laurie Brown: I said to Ron, "I need your help. Now they've got a second demand that a second person goes in. I'm afraid if I call the county executive, he's not going to trust that I can pull this thing off. Coming from you, it will mean a lot more. Can you make this happen?"

Meanwhile, the demonstrators were working on getting consensus on their end of it. There was this back-and-forth, all over the place with the various demonstrators who were speaking their piece. Finally, a consensus was reached, and they told their attorney, "Yes, try to make this happen."

I told them that it was the county executive who was going to tell us "yes" or "no." And eventually he called back. Right when he did all the demonstrators crowded around me and started asking, "Do we have an agreement? Is this going to happen?"

Right as I took the call my phone died. I was trying my best and then something so stupid like my phone dying happened.

All these demonstrators were saying, "Use my phone! Use my phone!"

I said, "I don't know what his number is!"

Ron Griffin: Did I give her my phone? I think I did. I had the number.

Laurie Brown: I got back in contact with him and I was about ready to start weeping. He said, "Yes, we agree."

I said, "They agree to it. The sheriff said, 'Yes, but that's it. Everything is off the table if there is another demand.'"

Ron Griffin: I'm standing there and I go, "Man, I'm getting thirsty. Does anybody want a bottle of water?" So I pop the trunk because I had cases of water in there. I said to John Sellers and everybody involved at that negotiation, "You know what? This deserves a celebration. Normally, it would be champagne, but I've got water." And my memory is they all warmly took the water.

Han Shan: I went in with Katya. She called me her paralegal or whatever. I remember thinking, "I'm a paralegal now—okay, cool." We went in to verify that people were actually being treated okay. Because before that, we were fucking doing sign language to people out windows. Crazy stuff. When we went in, we were able to talk to people. There were a few cases we were exceptionally concerned about but we left feeling satisfied that things were okay, that we were on the cusp of an agreement to get them released without charges. They were doing all this great organizing in jail, bonding, getting to know one another, singing songs, and developing this sense of solidarity. This was a real feeling of accomplishment and a great kind of culmination. They'd sacrificed and put their bodies on the line.

Laurie Brown: Katya and Han went into the jail, spent a little bit of time talking to people. After a while, they came into view in a spot where there was a catwalk and a bunch of windows. Katya gave the signal so that everybody could see it.

Skip Spitzer: I remember that Katya came out and reported that everybody was basically okay but that some people had been beaten. I think she said, "Good news and bad." She asked us all to sit down, hold hands before she told us that. I think a lot of us knew from experience, a lot of guards probably just don't like us—any number of reasons. But there was not a lot of anxious energy in Katya's report. "They are okay," she said, "but we have to get them out." We knew the negotiations would continue the next day.

Ron Griffin: They went in and basically found out that, yeah, your people are under arrest for these issues. No, they're not hanging upside down from the rafters and that kind of thing.

They wanted to stay through the night to show their presence. I said, "Okay. This is the line." And I pointed to a spot on the sidewalk. "You don't get any closer than this line. We're not going to sit here all night and babysit you and I better not get called out here."

I slept five hours the entire week. That's no bullshit. I'd get home at four in the morning and I'd be out at five thirty. So I'm tired, I'm done. I called Larry Mayes and told him, "Look, if I get home and I get a call to come back, my guys aren't walking off the bus. They're running off the bus. I'm going to wipe the protesters off the face of the earth. I'm done."

Laurie Brown: The demonstrators, bless their hearts, immediately started breaking things down. Eventually it was spotless. They cleaned up everything. They left no garbage. They were model kids—if you had a teenager, how you would want them to be. I don't mean to sound condescending but these were young people and they kept their word, left the place spotless.

That was the height of my career. I did a lot of things after that but I felt, at the time, that it took one hundred percent, every ounce of everything that I had learned about how to establish credibility, how to build trust, how to communicate clearly, how to get people to agree and resolve conflicts. That was the peak of the conflict and there couldn't have been a better outcome.

four waters: More communication is better than less communication. In the absence of communication, human beings create negative narratives. In the absence of communication, especially given what was happening with the rest of our law enforcement engagement, people had created stories. Yes, there were people in the jail who got hurt and, yes, things were not perfect, but for the most part, people were pulling together. There was a lot of support and camaraderie. I think that goes back to all the training. Even if not everybody in that group had the training, a few people did and they were able to pull people together.

FRIDAY, DECEMBER 3

Ron Griffin: Steven Thomas, the director of the county jail, comes back to town on Friday. He'd been away the day before and it was someone under him who was helping us with the negotiations. He comes back and sees protesters, a lot smaller group—fifty, sixty, seventy, eighty protesters—they had some of the coolest puppets you've ever seen. Big, tall rabbit puppets and everything, really, really cool.

Thomas goes up and he talks to the people. They said, "Well, we're protesting and we still have people in jail. Until they get released, we're going to show a presence."

He says, "Okay, and there's no law enforcement around?"

One of the protesters says, "No. We've negotiated with law enforcement. Some little guy, not very tall"—meaning me!—"some little guy made it real clear we could be here so long as we don't cross that line. He told us he'd wipe us off the face of the earth if we did." *Laughs.*

It was kind of cool because we made that shift. There were a lot of good people on the other side of the equation.

Lisa Fithian: We had to organize inside because we had a plan of noncooperating. On Friday, we were able to get collective meetings with the lawyers. They would move a bunch of us at a time into a big area where our lawyers would come in. If six hundred of us refuse to give our names, they have a problem, so they gave us that space to go through our process, dealing with self-care, making sure people are okay, deciding whether we stay or not stay. Eventually we were able to collectively say, "Let's commit to staying for three days—as many of us as possible, if we have to—three days."

Skip Spitzer: Katya basically said, "You guys have to do something, you have to take some action out here to strengthen their hand inside." We had been told pretty directly that she felt it was important for us to be problematic outside the jail, working up a sweat, which would give them the ability to make a deal on the inside to get everyone released. Katya specifically referenced that we needed to have facilitators and we needed to have a good process. So I thought, "Okay, maybe this is a time for me to get involved." I made my way up there and I offered myself, if people would have me, to help the group make a decision.

It took a while and it was a little chaotic. It's hard to do it all with the bullhorn. It's a difficult circumstance to make decisions together.

I didn't really have a plan. I walked up and started putting a plan together while I was waiting to get a bullhorn.

Denis Moynihan: The police had done a huge favor to the movement when they arrested people because the Direct Action Network did a very good job training people for jailhouse resistance. Everyone went out with basically two phone numbers written in Sharpie on their arm. One was for the legal defense line and one was for the media desk, which was where I was. The lawyer's desk was overwhelmed, so we would end up getting the calls. They separated the men and the women inside the county jail; there was no communication. They would call from the pay phone, a group of women protesters, and men would call the other line, and I would put the two phones together and they would have an organizing meeting through the phone receivers.

David Solnit: In my cell there was a Teamster organizer, a Latino punk from L.A., a North Coast activist—a real cross section. We could make phone calls out so I was in touch with the Independent Media Center folks who were setting up interviews. I would get the Teamsters organizer to do live interviews on TV from jail. They gave us the media numbers and we'd call places and they would have to accept the charges.

Nadine Bloch: The three activists who were running with me all day were the first people I told that I was pregnant. We were talking about, "Let's do a hunger strike." Now, I've done many a hunger strike because I've been in jail a lot, but this time I had to say, "Okay, look." *Laughs.* "Maybe I shouldn't do that. I can't do that and here's why." A lot of us were vegetarian or vegan and they're feeding us this crap, right? I've been in jail before, so I knew that if you're pregnant they give you things like extra milk because you're supposed to have calcium when you're pregnant. I met with the nurse and they gave me nothing. And when we were trying to negotiate for more vegetarian food the guard was like, "Do you think there's actually any meat in this stuff we give you?"

I'm like, "Thank you. And good for you—that's a good one."

It cracked me the hell up because he was being nice. He was like, "We can't give you any other food but let me just tell you there are no animal products in this food. Even though it's called a hamburger, it has nothing to do with hamburger."

Skip Spitzer: At one point someone's trying to speak outside the jail but it all gets disrupted because you see hands silhouetted on the glass in the jail. Somebody inside. Then all these hands. To see the hands sticking up to the glass felt like connection, and so, the spirit was good.

Nadine Bloch: We trained people to trust that there were people outside tracking us through the system and working in our best interests. It was also in our best interest to stay together and not give our names unless you had to. If you didn't have your diabetes medication, or you had to go—there were reasons to stand up and go and we would support people to do that. But generally, we were supporting each other to stay together.

four waters: By Friday I was inside the jail, doing legal support, trying to make sure that people were safe. Not everybody responds the same way even if they've had training. If someone is flipping out, we find ways to get them out or ways to get them the care they need. How people would get home or to a place of safety was important. Some people were injured. I watched a woman, a really sweet woman, sitting with her legs crossed on a concrete floor, handcuffed behind her back, and a sheriff deputy grabbed her hair, slammed her face into the ground, and broke her nose.

David Solnit: There was a point where some folks in local labor and the ILWU had said that if people didn't get released from jail, they were considering doing strike actions to protest. Part of me wonders what would have happened if we had been in jail for another week.

Skip Spitzer: We heard proposals, anybody could make a proposal. I think it was twenty-seven proposals. Then we broke up into affinity groups to discuss, relying on the model that we used to organize in the first place. These were impromptu affinity groups. Then we had a spokescouncil and we made decisions, we reached consensus on what we wanted to do. I think there was three or four parts to the program. I could sense that people liked and valued the structure. They liked the fact that they were part of the process. There were people complaining here and there along the way but overwhelmingly people were still there and responding. In some ways, the whole "repeat after me" format helps because you speak in a sentence fragment, but that means you can also think in fragments.

John Sellers: Seattle was the first time I ever saw the people's microphone get used. It was really magical when that started to happen.

Skip Spitzer: You say something and you're thinking about it while people are repeating it back, and you get a chance to consider how you're going to complete—what's the next fragment? More than once I changed the sentence that I started with. *Laughs.*

Nina Narelle: Recently I heard an activist talking about a protest where they were using the people's microphone, when one person will say something and then the crowd will repeat it. Someone said, "Oh yeah, that's from Occupy Wall Street."

I was like, "Sweetie, no, that happened in front of the jail at the WTO protests. I get that you learned it at Occupy—that's fantastic, I love that for you, keep on with the movement—but let your elder anarchists tell you that we used that approach because we didn't know that we were going to need a sound system in front of the jail."

Skip Spitzer: I felt alive, felt useful. I made mistakes along the way, things I said, I wish I hadn't. But in the end, it was a calm and thoughtful process.

One labor union organizer came over and said, "I just finally learned what democracy looks like." We had some favorable press, talking about the democratic process represented by the consensus process. There's something about the process that connects to the message. You're trying to live the world you'd like to see. Be the change you want to be. We were able to do that, that day.

Nina Narelle: The part of the story that often gets lost was that the protests produced enough of a delay, enough confusion, and enough stress that the African delegation and other delegations had enough room to block a lot of the work that was going to happen there. To me, those are the people who actually made it successful. Power shifted, even if just for a moment. That felt fucking big.

Tetteh Hormeku: We took what was happening in the street back into the meeting rooms. We went back into the negotiation center and began to tell our ministers, "You know, your citizens won't forgive you if you allow this thing to happen."

David Solnit: The strategy of disruption and disobedience is to create a crisis and to polarize things. For people within the U.S. to break from the idea that Americans support their government's corporate globalization policies was a big shift in how the world saw things. People in the United States are rebelling. That was huge.

Tetteh Hormeku: The ministerial was supposed to conclude at a particular time. But the WTO has a certain notoriety for extending deadlines.

Maud Daudon: The White House, the night before the meetings were supposed to end, had called and said, "Hey, can we extend the meetings by two to three days."

I said, "At your own peril, man. We are out of resources. People are exhausted. I'm really worried about public safety if you stay. I mean, I'm not saying don't but I am saying we can't guarantee a darn thing. It's taken everything we can muster to hold it together. People are exhausted." They were so furious at me. They were so mad! I was like, "I'm sorry, that's just the reality of the situation."

Vicente Paolo Yu: Towards the end, there were a lot more developing country negotiators outside of the meeting rooms than there were inside the rooms, oftentimes not knowing what was happening. You'd hear rumors or speculations swirling around, "Oh well, the Quad is meeting." "Oh, they're having a Green Room process in there . . ." It was that kind of dynamic. And as the days went on, you got this increasing sense of alienation coming from many of the smaller developing countries' delegations. There was an increasing sense of disaffection. "Why are they making decisions? We're also members of the WTO!" At the same time there was this feeling that you have these massive protests outside with tear gas and everything. We were seeing it on the television screens inside the conference center. There was a sense of frustration that the decision-makers were not listening to the protests. It felt like things were really coming to a head.

Pat Davis: Poor Charlene Barshefsky. She worked so hard. But Clinton came to town and told her that she had to include environment and labor agreements or we wouldn't do it. At the hotel where she was staying, you could hear her scream and hit the walls because of what he did. We couldn't come to any resolution when he said that. She couldn't continue to negotiate.

Mike Dolan: Michael Moore and Charlene Barshefsky realized there was a revolt among the delegates from the developing world—a lot of them in Africa, in Southeast Asia. They started enjoying the political—how shall I say—"emotional cover" of our protest outside. It helped them challenge the consensus that was developing in the Green Room.

Pascal Lamy: This conference was seen as failing because of what happened outside, which is absolutely not the reality. This conference was failing because of what happened inside—or did not happen inside. The media, you know, it's about pictures.

Tetteh Hormeku: As far as the African delegation was concerned, there was a sudden convergence between them and civil society saying, "Look, an agreement is not possible." The ministers were frustrated. Imagine your microphone is switched off, you can't have interpreters. These are ministers—I'm talking about full ministers. My minister from Ghana, for instance, I saw her at one point so angry, leaving the room, banging the chair. On one occasion, an important delegate came out to denounce the whole process and said that African, Caribbean countries would never sign anything as a result of these kinds of processes. Government ministers were marginalized, basically amplifying the voices of their colleagues from civil society who had been beaten up in the streets.

Lori Wallach: The developing countries were willing to shut it down. The cost of doing that—potentially getting foreign aid cut off and who knows what military interventions and commercial and other retaliations—it was at high costs to stand up.

Mike Dolan: Lori Wallach called me and she's just like, "We won. It's over. They're shutting down negotiations."

Tetteh Hormeku: They announced the closure of the meeting without a declaration. In other words, they didn't say, "We are currently speaking, we agree on our issues, we should continue"—nothing like that. They just said, "Okay, the meeting is closed." The sudden announcement that it was concluded was utterly surprising.

Mike Dolan: The rebellion on the outside was echoed in a rebellion on the inside. That's why, ultimately, the ministerial failed.

John Nichols: There was this remarkable moment where Mike Dolan and Lori Wallach came running out to say, "They just folded. They gave up." It's not very often that you see something that starts on a Monday and, by the end of the week, the protesters essentially achieved their goal.

Julia Hughes: In some ways, the U.S. team misjudged what was likely to happen and was unprepared and that made it easy for the other countries, for everyone else attending the ministerial to kind of say, "Whoa, wait a minute. We're not right, we're not making new commitments, not moving forward." We all felt lucky to just be getting out of there.

Helene Cooper: That Friday night, I was with the *FT* reporter, Mark Suzman—we ended up becoming friends that week. We had written our big stories that were about to launch and we were relaxing. Then we both get calls: the trade talks have collapsed. Like, "What!?" And the two of us go racing back to the convention center and we're both dying laughing because it failed! The protesters had totally won. I was supposed to leave to go back to Washington that Saturday. I stayed all weekend because I needed to write a huge story for Monday: "Protesters: 1, WTO: nothing."

Mike Dolan: We won and nobody could believe it. We won! The shouting, the screaming that you could hear—there just wasn't a dry eye.

Maud Daudon: Partly because of Ed Joiner's leadership, the police were remarkable about living in a state of deprivation and restraint at the same time because they had so many logistical problems trying to get food, trying to get water to the police on the street, get a place for them to sleep at night.

I think we finally struck a balance with the protesters at the very end of the week. It happened with a march led by Ron Judd.

Ron Judd: We had some good demonstrations, particularly leading up to the last day. We were trying to really make sure that the week of chaos and tear gas and rubber bullets and concussion grenades—that's what the headlines were about—were not the only thing people remembered. We wanted to try one last time to pivot back to what the original intent was: peaceful, civil disobedience, to talk about the policy issues associated with WTO agreements and how they hurt people and the planet. Part of that was taking back the no-protest zone and that led to some very interesting and challenging negotiations. The feds were calling the shots. There were too many international dignitaries here for them not to be in charge.

We had a conversation and my rap to them was "Look, none of us have wanted what has happened in the last four days. All of us have, at least on the last day, an opportunity to show the world that we can have large protests and be peaceful and not kick the shit out of one another with tear gas, concussion grenades, rubber bullets, batons—whatever—but you've got to work with us to do that. We're going to come down and we're going to come through your perimeter, back into the no-protest zone. If you block us, we're going to do battle. We hope that you will collaborate with us because we're there to do no harm. The fight is not with you. Your fight is not with us. Everybody, the city of Seattle, the state of Washington, the US of A, everybody needs to understand that we should try to end this week with a different message."

We went right in and there was a little bit of a standoff and they were six thick and it took everything we to have our folks get out of control. I gave a speech and talked to individual peacekeepers and everybody I knew. Ours is the practice of patience. Lack of patience when it's this hot on the street can lead to unintended consequences. We need to be the adults in the street. Finally, it was Jim Pugel and Maud Daudon and a few others who came down and I saw them on the other side. They motioned to an ear and called me and said, "Yeah, we're going to part waters here." The officers started moving aside and we marched through the thing and returned to the Labor Temple and had a big street party. *Long pause.* I'm going to choke up here so I apologize—I'm going to choke up because it's so powerful. That's where people laid in the streets and spelled out *democracy* with all the news cameras shining down on this big street party-protest we were having. The deputy mayor, Daudon, she called me and she was really in tears and she was saying, "It's been so hard and there's been so much hostility and damage," and she goes, "But you know when I saw *democracy* spelled out by people, I realized that's really what this week was all about. This is what democracy looks like. Sometimes it's ugly. And sometimes it's not. We all have a responsibility and role to play, one way or the other."

John Sellers: I thought we finally did something to put some points on the board right at the whistle at the end of the millennium. Maybe this is the sign of better things to come.

AFTER

Lisa Fithian: They ended up letting most of us go over the weekend.

Han Shan: People came out of jail with these shit-eating grins on their faces. You come out of jail and there's four hundred people waiting for you outside and you're fucking heroes. It was bear hugs and jumping up and down and chanting and cheering and dancing. Everyone was greeting each other as "Jane" and "John Doe." As tired and sleepless as everyone was, everyone understood that this was beautiful.

Maud Daudon: At the end of the week, I was at the Emergency Operations Center. Ed Joiner was there, of course, and Norm Stamper was there. I was like, "Norm, I have not seen you in days! Where in the heck have you been?"

He pulled me aside and he said, "I've got to tell you, I'm resigning. My heart was with the protesters, not with the police."

I was like, "You need to resign. You definitely need to resign."

Norm Stamper: By the end of it I realized that we were not at all ready for what hit us. I realized that I could not remain as police chief.

You know, I graduated from high school in '62. A good buddy of mine said, "Hey, Norm, let's go down and take the police test."

I said to him, "Why would I want to do that?"

He explained to me why he wanted to become a cop. It mostly had to do with job security and pay—it wasn't particularly inspiring. I did not have much love for cops in those days. I was playing in a rhythm and blues band. One of our sax players was Latino—it was a mix of guys.

One Sunday afternoon we were rehearsing and a cop came to the door. He said that we were making too much noise. He started giving a lecture on race, using the N-word, throwing it around like it didn't mean anything at all, as he talked about our singers. How can you talk that way about a fellow human being? I was pissed! It scared me. My emotional reaction to cops in those days was fear and anger. That's not a good combination. You do not have anger without fear. What makes you angry is what scares you. It gets twisted, and you have to dig down a few levels, but you'll probably get to it through some honest soul-searching.

But in '62 I was interested in getting married and needed a job and so I became a cop.

Five minutes later I was sucked into that culture. It's toxic and it will, in fact, transform you. I became very tainted in no time.

My father was a rabid racist. Every single racial or ethnic slur imaginable would come out of that man's mouth. I thought, "I ain't gonna be that way—I'm just not." Five minutes in uniform, I was. I used excessive force. I used racist language. For the first fourteen or sixteen months on the job, I was as bad as any of them. When I say "bad," in this case I mean that I was writing bad tickets, making false arrests, pulling people over for no legal justification whatsoever. While I never told any blatantly racist jokes characterized by slurs, I laughed at a lot of them. I spent a year undercover in Students for a Democratic Society. There is no excuse for that kind of an assignment in modern police work in America.

A principal prosecutor got to me. He slapped me upside the face, figuratively, after I had described a "drunk driver" who had been arrested who was not drunk. That was very definitely a false arrest. I had nothing to give a judge if he had demanded it.

This prosecutor who stopped me, he said, "Do you believe in the Constitution of the United States? Who the hell do you think you are standing here in the courthouse in your pin-striped suit with your hair slicked back, wearing glasses, looking really cool like a Hollywood star? Who the hell do you think you are? A real cop?"

Oh man, was that awful. I couldn't answer his questions. I just slithered down the stairs of the county courthouse and went down to police headquarters, expecting a call saying, "Officer, you're being taken off the streets for violating the law." It was wrong, just plain wrong to be a cop in a free, democratic society, ostensibly, to do the kinds of things that I was doing.

But the call never came. I'm forever grateful to that prosecutor for not busting me. He could have. That he didn't was really a turning point for me.

There was nothing in my background that said that I was cop material. Some of my critics say that I was playacting and performing. I would accept that, I really would. I was definitely performing the job of a police officer—the *role* of a police officer.

Maud Daudon: He was an unusual police chief in many regards. He wished he could be with the protesters, like he was on the wrong side. His heart seemed to be someplace else, and I never quite understood that. I certainly felt mixed myself but I didn't expect our police chief to feel that.

In my experience working with the police department, the best police officers were those who felt compassion for the people. With the psychological exams you have to have a heart but you have to have this incredible discipline that you kick into when you see danger, when you see a possibility of someone getting injured or hurt or killed. It's a weird combination, and very few people have that kind of core toughness but a really big heart. The best officers that I ever worked with were like that, they were kind of like social service workers with this discipline around weaponry and guns and I thought Norm had that.

Ed Joiner: When Norm decided to retire, I told him that his decision should not be tied to the WTO fiasco. I had the responsibility for our performance, not him. I worked with Norm for six or seven years. We had a number of significant differences relating to our policing philosophies but he always had my back.

Maud Daudon: When I looked back at the end of the week, it was shocking. I was so relieved when those delegates started to get on planes and leave. I was just so happy.

Larry Mayes: The fact that somebody didn't get killed still boggles my mind.

Celia Alario: I was one of the last people to leave Seattle. Part of the reason was that when the Independent Media Center closed, there were all of the tapes. There were already class-action cases forming. We had corporate media outlets that wanted video. We literally had requests like, "Do you have an angle from the southwest corner of Second?"

Jill Freidberg and I were closing down the Independent Media Center. We had all the tapes on a couple of racks on wheels, and as we went outside to bring them to my trunk with the intention of bringing them to her house, we were intercepted by some people who tried to push the cart away from us. We don't know who they were but they were in plain clothes. One of them offered to help, and then the other one just started wrestling for it. So we went back inside the IMC and shut the door and locked it and regrouped. Then we made a plan to get this stuff into my car, and we started doing it by the handfuls more aggressively. We got all the tapes loaded into the back of my car.

When we drove away, we got followed. We started driving around and trying to lose the car, which wasn't even trying to pretend they weren't following us. We were getting more and more nervous and trying to figure out what to do. I reached into my raincoat pocket and I had the business card of the guy who was the local head of the Teamsters, who I had befriended earlier in the week. I was like, "Oh my god, let's call the Teamsters."

They said, "Come over right away. Come to our office. We will help you. We will take care of you. You're going to be fine."

We pulled up to the Teamsters and we unloaded all the tapes into their office. We got the decks that Jill had rented and borrowed for digitizing. We essentially stayed, day and night, at the Teamsters, which was a place where we felt like we could be safe because the Teamsters work all hours and there were always people around. There were big burly guys who were going to protect us if we got into any trouble. We spent two or three weeks digitizing all of the tapes, which, in that era, had to happen in real time. We were reliving corner by corner, street by street, individual affinity group by individual affinity group, from different angles, the entire thing, because we were looking for video for the lawyers, looking for videos for the media. To see the place where pepper spray was first used and to see it from somebody shooting on the roof and somebody shooting from the ground—it was both riveting and totally traumatizing.

Harold Linde: I ended up staying in Seattle for a couple of weeks. I sublet a room and I was doing some writing. It was very cold and dark and I was processing, and had the sense of being alone, a different kind of alone. I went out, ended up at the movies. A film I didn't know anything about called *Fight Club* was playing and I went in. It's Brad Pitt and Edward Norton, organizing these interventions and actions to wake up the Muggles and institute change in this clandestine, highly technical training. I think it reinvigorated the notion or the possibility of democracy as more than just a thought but as an act, as an experience, as world-changing potential—all these people coming together for this reimagined Boston Tea Party, an expression of democracy and sovereignty.

Laurie Brown: I think it was devastating to Paul's reputation. I think it was a large part of why he wasn't reelected.

Pam Schell: There were some people who were in charge of political opinions, people that were respected, Democrats who said, "Paul, you have to apologize for what happened during the WTO meetings." Paul wouldn't do that. He didn't feel that he was responsible for the damage that was done. He wanted to get the damage cleaned up as fast as they could afterward but he felt that his motives absolutely should have worked. Maybe it made a difference in his reelection, I don't know.

Maud Daudon: It was only maybe a year and a half into Paul's term, and we never quite got our footing back. This major event went completely sideways and ate up his political capital. The cities that are the size of Seattle, there's a core group of people that really call the shots. Fortunately, I think it's becoming more transparent, more open, but particularly then you had to have business and labor lined up in your corner. He didn't have that anymore.

Pam Schell: We enjoyed the time he was mayor—we totally enjoyed it. It was a wonderful, wonderful time. He used to have lunches up in his office and different people would come and have a lunch with the mayor, and he'd have me come too, and we'd talk about whatever their issues were. I think back at it being a really good and interesting time, a little amazing.

Every once in a while—because I'm just a simple person—I'll still say, "Oh, yeah, we met with Nelson Mandela—and Clinton." It just seems a little bit unreal, like a story I'll tell.

Maud Daudon: The mayor got a ton of stuff done for the city, like a billion dollars of infrastructure investments done, libraries, community centers, parks, rebuilding the core things that make a city really tick.

Pam Schell: His real passion was that of an urbanist. He didn't know about it when he was young—that's why he originally became a lawyer. But he was always reading Jane Jacobs. That's what he loved.

Maud Daudon: When I was young and getting my business degree I actually interned at Paul's development company. We only had brief encounters then but I remember I was driving with him somewhere and he told me he had run for mayor earlier in his life and lost, and he said, "Probably just as well because my whole thing, if I become mayor, I'm going to be a kamikaze mayor. I'm just going to do what I want to do. I'm going to push as hard as I can to get stuff done. And I don't care if I'm reelected. I really just want to see good stuff happen for this city and I'm kind of tired of nothing ever happening."

So, when he was running again, I said, "Okay, Paul, I remember this conversation, you are going to be a kamikaze mayor."

He said, "Totally. Totally." And that's what he was. He really didn't care about the fallout and yet when the fallout actually happened it really hurt him, I think, to his soul.

I would see him years later, and he would say, "I've gotten over the WTO—but let's talk about the WTO."

It was the first thing he wanted to talk about. It was like, "Do we have to do this, Paul?" It was like therapy for him. It hurt him really bad.

It was really a pleasure to work with him in many ways and yet it was really difficult at times too. It was fun to see him grow in compassion during his time as mayor. He had a great heart and a great mind and, unfortunately, politics were not his forte—fortunately, or unfortunately, I don't know which.

Norm Stamper: I let Paul Schell know that I let him down. I let my cops down. Politics associated with policing major events in a democracy—it's interesting, multilayered, conflicting, contradictory, and inconsistent as hell. I felt heartsick. Schell was not my favorite mayor but I put him in a bad, bad spot. I know damn well I did. He really took unfair criticism because he was out there, day and night. He was a cheerleader for the city. He was a cheerleader for his police department. He said nice things about me and our people. It was unfair to blame a city administrator or politicians for the transgressions and failures of the theoretical experts on crowd control. It's just impossible to do anything worse than some of the stuff that I authorized.

Pam Schell: He was furious with Stamper. Paul just never forgave him because, I mean, what is the mayor supposed to do if the police chief isn't going to back you up?

Charles Mandigo: Shortly after the WTO, Nelson Mandela was coming into Seattle and he was flying into Boeing Airfield, which is underneath the jurisdiction of the sheriff's office. Prior to his arrival, there was a dispute between the mayor and Reichert as to who was going to do the motorcade and do the honorary type of stuff to escort Nelson Mandela from the airport to the city. It got into a heated argument.

Pam Schell: At the Nelson Mandela thing, Paul grabbed Reichert by the shirt collars and shook him.

Dave Reichert: The mayor, the governor, all of us are in a VIP room— for lack of another term. I came in after most everyone was there and we're all preparing for Mandela's arrival. There's media in the room. All of a sudden, Paul Schell comes up to me and called me an arrogant son of a bitch or something like that. I extended my hand and he took it. He told me that I need to stay out of his city and stop chasing innocent kids. I said, "No, they weren't innocent kids, Mayor."

He said, "Yes, they were."

And I said, "Well, maybe we need to have this discussion at another time and in another place. I'd be happy to talk to you."

He said, "Who the fuck would want to talk to you?"

I said, "If you don't want to talk to me about it then we won't talk about it."

He said, "You're an arrogant—" And he's still got my hand!

I said, "Mr. Mayor, I think we should end this conversation." I started to walk around him. He chest-bumps me and wouldn't let me walk around him. The Seattle police detective who's there is like, "Oh, crap." Because the mayor just—technically, by law—assaulted the sheriff. So I stepped back. He still won't let go of my hand.

I said, "Mr. Mayor, I suggest you not do that again."

"Oh, yeah? What are you going to do?"

I said, "Well, let's just go our separate ways."

I go to walk by and—boom!—he hits me again. This time I pulled him close to me and I said, "Mr. Mayor, if you don't let go of my hand, and if you do that one more time, I'm taking you to jail for assault." I whispered it in his ear. I may have said it loud enough for some people nearby to hear. The Seattle detective could see that something was going to happen here pretty quick. He grabbed the mayor and ushered him away from me and put him in a holding room by himself. Everybody in the room was kind of going, "What the hell just happened?"

Charles Mandigo: The relationships got so bad that there were a couple of occasions when I had to be the intermediary for information between Reichert and the chief of police. I'd actually get a phone call from one of them and they'd say, "Hey, I'm not talking to my counterpart. Would you relay this information?"

I once was talking to a sheriff for Los Angeles County and he said, "The difference between a sheriff and a police chief is that the sheriff only has to kiss half the voters' asses once every four years. The chief of police has to kiss the mayor's ass every day, all year."

Laurie Brown: There was a missed opportunity for people to get together and ask, "What did we learn from this? Is there anything that we can share with other cities so that they have a different outcome?" The listening stopped and there was no thought to evaluate the situation. It was all about who did what wrong and who we were going to hang out to dry for this.

Larry Mayes: It never needed to happen. With well-trained, well-equipped, coordinated officers out on the street in overwhelming numbers, with appropriate planning, it just didn't need to happen. What were the results? Millions of dollars in property damage, millions of dollars in lost business revenue, thousands of dollars in city cleanup, a number of injured officers and protesters. There were over six hundred arrests. There were officers out on the street extended hours, without relief, without food, without water, without proper gear. Communications were terrible. Did the city learn anything? No. Nothing. WTO was Paul Schell's Winter of Love. He called it a success and a great example of freedom of speech, and he justified that by saying nobody was killed. That was not because of good planning and execution. Seattle didn't learn anything. I don't mean the Seattle Police Department. I mean, the political leadership, the corporate leadership.

Maud Daudon: We had all these hearings in front of the City Council and people were called to testify about what they'd done, all of which was mostly political theater. There was some substantive good stuff but mostly political theater, which was unfortunate. There was no sincere after-action. It felt like more of a witch hunt atmosphere than it was a "we really want to learn from this" atmosphere. "It wasn't our fault, it was your fault"—we went through that.

Michael Ramos: Afterwards, there was all this assessment of the police. Once the event happened, it was news around the world. But everyone protesting—almost everyone—wanted to point to the issues for which we gathered: the WTO regime, its onerous policies, its inaccessibility, opaqueness, and the need to transform it. We were trying to redirect the conversation. But that wasn't the dominant narrative that we saw in the media.

Pat Davis: I was really disappointed in the media. We had talked to them a lot about what the issues were, what the trade situation was, all of those things which we thought were germane and also really important in Seattle. And there was none of that.

The city did a report blaming us, particularly me. But they had to blame somebody. And why not? We were the host committee.

I think the ministerial did dampen the city's enthusiasm, our feeling of how great we were with trade. The port always used to say we're the closest to Asia—because the world is round. I think we thought we were pretty great. But after that, we didn't parade ourselves quite so much. We still had Boeing. We still had Microsoft. We still had those big companies. But you didn't hear about trade so much.

Maud Daudon: The aftermath was, by far, the worst part. For me, it was so hard to hear the criticism of the Seattle police. I am not a law-and-order person. I'm kind of a centrist person but I had seen them up close in that week—and prior to it—and felt like that was such a misplaced criticism.

Even Paul's political advisers were like, "He should just start criticizing the police. He should blame the police."

I was like, "God, if you do that, I am so out of here. I refuse to be part of this anymore because that is wrong. The police were set up for failure."

Paul probably would have been politically smart at that point in time to blame the police. He didn't. He was the guy in front of the cameras all day—that was a tough job—and he never went there, he just said, "Look, I believe in our police force."

This is the irony: the business community burned him faster than anybody else. Like, "Why weren't you more aggressive?" It was so disappointing. They didn't even stand behind him and say, "Look, this was as good of a job as we could have done under the circumstances." They never said anything kind. It was just a finger-pointing exercise.

Norm Stamper: Council members were getting heat from their constituents: "They didn't plan." We planned and planned and planned, we did, but it was not good enough. If it had worked, it would have been a great plan but it didn't, so it was a bad plan.

Nick Licata: We had twelve hours of hearings; we sat for twelve hours listening to people. I would say the vast majority were more hostile towards the police. But there's a section of our people also concerned about what's happened to Seattle. "It's your fault," that kind of thing.

"Mr. Licata, they're smashing up downtown. You are personally responsible since you supported them."

"You welcomed protesters to Seattle. It's become a sewer."

We used information from the hearing but also did one-on-one interviews. We worked pretty intently. We wanted to make sure the report was complete. We wanted to do our homework for the public. It was a sincere effort.

Norm Stamper: The bottom line is that I blew it. It was the biggest mistake of my career. I tell people that. They say, "I heard you were really critical." Of course, I'm critical! You think criticism is a bad thing? Why don't we learn from every single one of these incidents, every single one of these chapters, not only in our personal lives but our careers and in the lives of organizations? If I have a defensive bone in me, I haven't found it yet. I like to hear about mistakes I've made—maybe not in the moment but after a while. I want to learn from what I've not done so well. The hardest but most important learnings in my life have come from having made mistakes and being corrected by people who were smarter and more experienced, more skilled than I was.

Laurie Brown: There were months of finger-pointing between the council and the mayor's office and the police department. The journalists were keeping it top of mind for people. I don't think it was for the public good. The citizens ended up having less confidence in their city leaders. It didn't stop for a long time. Rather than people looking for lessons that could be learned, they looked for ways to protect their reputations and move their own personal agendas.

Dave Reichert: Norm is very skewed toward the social arm of policing. I'm more of: the law says this, and I'm going to do it. My job is to enforce the law and be compassionate and provide service and protection to the community. I'm not a social worker.

I think Pugel and Stamper had to follow the orders of their mayor. But I have nothing but good things to say about the cops who were out there, just like our deputies and the state troopers. They stood their ground. They took a lot of crap. They were spit on. They were hit, pushed, shoved, and assaulted.

Maud Daudon: There was a big debate about Seattle being too lenient going into it. Should Seattle have just tried to establish the harder boundaries that we eventually got to? I don't think that the City Council would have been supportive of that and they would've pushed back.

Maybe politically that would have been a smart thing for the mayor to do. In the long run he could have said, "Look, I tried to take these measures and I got pushback from the community. I saw what was coming."

Michael Ramos: One of the police captains at the time was a Catholic and we attended the same church. Jim Pugel. I knew him. So they're human beings. The *National Catholic Reporter* covered the protests and Pugel's mom wrote a letter to the editor, defending the police actions in Seattle. It's a small world. But the system they were in needed intense scrutiny because of what they did—the over-the-top, brutal reaction is part of the system.

Charles Mandigo: There wasn't a decision as to any federal investigation of these people. It was looked at as a civil disobedience situation and if there was any follow-up, it was a local matter, not federal.

Jim Pugel: I know there was some misconduct. But for the most part, what I heard from outside agencies—not only the United States but in Europe—they go, "No one died!" Sure, there were a lot of feelings hurt. On all sides. But the downtown business community was pretty proud of us. And all the officers and firefighters and medic units.

Ron Griffin: We got lucky. The sheriff's office had very, very few lawsuits from the public. We had some internal issues that went on. I got called into the King County attorneys, because they had, like, eighteen snippets of video of what they thought was misbehavior and they wanted to find out from me if that was proper or not proper.

So I'm looking at the different vignettes of this activity, takedowns. I'm saying, "No, that was proper. Yeah, that was a little hard but it's okay. That was not too good." We're going through each one and they get to this last one. In the video the officer goes up and hits the person in the side of the head with a baton, like a cue stick, right to the side of her head. I go, "Oh, now that one's not good." And I've got five attorneys around me. Man, they're scribbling fast while I'm talking and I said, "Oh man, that's almost lethal force. That's terrible. It should not have happened that way." And I said, "But."

They said, "Yeah?"

"It's not my guy. Different agency."

Wow, were they relieved.

Dave Reichert: There was one thing that occurred during WTO where one of my officers, Van der Walker, the TV crews were filming him and a group of officers moving down the street. And in the street was a woman, bent over with her back to the deputies. She had a Red

Cross armband and she was leaning over a first aid kit and was about to give first aid to a protester who had fallen. She was opening the first aid kit and Deputy Van der Walker was marching down the street and approached her. I think they were yelling, "Move, move, move!" as they kind of step forward. She didn't move. I don't know if she didn't hear them because she was too intent on what she was doing to help this person but Van der Walker's foot came in contact with her rear end and knocked her forward. That's captured on film. So a complaint is filed and our Internal Investigations Unit conducts an investigation, views the video, and recommended that he be disciplined.

Our investigators determined Deputy Van der Walker kicked her and knocked her over. It was pretty obvious to us. But the union came in and argued with their attorney that it was not a kick but a trip. They replay this video and say he definitely tripped over her, he didn't see her. I wasn't buying it. So I fired him. The news media now is all over this. I was defending all the cops before who were doing all the right things. I didn't think this cop did the right thing. I thought he deserved to lose his job because he assaulted this woman. But the union had a hearing and the mediator, during the hearing, listened to all the evidence and afterwards said, "It's just not conclusive to me that it was a kick." So I was directed to hire him back. But I refused so they sued me. The case went through the appeals process and, eventually, I was ordered by the court to hire him back. I had no choice.

Jim Pugel: The biggest court case was over the large-scale arrests that happened at Westlake Center. There were individual lawsuits against me and the city for failure to train, failure to supervise. But thank god, we kept all our training notes and were able to show the judge, "Look, we tried."

I was in court for five years afterwards. The case over the Westlake arrests was in district federal court. Parts of it were appealed to the Ninth Circuit. Ninth Circuit kicked it back. We had to retestify and finally everyone said, "Screw it."

AIG was the insurer for the city of Seattle. The city is self-insured up to something like $5 million back then, per event. AIG, which later became famous for their collapse, they were on board for everything over the $5 million. And I remember sitting in the judge's chambers and the AIG representative was saying, "We'll just write a check."

And we're saying, "No! We didn't do everything they said we were doing!"

But they just kept saying, "We're done." And they wrote the check.

Dana Schuerholz: It was completely illegal for them to arrest me. I was a credentialed member of the press. I found a lawyer who was taking on different cases from the WTO. We deposed Paul Schell. I was sitting across from him. He had a lawyer, and I had a lawyer. The first thing he did was reach over to me and say, "I'm so sorry that you were arrested." His lawyer was like, "Don't say that!" *Laughs.*

Pam Schell: If you're a mayor, you're never supposed to apologize for anything, right? Because then a lawsuit is there right away, which is really so sad.

Dana Schuerholz: We went through the deposition. I did end up settling for some money, about $9,000.

Celia Alario: There are a number of people who have what they call—still, to this day—their WTO Jacuzzis, because the payout for a lot of those people who had been wrongly arrested was around $3,000 to $5,000. A lot of people bought hot tubs.

Nadine Bloch: I was one of the people who was part of the lawsuit. I got $3,000 and gave it back to the actions that we were doing.

Michael Ramos: The people who were harmed by police during the WTO, most of them had some kind of recourse. But many of the people who suffer from police violence, overreaction, or misuse of power do not have recourse. That was where we could have pivoted more quickly to understand the dynamics of racism and how that was endemic to the system, and to be able to foster change at the local level. We could have seized on the racial dimension of all this through conversation with our brothers and sisters, black and other communities, more readily. In the end, that came later. And they themselves initiated much of the protesting and awareness-building around police misconduct.

Laurie Brown: I have a little bit of PTSD talking about this. When I hear a helicopter overhead to this day it still gives me anxiety. I left the mayor's office in January after the protests.

Paul knew that I had decided to leave because I was so frustrated and disappointed, not that it happened but that people didn't seem to be focused on the right things after it happened.

Pam and Paul had this really wonderful place down in Palm Springs that I would go down to. We were sitting around the fire and the pool one night and he and I were the only ones there and I said, "Paul, I just have to get this off my chest. I have to ask you if you remember me coming in one week before WTO and telling you that I was really afraid that the city wasn't prepared, that we were going to be caught flat-footed and that the police department wasn't staffed up enough?"

He said, "Yes, I remember. What did I say to you? What did I tell you?"

"You told me to go tell Maud. I told you that I had already told Maud."

He said, "Yes, some things, we didn't do so well."

Pam Schell: He was depressed for a while. He was so depressed. He wouldn't talk to me about it so much. I think he wanted to get past it. But you don't heal as fast if you're just trying to get past it. *Long pause.* Inside, he was just devastated forever about it.

Ed Joiner: I remember afterward a meeting at the mayor's office and one of the comments was "You had several incidents where officers overreacted or did things they shouldn't have done."

I said, "You know, you can't expect perfection. It just isn't going to happen unless you're using robots. People have emotions and they're going to react to the stresses they're under." It was very hard on the officers. Particularly the ones that were among that two-hundred-man strike force, the crowd control teams. They were the ones that were confronted with protesters directly. You're getting rocks thrown at you, it's a really difficult situation for them. Very, very high stress. Officers do not like being in those situations but that's part of the job.

Looking at what I should have done: every time officers had a training class for crowd control, I met with them and really talked about calming down tensions. I tried to convey that these are supposed to be peaceful protests. We're not going in expecting violence. In hindsight, I should have had them better prepared for confrontations. That's counterproductive sometimes. You don't want to have them thinking, "Oh, we're going in to fight." Now you get them amped up and to me that's more likely to create situations. It's a psychological thing. Then if it turns out that you've got protests that are relatively mild, you might have officers overreact. It's a fine line. But in hindsight, I think I downplayed it too much—the threat.

Annette Sandberg: We participated in a number of conferences post-WTO about lessons learned. Everything from all the preplanning, maybe better ways of capturing intelligence, better communication, command, post structure—all of those things. A lot of cities did take lessons learned from what we did, mistakes that we made. We probably should have tried to break down that barrier that was becoming very apparent between SPD and the other parts of the law enforcement community. Say, "This is more than just a city thing. It's much larger." Get the governor's office and some of the feds in a room sooner and say, "We need to agree on rules of engagement going into this."

Maud Daudon: We had such a difficult time of it but I actually think it's only more complicated now, not less. You look at what happened during the pandemic and the aftermath of George Floyd and protests across the city.

Nina Narelle: Fucking police riots—that's what we should be talking about. We should be talking about the militarization of a city police department and how that has continued to happen.

Noam Chomsky: The militarization of police is going on all over the West, not just the United States. In England, the Tory government announced that it's going to ban protests if they make noise. In other words, stay home and keep quiet. A lot of techniques have been developed to kettle people and so forth. This is what you expect when protests begin to have an effect. The same in the '60s, as soon as the activism began to have an effect, there's a reaction. They try to contain and control it. In the United States, of course, it goes way back.

I mean, my own early memories are from the Depression and watching security forces beat up women on picket lines outside of textile factories. We have a very violent labor history, much more so than other countries, and it feeds into the current militarization of security forces. In fact, hundreds of American workers were being killed as late as the late 1930s. Even right-wing Europeans weren't fooled by the violence of the crushing of labor here. Right after the First World War, Woodrow Wilson's Red Scare was mainly kicking out of the country a lot of left-wing people, Emma Goldman, Alexander Berg, and many others, but it was primarily directed against labor. The labor movement was just crushed by police and vigilante violence organized by the government. You can see its effects today. When I travel abroad I can give talks at union halls. Can you do that in the United States? Can you find a union hall?

Ron Judd: We were successful even with the police overreacting. There was gain made in that overreacting because their overreacting and the militarization of Seattle sent a more powerful message around the world. "What the hell is going on in Seattle? I thought they were trade-friendly and they now made it a militarized zone—I've got to pay attention to this."

Hilary McQuie: In 2003 or 2004, I was doing medical marijuana organizing and I was up in Seattle for Hempfest, which is really not my scene at all—I hadn't been there in a long time. I go to this party and there's fucking Norm Stamper! And it was actually November 30th! I'm like, "Norm, do you know what day it is?"

He's like, "Yep, it's N30."

And I was like, "We've got to talk." *Laughs.* I asked him who called the shots at different points. It's not like he told me anything new but it was just nice to have that human interaction, human connection. He shared the analysis that the cops made it worse—especially the federal, especially after the 30th—that that kind of military takeover created a lot of unnecessary tension.

What I proposed to him—but honestly didn't follow through with—was that he get out and push back on the fact that all this footage from the Battle of Seattle was being used to justify expenditures for paramilitary equipment. This was a huge travesty and I thought it was an issue that he should consider taking on the road and offering a different point of view. I got his card and said I'd follow up and I didn't because, well, single mom, full-time work. But it was a really nice conversation. I really enjoyed making a connection with him because I always liked him.

Norm Stamper: For five years I defended most of what I did at the WTO protest, the tear gas against nonviolent, nonthreatening protesters—fellow Americans.

Then I did a lot of private apologies and, eventually, made a public apology.

What happened to me? WTO lit the fuse. It ignited me. It changed me. I started to become a left-wing advocate for police reform, there is no question about that. I became a gasbag of a police reformer, traveling all over the country, talking and writing about how toxic the system is.

I'm not an advocate for disbanding the police or defunding the police, as we heard in response to the George Floyd murder. I'm a radical reformist. We need fundamental changes, not tweaking, not PR, not cosmetic. It's got to be real fundamental change. We need to rearrange the way the molecules are organized. If you don't change the structure, you're not changing anything. Structures produce behaviors.

If you're really committed to an authentic community-police partnership, there isn't a protest that doesn't demand that the cops and the community get together and talk about how it should be handled. If we have a more solid day-to-day institutional relationship—and by that I mean the police department decides to cede some of its power to the people—we can make a different model.

I thought we had that going into the WTO. That's how naïve I was. I thought that we had rejected a PR version of community policing and embraced an authentic partnership with the community, not just blind supporters of law enforcement, but in some cases fairly radical critics of law enforcement. I thought that we were a lot further along in my efforts, my dreams, my visions of community policing, embracing the model as a fifty-fifty partnership. Sorry, cops, when you're at the WTO table as an executive in your city looking at various proposals you don't do this alone. You have a responsibility to sit with your partners and discuss policies, practices, tactics, weapons including tear gas, equipment, vehicles—all that becomes community property.

Cops are just not wired for that kind of relationship but I'm convinced that it has to happen if we're going to make any kind of difference. There is nothing that citizens as partners can't be involved in, including hiring. And I really do believe that representatives of citizen population should be paid.

We are the most violent industrialized society on the planet, no question. Police will always be facing really horrible situations. The more we can come together as an ostensibly free and democratic society and agree on how we want to be policed and then recruit, select, train, and equip a police force that deals with protests in such a way that the credibility of the cops is strengthened, not weakened, the better off we will be. That sounds like a pipe dream, I know. Am I really that naïve? Yes, I guess I am. I do believe that it is possible. But it will never work as long as the cops see the world as "we" and "they," "us" and "them." It won't work. "They" are the enemy.

four waters: I think it's important to know that the word *they* was used to set the whole thing up. The reason the WTO protest went all sideways is exactly that word. What happened was the feds came to the Seattle law enforcement organizations, both the city and the sheriff, and said, "'They' are coming. 'They' are going to kill people. 'They' are going to do property damage." This put tens of thousands of people into this giant bucket of people who were coming to hurt people in the city.

Since it is the job of law enforcement to protect people and themselves from the "they" that are coming to hurt them, this set up a dynamic where there was no parsing. Grannies in turtle suits were the same as the Black Bloc. Everybody became the same and everybody was treated as "they." It took me a long time to realize this. It explains a lot about the overreaction to what happened.

Vivian Phillips: I still believe that a white protest takes on a different level of significance. I hate to break it down to race, but it's still there. I cannot tell you how high my blood boiled watching January 6th. My gut says if, in fact, those had been black people storming any capitol, the bloodshed would have been enormous.

Working for the mayor's office cured me in many ways from any interest in public service. I realize the power is never where we really think it is. It's always disseminated into some other areas. I look at the police department. The police chief is not the person who holds the power. The power of the police departments is in the unions and the guilds. Until you can dismantle that system that supports the police department, you're just talking.

To understand the complexities of race in public safety, specifically in police departments, I believe, we have to understand the origins of policing in America. Very few people take the time to understand that policing in America originated with controlling slaves, that the KKK was at the origins of policing in America, that the propaganda about the danger of black people in America has lived beyond 246 years of slavery. When we talk about the blue code, what we're really talking about is the system that was created to keep people oppressed. Not to protect. That's some shiny bullshit that they put on the side of cars. Even if you enter with a desire to serve your community, you enter into a system that is hundreds of years older than you are. Otherwise, how do five black police officers beat and kill a black man in Memphis? How does that happen?

Vandana Shiva: You know the Seattle police were then taken to every part of the world, where they trained the local police. It becomes a seamless global, brutal force, putting down what is the fundamental right of people to speak for freedom, to speak for democracy.

Jim Pugel: I went around teaching other agencies that were having the 2000 Republican and Democratic conventions and then the International Monetary Fund in D.C. Because of what we experienced in Seattle, all these other agencies were a lot better prepared. I taught a class at the FBI Academy at FBI Headquarters. Very interesting to dissect it after it was all over.

Ron Griffin: I started to get inquiries about tactics from police departments. I actually have a slide show. I went out and did this around the country. I went down to California a couple of times, went to Alaska. I talked about different tools, putting the names of the deputies on the back of the helmets, along with their rank, so I could see rank and I

could see names of people when we were in the chaos on the street—
that kind of stuff.

Jim Brunner: I do remember a lot of other cities looking at Seattle
and the lesson they drew was: just smash it. Smash the protests and
instigators before they're able to do anything. Smother it. Which, I
think, leads to questions about the militarization of the police forces.

Helene Cooper: I had some Seattle flashbacks in 2020 with George
Floyd and the protests in Washington. But it's so different now and
part of it is because of the color of the protesters in Seattle versus the
Black Lives Matter people. They had it great in Seattle compared to
the shit that we saw with helicopters overhead, calling in the National
Guard, and shit like that in 2020.

Ron Griffin: I've been retired six years now. I left just shy of thirty-
seven years. I truly could not do it right now. The politics involved
and what's happening with the whole law enforcement piece, I'd have
a very difficult time. Here in the state of Washington, they enacted
some legislation. It's just stripped law enforcement of the ability to do
their job. They actually prevent you from doing police pursuits, minus
a Class A felony. For example, the city of Baring, they get an alarm of
a burglary in progress. They arrive. They got the bad people sitting
right in front of them and the bad people run and jump into a car
and speed off. The law says you can't pursue that. The idea was "Oh,
well—use your investigative leads and track them down later." But the
car was stolen and didn't have any plates; they hid their faces—we're
never going to catch them.

The other big problem is the possibility of taking away indemnified
immunity. No person in their right mind would be in law enforcement without that protection. You've got law enforcement folks that
are being prosecuted for murder and when you read the cases, you
just shake your head. Yes, there are some bad, bad, bad things. I don't
condone that at all. But if you don't have protection at a murder trial,
you're going to spend half a million dollars minimum. Why would
you risk your house, your family, and everything to do the job? This
country, we're not done yet. WTO set the stage for issues for years
and years to come.

John Sellers: We nonviolently shut down the most powerful business meeting that has ever happened on the planet and we did it with people power and discipline. Fifty angry white kids from Eugene are now most of the story. In the moment, they were just a tiny part of the story. Much of the story was stolen from us, much of the Battle of Seattle—because it is largely considered a battle. The protesters came to Seattle, smashed up corporate property, the cops kicked the shit out of them, and they got what they deserved—that's the Battle of Seattle. That's really sad. They've rewritten history because that's not what happened but that's the dominant story.

John Nichols: What was the story of Eugene Victor Debs and his principled opposition to World War One? He got arrested, went to jail. They jailed him in the Atlanta penitentiary. What was the story of the civil rights movement? A noble, nonviolent movement seeking to overturn hundreds of years of enslavement, segregation, Jim Crow, all of the violence and cruelty. And what did it become? A story of Bull Connor turning the fire hoses on young protesters. It's the story of the police not protecting civil rights activists, and, in fact, maybe even being involved in violent assaults on those activists. The Vietnam War protests—again, people seeking to change U.S. foreign policy, proposing a whole new approach to the world, an end to the Cold War, a beginning of an emphasis on diplomacy and peacemaking—being confronted with police officers, National Guard troops. And you finally end up with Kent State and Jackson State, where you have people being shot in the streets.

This is what happens when grassroots movements, that are often led by young people and that really seek to achieve a great deal of change in a very short amount of time, the reaction of power is to say, "No." And the way that power says "no" is with excessive policing. When you seek to change economic and social and political realities, the people who have a lot of control over those economic, social, and political realities are going to respond in a very intense way. They're going to use policing as a tool to try and shut you down, to try to maintain a status quo. It happened in Seattle, there's no question.

four waters: It's really easy to talk about tear gas and rubber bullets and people having their faces smashed in jail and all those things but what happened was really remarkable from an organizing standpoint. We were not training 24/7, but we were training in teams a lot of hours every day. Training in teams really helped because even if everybody wasn't completely trained, enough people in that group were sufficiently trained that they could deescalate. We had this giant organization that was amazing and diverse. We had seniors and grandmas, we had the steelworkers, we had college students—all these different people.

John Zerzan: Seattle was a win. That was cool. Let's go from there. People did go on. In Eugene, we established an information shop. We had a weekly live show on cable-access community TV. We had a pirated radio station. We had all kinds of stuff going on. But that post-Seattle winter, I was quite surprised, to tell you the truth. It wasn't so joyous. It was more nihilist. I was surprised to see it got to the point that there were fight clubs. Not all the time, but even women punching each other. What are you doing? What are you thinking? This is time for a party, not for getting more digressive. That's what it looked like. We were on an upsurge, but when you'd go to these parties, it didn't seem like it. I was baffled by it. That was the moment to be happy but, in my experience, it wasn't really that way too much.

Helene Cooper: I think that it was a movement that was really gaining strength and then September 11th happened, and I think September 11th killed it.

John Sellers: Lockboxes were hugely popular in the '90s. Then 9/11 came along and they started calling us terrorists. I guess they had always called us terrorists but after 9/11 people started believing them, so we stopped doing so many things like that.

Kevin Danaher: The next year we had meetings in the AFL-CIO headquarters in Washington, D.C., where I actually got up out of my seat for John Sweeney, head of the AFL-CIO at the time. He was an Irish guy, bald, overweight. He sat in my seat and around this massive conference table are anarchist groups, environmental groups, church groups. It was a huge umbrella coalition that was going to come out in the fall of 2001 in Washington at the Annual World Bank, IMF meeting and shut it down like we did in Seattle. It was the first time that the AFL-CIO had agreed to get arrested. Top leadership was going to blockade, sit in the streets with the rest of us and get arrested. Then September 11th happened. The AFL-CIO said we can't participate. They backed out. We had the protest but it wasn't anywhere near as effective as it would have been with the AFL-CIO.

Denis Moynihan: On 9/11, I was dressed up because I was going undercover to observe a Zurich security company conference on how to deal with protesters. I was about to go down to glean what I could from this. I was harnessing, to the extent that I could, the straight, white-looking, suited male. I could blend. But it was 9/11. So, yeah, that did not happen that day.

Hilary McQuie: When 9/11 happened, everyone's like, "Oh, we're not going to let this stop us, this doesn't change anything."

I was like, "Yes, this changes everything. We are not going to be able to do the same kind of organizing we've been doing." And we weren't able to do it the same way anymore.

Medea Benjamin: Not only did it become hard to do those kinds of protests but people then started to turn their attention away to try to stop the invasions. That's where I've been stuck for the last twenty years.

Lisa Fithian: September 11th took us back to war, shifted the whole damn thing with the Patriot Act and Homeland Security. That's what I think Seattle brought in and 9/11 accelerated: a new era of police militarization and repression that we've been living with—and it's getting worse.

I did a lot of antiwar work when I was coming up. Antiwar work is really hard to do because they can always win on patriotism on a certain level. They can change that narrative. They know how to control that playing field. There's a way in which I feel like war and militarism is the belly of the beast but capitalism is the heart of the beast.

Kevin Danaher: We had an agreement with *60 Minutes* that they would do a show about the organizing of the protests but, instead, they shifted to property destruction. I did a half-hour interview with a

New York Times reporter and the only quote they used was where I said, "Expecting the WTO to reject capitalism would be like the Cuban government rejecting socialism." That was the quote they used from me. I realized that with corporate media, you're not going to get the kind of coverage that you really want.

Jim Hightower: I think a particular role that we played on the radio was to restate what happened because the media had pretty much trashed it. There was a lot of effort to try to change that narrative, get it away from the idea of those few anarchists and back to the bigger picture of the arguments that were being made. I was on other people's shows. Charlie Rose. He wouldn't have me on at first. But Bill Moyers was on and Moyers said, "You need to have Hightower on." Sure enough, because of that, we got an invitation. Ralph Nader, me, and Bill Greider were on together for thirty minutes. And the next week, Rose had Bill Gates for an hour. *Laughs.* Just to say, "That Hightower thing, that was silly."

Kevin Danaher: You will never hear the word *capitalism* on Main Street TV or radio. I listen to NPR all the time and I never hear the word *capitalism*. That's the name of the economic system. It's not "free enterprise"—that's ideology. It's capitalism. That's what it's called. Under communism in the Soviet Union, people were allowed to use the word *communism*, but we're not allowed to use the word *capitalism*. Try it sometime in a mixed group; use the word *capitalism* in a couple sentences and see how people back away from you.

Celia Alario: There was a moment where the promise of the Independent Media Center was crucial. Instead of there being one IMC in Seattle there were soon hundreds of them.

Denis Moynihan: The Indymedia movement was inspiring and wonderful but it failed in that it's now defunct, essentially. I'll raise hackles by saying that but it's defunct. All the content, twenty-plus years is largely gone. A lot of the Indymedia sites are dead. Hopefully the NSA has it. *Laughs.* But there's no money to sustain it. I'm sure there's hard drives and compromised servers that have all this great content scattered around the world. It went everywhere and then it collapsed.

I was just at a celebration of the IMC that's based in Troy, New York. It's called the Sanctuary for Independent Media, and they actually bought a church. There's another IMC in Urbana-Champaign, Illinois. One of the hallmarks of both of those still-viable IMCs is that they bought a building. You really have to raise money and have a board of directors, and actually have brick and mortar. I'm a little sad that most of it's no more.

Noam Chomsky: Now you have the right-wing media empire that was developed first with talk radio, then with Fox News, Breitbart, the rest of them. It's a huge media propaganda system that didn't exist in the past, and for many people, that's all they know. Listen to Tucker Carlson or any of these other guys, they always sound supremely confident. They've got all kind of facts and figures and why not believe it? Especially when you don't trust institutions anyway, for good reasons, because they're of no use to you. So, you hear it and why not believe that? And you end up with a population that's off in outer space.

One of the effects of the internet and social media has been to wipe out local media. There used to be very good local newspapers. *Boston Globe* was quite a serious newspaper. In fact, it did the best reporting on the Central American wars. Now the *Boston Globe* just has wire services and local news. Same with *San Francisco Chronicle, Detroit Free Press, Los Angeles Times*, they just declined. That's had a very negative effect on reporting. Everybody used to have news bureaus all over the world.

Vandana Shiva: We are living in times where you can have a rally of one million people and the mainstream media won't cover it.

David Taylor: Twitter made organizing worse, because it broke down the interpersonal connections and the dependencies of people and the trust networks of people. With Twitter, you can put a tweet out and thousands of people would show up but those thousands of people aren't operating in this group of ten or fifteen people that are high trust, high focus, high commitment. It doesn't have the same impact. And I was a victim of it. I created the tools. I did all the tech infrastructure for the People's Climate March in 2014. We had 2,000 distributed events and sent a half million text messages around the world. Yeah, it scales better but those people just all got email messages, they never came back together in communities and then had local action groups in their community. Being able to put the things out on social media, people show up but the decision-making ability and the accountability and the infrastructure has all gone away in these mass mobilizations. In some ways, it's what made Occupy so chaotic.

WTO and Occupy were both based on decentralized, nonhierarchical organizing but the affinity group and spokescouncil model has accountability and structure and decision-making ability, while the Occupy model is whoever's there and takes the mic does it.

The people who traveled to Seattle together and did the affinity groups, they all went to their communities and kept organizing together. If the same people could have come together, meeting face-to-face, and built those bonds and those peer relationships in those 2,000 cities that participated in the climate march, the impact would have been exponentially stronger.

The technology enables us to scale but it doesn't enable us to deepen and we don't invest in deepening. The deepening is hard and expensive and difficult and we get lazy about it. If I had gotten a text message to show up to the WTO, I would've showed up but I spent six months of my life—I've spent the *rest* of my life doing political organizing. I don't think I would've had that personal transformation unless I had that depth. Personal transformation on the individual level is a huge part of what creates the level of political commitment for people to keep doing that work over time. Tech facilitates the process but it doesn't facilitate the connection and the commitment.

Jim Hightower: The Occupy Wall Street movement, of course, came out of Seattle. And then the Occupy protesters got criticized: "They won nothing, they've made this big fight and they won nothing." In fact, they put Wall Street on the political table in America for the first time since the 1920s, and suddenly it was okay to go after Wall Street. Then we had candidates begin to do that. So that was a huge step forward. And that came right out of Seattle. The same arrogance that led to Seattle then led to Occupy Wall Street, and then led to the movements that flowed out of that.

Noam Chomsky: Power systems are not going to abandon their power freely. It has to be taken away from them, and that's going to be by constant struggle. Seattle set the stage for the Occupy movement, and Sanders's movement pretty much came out of Seattle. The idea of radical inequality, which had barely been discussed before, became kind of a cliché after Occupy—one percent, all those things matter. That's constant struggle. Carry out an action, you might not get immediate consequences but it lays the basis for moving on.

David Solnit: Occupy demonstrated some continuity with Seattle in that they had language of the ninety-nine percent and the confrontational tactics but they launched themselves with a single tactic, a bad decision-making model. They were wildly successful in terms of creating a space to demonstrate rebellion but in terms of building a long-term movement that can actually shift things, they had some bad DNA and hadn't learned lessons from Seattle.

Those of us in the Direct Action Network didn't do a great job of analyzing what we did and putting it out there.

Lisa Fithian: If you want change, go shut down a building. Use your power while you have it. It's not enough to just show up. It's like the Women's March after Trump was elected. Million people in D.C. We were just meandering all over, after going to the trouble and expense of mobilizing all those people. One thing I've learned is that no matter what your primary strategy is for organizing, whether it's electoral or regulatory or community organizing, when you're in a fight, if you can figure out how to bring direct action into your tactics your chances of winning are so much greater. It pressurizes things in a way that helps.

Jello Biafra: I still stress that everybody can become the media now and it's both the best part and the worst part of the digital age. It also means going one-on-one and not just blogging to echo chambers of people who agree with you, but going out in the world and actually talking to people. That's really what becoming the media is. One-on-one, eye-to-eye, face-to-face with people who don't agree with you—family, school, work.

Dan Seligman: I think that the failure of the Democratic Party, dismissing the protests in Seattle, laid the ground for a whole series of problems: the political eclipse of the United States by China, Trump, hollowing of the middle class—it's a wide cascade of adverse effects. There's a whole string of consequences that flowed from the process of globalization, the policy process that the Clinton administration picked up and accelerated. I think we're living in a world that was created in the decade of the '90s. I view the Seattle protests as kind of the cry in the night, you know, this is coming—beware.

Noam Chomsky: The general effect of Seattle was to bring to large public attention the really harmful effect of the Clinton neoliberal globalization programs, an extension of Reagan's class war, carrying it forward against the American working class, and the poor, and the middle class. It began to give an appreciation of what is being done to us. It was in the carefully designed industrialization of America. You find it in the Rust Belt, the voters for Trump. Voting for Trump is suicidal but you can easily understand it. They've simply been betrayed by everyone, particularly the Democrats. But at the time of Seattle, this was not much discussed. Take a look at the nature of NAFTA and the WTO arrangements. It was implicit in their design that these would-be investor rights agreements with enormous protection for private power and it would crush the American working class. It was the nature of their design.

One thing this leads to is a correct sense that we can't trust the institutions, and that can go in two directions. One can open the door to demagogues of the Trump variety, saying, "Follow me, I'll take care of you, on to fascism." The other way it could lead is to, "Let's get organized and act, do something constructive to overcome this." There's a little of each now. Too much of the first, unfortunately—Seattle certainly opened the door to that.

Victor Menotti: The progressive critique of globalization, the WTO, it's just been totally forgotten. Today, if you do criticize it, you're quickly viewed as a Trumpist in some way.

Nick Licata: Republicans talk about globalization. Democrats do as well but they're not as overly critical because there's still a portion of the Democratic Party and liberals in general that say, "Globalization has negative impacts but, overall, it's good, so we have to learn how to work with it, enlarge it."

Ralph Nader: When I was running for president, I made the trade thing front and center. It was off the table by both Republican and Democratic candidates.

John Nichols: There's no question that Ralph Nader's 2000 presidential campaign extended from what you saw in Seattle. People can like Nader or dislike him, they can agree with him or disagree with him, but there's simply no question that his 2000 campaign was essentially Seattle taken to the ballot box, to the polling place—with success or failure, depending on how you measure such things. He wasn't alone. There were a lot of members of Congress, like Dennis Kucinich and Paul Wellstone, who came and who were moved by what they saw.

Dan Seligman: The Clinton model went a different direction. Mistrust of the Clintons is rooted in that shift. It's not just made up out of blue smoke. I was talking to this guy who is a construction supervisor in my neighborhood and asked why he hated the Clintons so much. He ticked off a bunch of things about trade, NAFTA. He wasn't super-educated but he was right about the essence of what they did and why he didn't like it and the effect on his family and that his kid can't get a union card and he can't hand down to his family what he had.

Clinton redefined the role of the state. The FDR state was really about leaning against the excesses of the market. And Clinton, in a big way, accelerated the marketization of society. The '90s are a consequential decade as a result. The parties themselves have changed in their composition.

Noam Chomsky: There was a fairly substantial constituency of white working class who voted for Obama, believing his promises. Didn't take long to realize it was a total fraud. By 2010, two years later, in the election in Massachusetts for Ted Kennedy's seat, who had died, even union workers didn't vote Democratic. They'd realized that Obama had just screwed them, and after that it goes straight off to Trump.

Denis Moynihan: It's unfortunate that the greatest WTO critic is Donald Trump, who is using this kind of nativist argument. Not the type of arguments we were making, that this is ruining the planet and subjugating people around the world to almost slavelike conditions. He is essentially making racist arguments against global trade. The critique of global capitalism is almost owned by the far right now.

Lori Wallach: When we look at the broader fight about corporate power, I think Seattle was a moment when, in the U.S., people who had been 1980s-Reagan-focused suddenly had this breakthrough where it wasn't just the radical lefties who were saying, "These corporations have too much power." It wasn't where we are now, where you can get the two-time Trump-voting Texas Republican white man and a hippie chick from Seattle and they both agree that these corporations have too much power. That was not where we were then, but I think it was the beginning of that.

Colin Hines: What globalization does is it increases people's insecurity, which, of course, is the populist dream.

Medea Benjamin: I've got a lot of relatives who think very differently than I do. To this day they are Trump supporters, but I love talking to them because I love hearing how they feel and why they feel that way. It's important for us to listen and understand, especially when the Democratic Party has lost so much of its working-people base. We've got to be much more open to listening and understanding where people are at and not expecting that everyone will agree with us on one hundred percent of our issues.

Mike Dolan: I have always been willing to discuss the left-right coalition that was in Seattle. I think it addresses a lot of the polarization today. It redefines populism in some ways. There's a third rail in the progressive conversation about anticorporate globalization and free trade, and the third rail is "Well, Trump didn't do everything wrong, getting out of NAFTA." There is a populist response—both on the conservative side and on the progressive side—to globalization and it's still part of the conversation today.

The year after Seattle, when it looked like China would join the

WTO, that was a big fight where left and right came together, where the Teamsters invited Pat Buchanan to stand up on their podium in front of the Capitol. Look, I worry about Marine Le Pen and I worry about the immigration angles and racism, I worry about all the rest but I just think that if the anti-globalization movement is going to have legs, politically, we have to figure out what the left-right coalition looks like. I think that in the spirit of Seattle, you have to open up the tent and find the common ground in fighting corporate globalization.

four waters: It's so easy, especially right now, to say things about an entire bucket of people instead of treating them like humans. When you do that to someone, they respond the way you would respond if you were put in that place. I think that speaks a little bit to what's going on now, which is that liberals and conservatives aren't speaking to each other as human beings, they're speaking to each other as buckets of issues. We need to back up a little bit, which is not easy because when you're angry, you want to punch somebody, but back up and have a different conversation. There are people that you're not going to change who are just cruel and egotistical and narcissistic and focused on their own ideas, but most people are human and if you treat them like humans, you can build a relationship with them.

Colin Hines: The thing that's worrying sometimes about young activists is they're not concentrating on the power structure and the systemic change, which is what you've got to do. There are still a lot of culture wars, which I think is a very clever move by the right. In the U.K., the right is always saying something about the "woke culture." I've got kids now in their thirties and I'm in my seventies. Often we have these discussions and the phrase they use is "You can't say that."

And I think, "Well, actually I can say that." *Laughs.* "And here's why I think so . . ."

But it is a worry because we aren't going to get big changes just from one little sliver of society doing it. We have got to get the majority of society, particularly when people really are realizing things are bad. They don't trust governments anymore. They certainly don't trust banks anymore. The old "free market" stuff is disappearing. I've always said that you need everything from left to small-*c* conservatives. I like small-*c* conservatives! They're localists. The word *conservative* has the word *conserve* in it. It's obviously been utterly corrupted and stolen by the elite bastards, the millionaires and billionaires that run our place.

Obviously, it's cozier to be with people who say the same things. But you've got to extend out and get a wide swath of people interested. You won't do that by tutting at them. The culture stuff is whipped up a lot by the different world of communication now. Just think about how fast things can be perverted and misused.

Medea Benjamin: I think this whole idea that we have to be homogeneous in the way we talk about things is ridiculous, learning the right language to use, being afraid to say something wrong. I had daughters in college who were afraid to speak out in their classes because they were afraid that they would use the wrong language and then be "canceled."

The whole cancel culture and the #MeToo movement, everything went too far. What's so hypocritical to me is that we say that we want prison abolition and people are not as bad as the worst deed they've committed and yet we are willing to cancel people for one thing they did wrong. Their crime makes them not part of our community anymore. Where is the redemption? Where is the forgiveness? How are we educating people and moving them along? There is a lot of rigidity that keeps us from working together. Groups are more fractured now. They're working on more individual issues. For all the talk about intersectionality, there is not as much as there was back then.

Noam Chomsky: The United States does not have a continuing left tradition. Everything always starts from Europe. In Europe, you have the socialist parties, communist parties, labor unions that have a tradition—you remember how you did things in the past, you can learn from it and do it the next time. In the United States, everything starts from zero. Just mostly young people saying, "What can we do? Let's try this, let's try that." Every single movement is like that. Extinction Rebellion in London, when they went after closing the subways, that harmed their movement. They were harming people who just had to get to work, and that turned people against what they were doing. That was the wrong kind of tactic. You have to constantly think, what's the effect going to be on the audience that you're trying to reach?

four waters: I think part of the challenge now is that there is less training. That's the difference between what protests look like now and what protests looked like then. The most important thing you can do is teach people what the mechanisms look like behind the scenes so they understand what is important, what is being judged, where the levers of power are, how they can engage with those levers of power, how they can get around those levers of power, how they can reproduce those levers of power in ways that produce a strategic result.

David Taylor: One thing I really wanted to do after Seattle was form more consistent infrastructure across the national Direct Action Network but the people that were involved did not want to because they were so antihierarchy. I was like, "But this is how we have to build power." So I think the anarchist, direct action organizing is not capable of building power; they're capable of executing tactics. Power-building in the radical communities is deeply important and it's a very hard political project. We weren't able to do it because the fear of hierarchy and power consolidation was so great but you're not going to win anything without building power on the radical left. The radical left managed to do that all over South America and all over other parts of the world, but the movements never have been mature enough in the United States. They were mature enough to have moments of tactical success that were important but never moments of political consolidation like you've been able to see in places like Argentina or Ecuador, or all of these other Latin American movements. Part of that's because we don't have the political traditions; part of it is just a lack of maturity within the movements.

Ralph Nader: Year after year, the left, they couldn't get over their giddiness about Seattle. "Oh, remember Seattle." It's what I call the self-enforced satiety of the left. What they do is generate one good demonstration and they lunch off it. They've incorporated it as part of their civic ego, and they can't let it go. They keep regaling it as though it were Lexington and Concord. Then they went fishing. That is a trait of the left. They get a big demonstration and they're so giddy about it, months later, they don't know how to extend it.

Most of the people on the left never want to admit they're powerless. Because they are powerless. The first trait you have to have as a civic advocate when you're powerless is to publicize it. That's the only way you can turn it around. One, it drives you. It shames you. In the other direction, it says to Congress, "Why are you rendering the people powerless? Why are you rendering the victims of these agreements powerless?" The hollowed-out communities in the Midwest, the workers who lost their jobs. The left cannot admit it and, as a result, they remain powerless. They brag about the most minimal victories.

James P. Hoffa: I'm from Michigan so you have a tradition of unions. You have the UAW, you have the Teamsters. For many people it's "My dad worked with the Teamsters." Or "My dad drove a truck." Or "My dad worked at Ford or Chrysler or General Motors." There's a tradition that they know about but that's not the case when you hit other parts of the country where there's right-to-work laws or a lack of any tradition of unionism. When you meet somebody that has no union ideas about his family, the father never talked about it at the dinner table, then they don't know anything about it. And we don't teach labor in history. People don't know about unions. I've had people say, "What's a Teamster? What's a union?" I've run into that a number of times. We're not teaching it, it's not getting out.

Hilary McQuie: I think some overemphasized the direct action and didn't understand the value of the inside-outside piece, didn't understand the value of the NGOs and all the public education that they did to set the stage so that the community actually understood—having yard signs and all that kind of classic organizing, which was really present. The direct action stuff is so sexy and it gets all the cameras. But people didn't understand all the different pieces that went into it.

Pascal Lamy: History will say that Seattle failed because the demonstrators were against people who were ready to agree. That's totally nuts! The people inside were not ready to agree. There was nothing like a sort of taking of ground outside that created a dynamic indoors.

Mike Dolan: The reason why Seattle's a turning point in the larger conversations around globalization is because of those synergies, that amazing alchemy of inside and outside and all those different perspectives.

I would never suggest that I'm the reason why the WTO failed in the fall of '99. Nobody gets to say that. If it had just been me and there hadn't been a Solnit or a Sellers, then it just would have been permitted marches and symposia and those good radio shows. It wouldn't have been nothing but it wouldn't have been what it was.

Similarly, if it had just been the Black Bloc and the Ruckus Society and nothing going on in the inside and no NGO involvement, engagement like that, then it would have been just that. The reason why it couldn't be dismissed by the international press is that it was all of those things. That's where the alchemy is. The whole was greater than the sum of its parts.

Nadine Bloch: A lot of people are what I call "sunshine activists," like, "It's easy to show up, you can pay your fifty bucks, spend the night in jail. That's the worst that will happen to you," or "Sign this petition and it will be really meaningful." We don't support people in understanding the real risks because in the U.S. we're so privileged in the lack of repercussions particularly as white people. Black folks, folks of color, trans folks, other marginalized folks know that's not quite true. This has been a problem in the privileged, middle-class, upper-middle-class, white activist community for a long time.

four waters: The WTO protest was a white movement. That is not exclusive to the WTO. One of the more shocking things to me when I got to Humboldt during the Timber Wars was realizing that most of those activists were on hiatus from college. They all came because they had the choice to not work, to leave college and to spend time protesting. To have that inherently means that you are not from a disadvantaged household. If you have to earn your living and you are responsible for your family, that's totally not an option.

Nina Narelle: It was overwhelmingly white. A lot of people who were connected to Ruckus, much like the environmental movement itself, it was largely white, middle-class, highly educated people who were pretty radicalized around issues with the environment, climate change, and deforestation. Without having a really explicit racial justice analysis or any racialized awareness at all of what social justice movements should look like, inevitably it was mostly white people organizing other white people.

Shortly after Seattle, we had a camp outside of L.A. in advance of the Democratic and Republican National Conventions. The idea was to have a camp where all the community organizers could come and see how things were done in Seattle. We said, "We have resources, equipment, direct action training, radios, medics. How do you want to do it?"

They said, "The fuck?" It was all communities of color. They were like, "First of all, get your shit together. Second of all, how dare you think that you're going to come into our communities where we fucking organize with your fucking white dog-and-pony show. Get the fuck out of here! Also: we need you. We need all your resources. We need all the fucking attention. Get your shit together right the fuck now because we need a movement for social justice. What are you doing? You're a mess!"

I was like, "You're right! You're fucking right!"

I'm so grateful for that experience and particularly for the organizers, the people of color working in communities of color who either directly through conversations or through their movement-building work were like, "I need you. I need you to get your shit together!" It wasn't like I was canceled. They were like, "In fact, if you collapse into a corner, we will be pissed because we don't have time for that!" I'm so grateful for the people at that point in time in my life who were just so fucking direct and clearsighted.

John Sellers: There was a lack of racial diversity in the streets of Seattle—but not a complete lack. There were a lot of people of color there and I don't want to erase them. The anti-globalization movement, the global justice movement in the United States which was calling itself the global justice movement, was pretty white, honestly. Getting called out afterwards was important. We grappled a bunch. When you say, "This is what democracy looks like" and you're mostly white people, it sends a weird message to everybody else.

We started working to bring more racial diversity into Ruckus itself. We got some things right in that process. We got some things wrong. We got called out. We had interventions. We had some camps that were pretty challenging for people of color, for white people who were getting called out. We kept fucking up, then doing the right thing, fucking up, then doing the right thing. We kept going forward.

Yalonda Sinde: It wasn't as diverse as it could have been in terms of the larger picture. But there were parts of the march that you could see the diversity on different blocks because the way it merged is that people were coming in from different parts of the city. So it looked like different races of people were separated. But after a while they mushed all together. But if someone went to one side of town and saw, "Okay, here's the Nature Conservancy," they see that section and are like, "Oh, where's the diversity?" Look at the other block!

Michael Ramos: There's a poet named Patrick Chamoiseau. He wrote a book called *Migrant Brothers* and he talks about what he calls in terms of immigration policy—and I would call in terms of the trade regime—"dis-humanity." It's not just inhumanity. It is really actions that counter our humanity, at the individual level but also at a collective level. In the face of that, he posits a new term—he's a poet, after all—called *globality*. It's that sense of global awareness, that we're all connected, even if we think we're not. What we do in our policies affects people in other parts of the world. Unless we're listening to them, we will have missed something necessary for our own humanity and what we need to bind ourselves together as one common people. The protests helped make that connection between the dis-humanity that's practiced in WTO policies and the globality to which we aspire.

Ralph Nader: In subsequent meetings of the same trade reps, the protesters couldn't even get within half a mile. They went to Canada and barricaded half a mile away from the venue. Then they went to Doha. They never got close again. The governments and corporations decided that they were not going to let protesters stand near the venue or march or picket or sing or roar.

Victor Menotti: The WTO will never be invited to the U.S. or never again have such a summit in a place that isn't totally secure, like Doha, where they went two years after Seattle. Shrinking the space for civil society participation is definitely part of the plan. All that street heat changes the way decision-makers behave. It's like they know they're not acting in the dark. They know their decisions will be scrutinized. They know there'll be some degree of accountability.

Vicente Paolo Yu: The next ministerial in Doha was a completely different game. You simply could not risk protesting outside unless you wanted to be thrown into a Qatari jail.

Of course, the difficulty with Doha was that it had just happened after 9/11 and so you also had this whole dynamic about the U.S. saying, "We cannot afford to let this collapse," and then a lot of the things that the U.S. also wanted got into the Doha ministerial declaration because you also had this dynamic at the time of "If you're not saying yes to what the U.S. wanted then you're essentially agreeing with whoever attacked the U.S. on 9/11."

The positioning of the U.S. at the time was these issues are crucial for the global trade multilateral system because this will show that civilization continues, that the world continues and we are not bowing down to terrorists. Therefore, you know you have to make Doha a success. That was the whole dynamic.

Pascal Lamy: During the Plan B conference that took place in Doha a few years later, I got the mandate on fishery subsidies which led, twenty years later, to the fishery agreement. But we did not get the social side included in the agreement. We did get overfishing included because overfishing is a problem for everybody, whereas social rights—social security systems and unemployment benefits and maternity leave—is something that is much more of a local problem than depleting fishery resources.

I think the explanation for the failure of Seattle is that countries did not agree. The WTO works on a very expired model which I think is being redeveloped, which is that if there is no consensus then you can't move. In simple terms, Seattle failed because there was no agreement. The reason there was no agreement was because the principle, at the time, was that until everyone is agreed, nothing is agreed.

Vandana Shiva: The next ministerial was totally under military operation. I went but our visas were given from Geneva. They weren't given from Qatar. At the Doha ministerial, it was U.S. military ships and there were constantly helicopters going overhead. It was really a military operation. By then the suicides of farmers had started in India. The suicides of farmers in India, that became big in Doha.

Lisa Fithian: We won again in Cancún in 2003. A lot of it because of the sacrifice of the farmworker, Lee Kyoung Hae, who killed himself. It's really important for people to understand that we don't have to accept things the way they are.

Vandana Shiva: In Cancún, there was this giant-sized fence separating the civil society representatives from the government and corporate delegates at the ministerial, and Lee climbed on top of the fence. He had a suicide note and he stabbed himself to death. He said, "I commit suicide so that the world wakes up to watch the WTO." And he had a placard saying, "WTO kills farmers."

Vicente Paolo Yu: Korea overcommitted in terms of liberalizing their agricultural sector, which essentially led to their wiping out a lot of small Korean farmers. I remember seeing the protests there in Cancún. They were very, very impressive. The Korean protesters were among the most impressive that I saw because they had this tactic of smashing through police barriers where they used humans as battering rams. When I spoke to some of them, they said they learned it during protest days against the South Korean dictatorship, Park Chung Hee, back in the '70s. They would form an attack column of fifty strong, arranged in ranks, and the first two ranks of people would be lifted up by the people behind them with the first two ranks lifting their legs up as battering rams. They would run full tilt at the police shields and would smash through and then you'd have this next cohort coming in and widening the breach. It was quite impressive.

José Bové: I went with them, the people of Korea, when we blocked the WTO meeting. The farmers' movement was really in the center of the organization and I think this will be a new thing in the world, the capacity of the farmers to have very strong links together even if they were living in completely different countries. Because we were fighting for the same ideas to change the agricultural policies, to take the "free trade" out of agriculture. It's like what happened in the nine-teenth century when the workers of the world tried to build together international movements of workers. We made the same thing at the agricultural level. And what we are seeing now with the climate change, with the problem of water, the problem of pesticides, and the problem of the big companies that have food patents—thirty years ago, peo-ple and the government were thinking that we were completely crazy talking about these subjects. It's fact now at the international level, the scientists recognize clearly what we were saying.

Lori Wallach: The WTO is on life support. It's an organization that has never reestablished its legitimacy from Seattle. We blew up the agreement, things that we were told, "It's happening, there is no alter-native, get the fuck out of the way!" The myth that the U.S. popula-tion was the beneficiary and that they loved it—the PR that was being sold around the world—the whole idea of the golden handcuffs, "It sucks, but it's going to make you rich"—you could see all around the world that that was a cracked ship because there were 50,000 people, mostly Americans who don't protest about anything, out in the driving rain on the warpath over an acronym.

Celia Alario: It was such a miscalculation on the part of the World Trade Organization. It was such a massive overstep. What they were asking for was so egregious that it was mythic. They painted them-selves into a Star Wars–style mythic battle. Anybody who cared about pretty much anything were the rebel alliance, and they were the bad guys.

Pascal Lamy: The people demonstrating in the streets were basically demonstrating that trade is bad for developing countries but years later it's pretty clear that trade was good for developing countries and maybe less good for developed countries that do not have a social wel-fare system.

We've had over two decades of distance. The paradox of those who, at the time, said—sometimes violently—to stop opening trade because it's terrible for developing countries got it wrong. We have a problem that exists: the road to hell is paved with good intentions.

Ralph Nader: The WTO is in total shambles. It's a treaty that looks like Swiss cheese. Everybody is violating it with total impunity. They're not even bringing cases against each other anymore hardly. That's the way to get it repealed—and that should be the strategy, to repeal it, get rid of it.

Victor Menotti: It's still there. The WTO regime exists and it survives. That system of rules is what drives capital and commodities every day. It's still hanging over policymakers' heads whenever they have to think about what they need to do to protect jobs or environment or save the planet or a fair economy.

Helene Cooper: The whole free trade movement, I thought it was a juggernaut that couldn't be stopped. I think Seattle taught me better. That it could be at the very least slowed. It's definitely been stymied in many, many ways and it's partly because of the environmental concerns and the labor concerns. The WTO is weakened. You have so many workers who feel they've been betrayed by NAFTA and by the WTO and by seeing their jobs go overseas.

Noam Chomsky: Right now the WTO is eroding, largely under U.S. pressure. The U.S. is moving towards a kind of nationalistic mercantilism, which is hitting Europe very hard. The U.S. is violating straight out many WTO provisions by now, and I think the whole world is on a cusp where it's not clear where it's going to go.

James P. Hoffa: Much to our favor, jobs are coming back to the United States because they don't want the instability of these long supply lines that were interrupted by Covid, interrupted by the Ukraine war, interrupted by the instability in China and all the sanctions on Russia. The world's in turmoil right now because there's so many things going on. You see a lot of people have a new word, it's called *reshoring*. There used to be "offshoring" and we're now calling it reshoring. It's a Wall Street buzzword. People are saying, "We want to have our supplies close by."

Pascal Lamy: The protectionism which the U.S. has now taken, they have, de facto, left the WTO. There is zero difference between Trump and Biden on the view they have of the WTO. Plan A is to have the U.S. back in the WTO in a more meaningful way. The Inflation Reduction Act, Chinese-like green plan is a bad thing. Green with subsidies is what the U.S. and China should not do because it's unfair competition and violence on the playing field.

Lots of people think that one day we will have a system where you have an understanding among countries that trade opening remains the way to go, that protectionism is not the thing to do.

José Bové: Ten years after Seattle I was elected as a European Parliamenteur for the Green Group at the European level. I was there as a farmer, so my mobilization side of the European environment was clearly on the agricultural issues—GMOs, food sovereignty, fighting against the big lobbies, against globalization.

I went to Canada to a meeting—links between farmers, unions, workers, and so on—and they blocked me saying, "You're not allowed to come inside Canada." It was quite interesting because I was member of the European Parliament. Of course it was a big mess in Canada because I was not allowed to come in and everything was waiting for me—a conference and meetings and so on—and at the end they had to let me come in.

Then in 2006 I had a meeting in New York with all the organization and the workers from Monsanto and people fighting against GMOs and I was officially invited and when I was at the airport, they refused to let me come inside the United States, saying that I'd been sentenced so many times for the dismantling of McDonald's and for GMO demonstrations in past year and so now I was forbidden to come inside, and they kicked me out, put me in the plane to go back.

After the free agreements between the United States, Canada, and Mexico, these countries decided that I'm not allowed to come inside of their countries. As Canada is a member of the Commonwealth, all the countries in the Commonwealth say that I'm not allowed to come inside of their countries, even if I ask only to get in an airplane and to take another plane for another country, I'm not allowed to do it. This is completely crazy. This is still about free trade and the big business of the international companies.

Ralph Nader: Corporations always know how to bounce back. They have the stamina of being an artificial entity driven by one value system: maximum sales and profits.

Tetteh Hormeku: We still have the transnational corporations from the North, still trying to protect their interests and operate in the South. And we have the groups in the South saying, "No." As to whether or not civil society organizations and citizens have still got a fire in their belly to continue to resist, that is the issue. But the top corporations are not sleeping. They are there to open many, many more avenues. We used to only have big cars and big pharma. Now we have big tech—big this, big that. They all want the same thing. They do not change. So we also have to continue and make sure that we keep on fighting against that.

four waters: As globalization has become more of a thing, wealth has consolidated and power has consolidated and it has become a bigger issue by a long shot than it was at the WTO protest. Yes, we shut down the meeting but we did not change the trajectory of this problem in general. I think that it's significantly worse. The nexus between globalization and climate change, planet overpopulation and how we deal with the care and capacity of the planet will be one of the most challenging conflicts over the next one hundred years.

Jello Biafra: You can visualize the tank of new corporate feudalism which has been slowly but surely moving forward and crushing as it goes—at least since Reagan, maybe even since Carter. Every once in a while, they step on the gas. Like with 9/11, they step on the gas. Trump gets in, they step on the gas; January 6th and a whole new crop of reactionary, wannabe neo-Nazis, they're really stepping on the gas. What choice do we have but to fight like a cat in the corner?

Mike Dolan: I'm not sure that participatory democracy at a grand scale is going to achieve the solutions to global warming, for example, in a process. I don't know if we have time for all the process. But if we can localize down to the county and state and regional levels and shorten our supply chains, if we can bring our economies into some sustainable, coherent local control—that's what both conservatives and progressives can agree is good. I try to find the floor, the thing that we agree on. We can talk about it in a way that makes sense to both of us. That's always the challenge in any political conversation.

Seattle represents a moment when the elite Washington consensus around neoliberalism was really genuinely shaken. That whole order was challenged successfully at an intellectual level—not to mention at the street—but at an intellectual level for the first time in the U.S. in a real way. If the conservative side wants a piece of that, you're welcome to it. It's no longer a D-versus-R issue. It becomes a corporate-versus-anticorporate issue.

Suzanne Savoie: We had an opportunity to bring globalization to the world, and we did. We succeeded bringing attention to issues that were not getting attention. We were part of a global movement, not just sitting at home feeling very disempowered by all the powers in the world that you have no control over. You actually felt like you were there with other people, making an impact. It was a very powerful emotional experience that felt very positive at the time. People speak a lot about intersectionality these days and the WTO protests were the epitome of intersectionality. There were so many different groups, from indigenous tribes and different cultural groups, labor issues, environmental issues—the intersectionality was very strong there.

Vandana Shiva: It was wonderful because no one engineered this convergence. It was an emergent phenomenon. It brought people of concern together who would never have worked together. That was what was to me the miracle of Seattle. The miracle of Seattle was the way organisms evolve. Molecules and cells get together and before you know it, you have a tree. Before you know it, you have a human being. That's what Seattle was.

John Nichols: Seattle ushered in a new era of protests, a new vision for how you did protests. It wasn't just the core circle of activists around a single issue. You now expanded and you have very broad coalitions, and you have respect for the people that were in those coalitions. You basically taught people how to get along, how to work with one another. It's the concept of Teamsters and turtles. That new vision of how to do protests was, in some ways, as important as any identifiable accomplishment. People started to think differently about how they organized and how they protested and maybe imagined that they could win.

Jello Biafra: You know, we're never going to "win." It's an ongoing thing. Freedom isn't free. Right when you think you've won, here comes Trump and Satan and the rest of them to roll it all back again. You've got to fight all over again just to make sure somebody can learn about their own people in a schoolbook. It's just nuts.

Some people just don't want to get involved. They just think it's going to take too much out of them. But doing something is better than doing nothing. Always.

Chie Abad: Keep fighting with corporations and all injustices. Keep working. Spread the word. Educate, agitate, motivate, and then organize. There's no victory. You have to keep working.

Lisa Fithian: Many people in this country don't really have a good sense of what freedom is. White people, they don't. There's a freedom that we have as white people that makes us not even aware that we have some freedoms. I feel like Seattle gave people a sense of freedom and power and life, that I'm sure motivated thousands of people towards a lifetime of continuing in this way. Ain't no power like the power of people because the power of the people don't stop.

Lori Wallach: The part of globalization that is great is the people's globalization.

Colin Hines: When I'm out to chat with young people at demonstrations, it is very heartening. No, they don't know about Seattle, but they *care*. I think it's important to know what's happening in the past but the first step is the *caring*. I'm always kind of optimistic. Recently, I was trying to get some money to do some research and one of the people from a trust said, "Well, you've been doing this for a very long time"—putting it mildly. *Laughs.* "Don't you ever get depressed about how you can keep going and nothing seems to be working?"

And I said, "Well, I like musicals. And I always think of the concept of 'ram dam.'"

He looked at me quizzically.

I said, "There's a wonderful song called 'High Hopes.' And the ram dam principle is as follows: 'Just what makes that little old ram think it can punch a hole in the dam? Anyone knows a ram can't . . . but he's got high hopes.' Then, it ends brilliantly: 'Whoops, there goes a billion-kilowatt dam.' That's what keeps me going."

Nadine Bloch: There's a lot to say about that breakdown of connections between movements. I think there's a lot of ageism today; people don't want to listen to the old folks. I think, also, there's a lot of old folks who want to tell young folks how to do shit—I'm not interested in that. I am interested in people listening so that they can pick what works. The thing that changes the world is the ability to access the lessons in the stories you hear and apply them to your own context.

Yalonda Sinde: People are going to tell the story how they want. There's not a whole lot we can do about it other than push back and say, "We were there. There were tons of us. Where were you?"

VOICES

Chie Abad worked in a sweatshop in Saipan for several years before immigrating to the U.S. and joining Global Exchange as a "no sweat" activist.

Celia Alario helped set up the hotline for mainstream media in the Independent Media Center; also filed radio dispatches throughout the week.

Medea Benjamin cofounded Global Exchange with her then-husband, Kevin Danaher. She went on to run for a California U.S. Senate seat on the Green Party ticket and later founded Code Pink.

Jello Biafra helped bring together the No WTO Combo to perform during the protests; he is best known as the lead singer for the Dead Kennedys.

Nadine Bloch worked with the Ruckus Society before going on to found Beautiful Trouble, a nonprofit that provides resources for activists and organizers in eight languages.

José Bové is a French farmer who disrupted the construction of a McDonald's near his hometown before traveling to Seattle to join the protests.

Laurie Brown was a special assistant to Mayor Paul Schell; previously she worked as a union organizer.

Jim Brunner was a new hire at the *Seattle Times* when the protests began. He is now the political reporter.

Noam Chomsky is a linguistics scholar and well-known critic of capitalism.

Patrick Collins was an operations officer when Governor Gary Locke activated the National Guard in Seattle.

Helene Cooper was a reporter with the *Wall Street Journal* covering trade; she has since moved to the *New York Times* and covers the Pentagon.

Charles R. Cross was the editor of the *Rocket* and has written acclaimed biographies of Jimi Hendrix and Kurt Cobain.

Kevin Danaher cofounded Global Exchange with his then-wife, Medea Benjamin; he went on to found Green Festivals and became the executive director of the Global Citizen Center.

Maud Daudon was the deputy mayor during Paul Schell's administration; she went on to become the president of the Seattle Metropolitan Chamber of Commerce.

Pat Davis was the chairperson of Seattle Host; previously she was the first woman elected port commissioner in the state of Washington.

Aaron Dixon cofounded the Seattle chapter of the Black Panther Party; when the chapter closed he started Central House, a nonprofit that provided housing for teenagers in distress.

Elmer Dixon cofounded the Seattle chapter of the Black Panther Party; he went on to do work with Executive Diversity Services for more than thirty years.

Mike Dolan was the field director for Global Trade Watch, which was part of Public Citizen. He also helped conduct field work for the Citizens Trade Campaign.

Lisa Fithian was an organizer with the Direct Action Network; she later wrote *Shut It Down: Stories from a Fierce, Loving Resistance*.

Jim Flynn was an organizer with Earth First! His experience being pulled from a tree in a Eugene, Oregon, protest is documented in the film *If a Tree Falls*.

Jim Hightower is a longtime radio host and the author of *Hightower's Lowdown*, a newsletter.

Colin Hines was a cofounder of the International Forum on Globalization; he later became a coauthor of the "Green New Deal" in the United Kingdom; it eventually found its way to the U.S.

Matt Griffin founded the Pine Street Group and still works in development in Seattle.

Ron Griffin was a captain with the King County Sheriff's Office. He reported to Larry Mayes.

James P. Hoffa served as the president of the International Brotherhood of Teamsters until he retired in 2021.

Tetteh Hormeku was the coordinator of the African Trade Network. He is now the head of programs at the Third World Network–Africa.

Julia Hughes served as vice president of the United States Association of Importers of Textiles and Apparel. She is now the president of the organization, which has been rebranded as the United States Fashion Industry Association.

Deborah James was an organizer with Global Exchange, focused on fair trade campaigns; she went on to serve as director of International Programs at the Center for Economic and Policy Research.

Ed Joiner was the assistant chief of police for Seattle. Jim Pugel reported to him and Joiner reported to Police Chief Norm Stamper.

Ron Judd served as president of the King County Labor Council; he went on to serve as external affairs director for the state of Washington.

Tracy Katelman had worked with several environmental groups before partnering with Don Kegley to run the Alliance for Sustainable Jobs and the Environment.

Don Kegley had a long career as a steelworker before working with Tracy Katelman to run the Alliance for Sustainable Jobs and the Environment.

Steve Koehler is the founder of Koehler & Company, a prominent Seattle-based property developer. At the time of the protests, he was the chair of the Seattle Downtown Association.

Dennis Kucinich served in the U.S. House of Representatives for sixteen years; he later ran for president.

Pascal Lamy was the EU trade commissioner and later went on to become the WTO director general.

Nick Licata served on the Seattle City Council for eighteen years before retiring in 2015; he continues to write about issues around globalized capitalism.

Harold Linde was an intern at the Rainforest Action Network when he arrived in Seattle, where he was introduced to direct action. Since then, he's worked on campaigns and with several nonprofits, often as a media producer.

Gary Locke was a two-term governor of Washington State; he went on to serve as the U.S. secretary of commerce and as ambassador to China.

Michele Manasse has owned Fireworks, a Seattle-based retail store with multiple locations, since 1983.

Charles Mandigo was the assistant specialist in charge for the FBI office in Seattle.

Larry Mayes was the deputy chief for the King County Sheriff's Office. Ron Griffin reported to him and Mayes reported to Sheriff David Reichert.

Hilary McQuie organized around several issues with different groups before joining the Direct Action Network in Seattle.

Victor Menotti worked with the International Forum on Globalization and went on to become its executive director.

Denis Moynihan worked with Celia Alario to run the mainstream media communications at the Independent Media Center; he went on to cofound Democracy Now!

Ralph Nader founded Public Citizen and went on to launch multiple presidential bids.

Nina Narelle worked on several social justice campaigns before working with the Direct Action Network in Seattle.

John Nichols is an author and the national affairs correspondent for the *Nation* and associate editor of the *Capital Times*.

Vivian Phillips served as Mayor Schell's communication director. She went on to serve as Seattle arts commissioner.

Jim Pugel was a captain with the Seattle Police Department and the field commander during the protests. He reported to Ed Joiner. More recently, he ran an unsuccessful campaign for Seattle City Council.

Michael Ramos was an organizer with the Washington Association of Churches. He went on to become the executive director of the Church Council of Greater Seattle.

David Reichert was King County sheriff until 2005, when he left the post to run for Congress. He served in the U.S. House of Representatives for fourteen years.

Annette Sandberg was the chief of the Washington State Patrol for six years—and the first female to hold the post. She runs a transportation regulatory compliance consulting company.

Suzanne Savoie spent many years working with Earth First! and other environmental groups. She went on to work with the preservation and distribution of native seeds in the Klamath-Siskiyou Mountains.

Pam Schell was married to Mayor Paul Schell until his death. She has devoted much of her time to the Seattle arts community, serving on the board of directors for several theaters.

Paul Schell was the mayor of Seattle from 1998 to 2002. He died in 2014 at the age of seventy-six.

Dana Schuerholz cofounded Arts and Revolution with David Solnit. In 2007, she founded the Vashon Green School.

Dan Seligman was the Responsible Trade Program director at the Sierra Club until 2004. In 2020 he began working for Ceres, a sustainability-focused nonprofit.

John Sellers was the executive director of the Ruckus Society until 2006. In 2009, he founded other98.com, which specializes in "meme warfare."

Han Shan was the program director for the Ruckus Society. Today he makes art and lives in Italy.

Vandana Shiva was a founder of the International Forum on Globalization. She is the author of several books and continues to advocate for food sovereignty, remaining a leading voice in the anti-GMO movement.

Yalonda Sinde served as the executive director of the Community Coalition for Environmental Justice until 2006. Since then, she has worked as a nonprofit organization consultant.

Skip Spitzer was working with Pesticide Action in North America when he joined the Direct Action Network. Since 2010 he has done tech consulting work for nonprofit organizations.

Norm Stamper was the chief of police for the city of Seattle. Since resigning from that position, he has become a leading advocate for police reform.

David Solnit cofounded Arts and Revolution with Dana Schuerholz. Since 1999, he has continued to work on direct action campaigns all around the world, with a continued focus on the Bay Area in California.

David Taylor was an instrumental student organizer within the Direct Action Network. He continues to work on direct action campaigns as a tech consultant.

Kim Thayil played the guitar for the short-lived No WTO Combo. He is best known as the lead guitarist for Soundgarden.

Lori Wallach founded Global Trade Watch, which she ran for decades as a division of Public Citizen. She continues to be a leading voice when it comes to scrutinizing the WTO and international trade agreements.

four waters served as legal support during the WTO protests. She founded four waters media, a communications consulting office.

Vicente Paolo Yu is a lawyer specializing in international trade and environmental law; after Seattle he worked as a consultant for various United Nations agencies and as a senior legal adviser with the Third World Network.

John Zerzan is an anarchist and primitivist who continues to write and advocate for a reimagining of society, rooted in a hunter-gatherer framework.

ORGANIZATIONS

AFL-CIO, or the American Federation of Labor and Congress of Industrial Organizations, is the largest federation of unions in the United States. It includes sixty member unions ranging from government employees and transit workers, to educators and various trades.

Africa Trade Network is a network of allies developed under the auspice of Third World Network–Africa, for the purpose of elevating civil society concerns about international trade.

Alliance for Sustainable Jobs and the Environment was one of the original "blue-green alliances." It was collaborative organizing between environmental groups who were fighting against the actions of the Pacific Lumber Company and steelworkers who were striking against Kaiser Aluminum—both companies were owned by Charles Hurwitz.

Art & Revolution was founded to incorporate culture, art, puppets, and theater into mass mobilizations. It was cofounded by David Solnit and Dana Schuerholz.

Black Bloc is a term used for an informal group that moves through a protest together, uses face-coverings, and engages in property vandalism as an act of civil disobedience.

Central House was a nonprofit founded by Aaron Dixon. It provided transitional housing to minors in need.

Citizens Trade Campaign is a "national coalition of environmental, labor, consumer, family farm, religious and other civil society groups." It was founded in 1992 in an effort to improve the North American Free Trade Agreement (NAFTA).

Community Coalition for Environmental Justice was a "people-of-color led" environmental justice group based in Seattle. It closed in 2014.

Confédération Paysanne is a union organized by small farmers throughout France.

The Diggers were a seventeenth-century group of English political and religious dissidents who advocated for agrarian socialism. The name was revived by a theater group that performed from 1966 to 1968 in the Haight-Ashbury neighborhood of San Francisco.

Direct Action Network was the informal coalition that formed from the various disparate organizations and informal groups who wished to use direct action to shut down the 1999 WTO ministerial.

Earth First! is an environmental advocacy group, with anarchist leanings, noted for some of its more militant direct action tactics.

Executive Diversity Services is a consulting and leadership development office Elmer Dixon began working for shortly after the Seattle chapter of the Black Panther Party closed.

Extinction Rebellion is a global environmental movement, headquartered in the United Kingdom, that employs direct action tactics to draw attention to the climate crisis.

Food Not Bombs is a loose network of collectives that distributes food to communities in need.

Friends of the Earth is a Washington, D.C.–based environmental nonprofit organization.

G8, or the Group of 8, was an intergovernmental political forum that brought together the world's largest economies for regular meetings from 1997 until 2014. The group expelled Russia in 2014 and became G7.

Global Exchange is a nonprofit dedicated to the promotion of "human rights and social, economic, and environmental justice around the world." It was founded in 1988 by Medea Benjamin and Kevin Danaher.

Global Trade Watch is a trade-focused, consumer advocacy organization that Lori Wallach founded in 1995, under the auspices of Public Citizen.

Greenpeace is a Canada-based global campaigning network that employs direct action, lobbying, and research to reach its goal of ensuring "the ability of the Earth to nurture life in all its diversity."

Highlander Research and Education Center is a social justice leadership training school that dates back to 1932 and was critical to the civil rights movement, training Rosa Parks and countless other activists in civil disobedience. Han Shan refers to it in the text as the "Highlander School."

IMF, or the International Monetary Fund, is a financial agency under the auspices of the United Nations that oversees a borrowing fund for countries seeking help to meet fiscal obligations.

Independent Media Center, also known as Indymedia, is a "network of activist journalist collectives that report on political and social issues." The first iteration of IMC came out of the 1999 WTO protests.

International Brotherhood of Teamsters is a labor union for Teamsters, or professional drivers.

International Forum on Globalization is an alliance of activists, economists, researchers, writers, and scholars that formed in response to economic globalization. It is well-known for its "teach-ins."

Koehler & Company is a Seattle-based real estate development company founded in 1976.

Natural Resources Defense Council is an environmental advocacy organization headquartered in New York City, with offices around the world.

National Wildlife Federation is the largest nonprofit conservation education and advocacy organizations in the U.S.

No WTO Combo was the short-lived band formed to perform during the 1999 WTO protests. Its members were Kim Thayil, Jello Biafra, Krist Novoselic, and Gina Mainwal.

People's Global Action is the name that was given to worldwide coordination, which began in 1998, harnessing direct action social movements and grassroots campaigns in resistance to capitalism.

Pine Street Group is a Seattle-based real estate development company that was at the center of much of the redevelopment of the downtown business district in the 1990s.

Public Citizen is a nonprofit progressive consumer rights advocacy group and think tank founded in 1971 by Ralph Nader.

Rainforest Action Network, or RAN, is a San Francisco–based environmental protection nonprofit founded in 1985.

Reclaim the Streets is an informal resistance movement that opposes the "dominance of corporate forces in globalization" and promotes community ownership of public spaces.

The *Rocket* was a biweekly music magazine, focused on the Pacific Northwest, published from 1979 to 2000.

Ruckus Society is a nonprofit organization that specializes in training activists in direct action skills and strategies.

Seattle Host was a six-person committee, formed by members of the Washington Council on International Trade, that was in charge of organizing the logistics for hosting the 1999 WTO ministerial.

Sierra Club is an environmental organization with chapters in all fifty U.S. states. It was founded in 1892 by John Muir.

Student Nonviolent Coordinating Committee, or SNCC, was a civil rights organization founded in 1960 as an outgrowth of sit-ins at segregated lunch counters, often led by students.

Third World Network is a nonprofit network of organizations focused on issues facing developing countries, particularly as those issues relate to North-South affairs. It is headquartered in Malaysia with offices in other regions of the world.

UAW, or the International Union, United Automobile, Aerospace and Agricultural Implement Workers of America, is one of the largest unions in the U.S., representing workers in automobile manufacturing, automobile parts, health care, casino gambling, and higher education.

United Farm Workers is a labor union for farmworkers throughout the United States, founded in 1962 by Dolores Huerta, Philip Vera Cruz, and César Chávez.

United States Fashion Industry Association is a lobbying organization that represents clothing brands, retailers, importers, and wholesalers.

Washington Council on International Trade is an organization that advocates for "trade and investment policies that increase competitiveness of Washington state workers, farmers and businesses."

Wobblies, or the Industrial Workers of the World, is an international labor union founded in Chicago in 1905 with ties to various socialist and anarchist labor movements.

World Bank is an international financial institution that provides loans to low- and middle-income countries.

World Wildlife Fund is a Swiss-based international nongovernmental organization that works to preserve wildlife and reduce the human impact on the environment.

Yippies, or the Youth International Party, was founded in 1967 as an offshoot of the antiwar movements of the era. It is known for its pranks and theatrical approach to direct action.

Zapatistas have a long history of revolution in Mexico. On January 1, 1994, the Zapatista Army of National Liberation coordinated an uprising in Chiapas state, protesting the enactment of NAFTA.

ACKNOWLEDGMENTS

Thanks goes to:

Everyone who gave their time and energy to contribute to the story. I'm grateful to each of you for your generosity and for trusting me. Not all interviews are included in the book but everyone I spoke to helped deepen my understanding of the events. Thank you. Extra gratitude to those who let me interview them in English, even though it's not their mother tongue.

Emily Simonson, Laurie Brown, Celia Alario, Mike Dolan, Yolanda Sinde, David Solnit, Lori Wallach, Victor Menotti, Harold Linde, David Reichert, Norm Stamper, Colin Robinson, Matt Griffin, Susie Plummer, and so many others who helped connect me with some of the voices in the book.

Carolyn Cole, Harold Linde, Dana Schuerholz, Steve Kaiser, and Tony Gale for sharing photography.

Lori Lawton for reliably turning around transcripts; for being so responsive and supportive.

Jonathan Karp, Priscilla Painton, Irene Kheradi, Tom Pitoniak, Matthew Monahan, Alyssa diPierro, Amanda Mulholland, Phil Metcalf, Paul Dippolito, Beth Maglione, Rebecca Rozenberg, Tzipora Chein, and everyone at Simon & Schuster who helped make this publication possible. Especially to Sean Manning for his partnership in conceiving and editing this book.

Chris Parris-Lamb for always providing vital counsel.

Shug, who was always teaching me how to interview, even if she didn't know it.

Gigi, who has redefined love and my connection to humanity.

And most importantly Tasha, for being the best partner I could ask for. Thanks for letting me make my way through this life with you. You make it all worth it.